Formal Approaches to Computing and
Information Technology

Springer
*London
Berlin
Heidelberg
New York
Barcelona
Hong Kong
Milan
Paris
Singapore
Tokyo*

Also in this series:

A Theory and Practice of Program Development
D. Andrews
ISBN 3-540-76162-4

Constructing Correct Software: *the basics*
J. Cooke
ISBN 3-540-76156-X

Proof in VDM: Case Studies
J.C. Bicarregui (Ed.)
ISBN 3-540-76186-1

Program Development by Refinement
E. Sekerinski and K. Sere (Eds)
ISBN 1-85233-053-8

Industrial-Strength Formal Methods in Practice
M.G. Hinchey and J.P. Bowen (Eds)
ISBN 1-85233-640-4

Marc Frappier and Henri Habrias (Eds)

Software Specification Methods

An Overview Using a Case Study

Springer

Marc Frappier
Département de Mathématiques et d'Informatique, Université de Sherbrooke, Sherbrooke,
Québec J1K 2RI, Canada

Henri Habrias
IRIN, 2 rue de Houssinière, BP 92208, 44072 Nantes Cedex 03, France

Series Editor
Professor S.A. Schuman, BSc, DEA, CEng

FACIT series ISSN 1431-9683
ISBN 1-85233-353-7 Springer-Verlag London Berlin Heidelberg

British Library Cataloguing in Publication Data
A catalogue record for this book is available from the British Library

Library of Congress Cataloging-in-Publication Data
Frappier, Marc, 1965-
    Software specification methods / Marc Frappier and Henri Habrias
      p. cm. - (Formal approaches to computing and information technology, ISSN 1431-9683)
    Includes bibliographical references and index.
    ISBN 1-85233-353-7 (alk. paper)
      1. Formal methods (Computer science 2. Computer software—Specifications. I.
Habrias, Henri. II. Title. III. Series.
QA76.9.F67 F73 2000
004'.01'51—dc21
                                                                              00-061256

Apart from any fair dealing for the purposes of research or private study, or criticism or review, as permitted under the Copyright, Designs and Patents Act 1988, this publication may only be reproduced, stored or transmitted, in any form or by any means, with the prior permission in writing of the publishers, or in the case of reprographic reproduction in accordance with the terms of licences issued by the Copyright Licensing Agency. Enquiries concerning reproduction outside those terms should be sent to the publishers.

© Springer-Verlag London Limited 2001
Printed in Great Britain

The use of registered names, trademarks etc. in this publication does not imply, even in the absence of a specific statement, that such names are exempt from the relevant laws and regulations and therefore free for general use.

The publisher makes no representation, express or implied, with regard to the accuracy of the information contained in this book and cannot accept any legal responsibility or liability for any errors or omissions that may be made.

Typesetting: Camera ready by editors
Printed and bound at the Athenæum Press Ltd., Gateshead, Tyne & Wear
34/3830-543210 Printed on acid-free paper SPIN 10774562

In memory of Philippe Facon

Preface

Objectives of this Book

This book is an introduction to a set of software specification methods. Its targeted audience are readers who do not wish to read pages of definitions in order to understand the basics of a method. The *same case study* is used to introduce each method, following a rigorously uniform presentation format. Special care has been devoted to ensure that specifications do not deviate from the case study text. As much as the method allows, what is specified is what appears in the case study text. The benefits are two-fold. First, the reader can easily switch from one method to another, using his knowledge of the case study as a leverage to understand a new method. Second, it becomes easier to compare methods, because the same behavior is specified in each case.

Each method presentation follows the same pattern. The concepts are progressively introduced when they are needed. To illustrate the specification process, questions that the specifier should raise during the analysis of the case study are stated. Answers are provided as if they were given by an imaginary client. The question/answer process guides the derivation of the specification. Interestingly, the questions raised depend on the method, which is illustrative of the differences between them. When a question is raised in one method and not in another, the reader has an issue to resolve: does the other method allow this question? If so, what should be the answer? As such, this book is a trigger to stimulate the reader's curiosity about specification methods; it does not intend to provide all the answers. More elaborate materials are referenced in each chapter for a deeper coverage.

About Specifications

Some Definitions

A specification *method* is a sequence of activities leading to the development of a product, called a specification. A method should provide enough guidance on how to conduct the activities and on how to evaluate the quality of the final product. A *specification* is a precise description, written in some notation (language), of the client's requirements. A notation is said to be *formal* if it has a formal syntax and a formal semantics. A notation is said to be *semi-formal* if it only has a formal syntax.

Several characteristics of a system can be specified. One may distinguish between functional requirements, efficiency requirements, and implementation requirements. Functional requirements address the input-output behavior of a system. Efficiency requirements address the execution time of a system. The client may be interested in specifying a time bound for obtaining a response from the system. Some authors argue [1] that a specification without time bounds is not an effective specification: indeed, strictly speaking, if the specification does not include a time bound, the implementation may take an arbitrary duration to provide a response. It is impossible to distinguish between an infinite loop and a program that takes an arbitrary time to respond. Implementation requirements address issues like the programming language to use, the software components to reuse, the targeted hardware platform, the operating systems. The methods described in this book address functional requirements.

Specifications as Contracts

A specification constitutes a *contract* between the client and the specifier. As such, the client must be able to understand the specification, in order to validate it. Typically, clients are not sufficiently versed in specialized notations to understand a specification. There are several ways to circumvent this lack of familiarity. The least is to rephrase the specification in the client's natural langage, avoiding ambiguities as much as possible. If the specification is executable, scenarios can be tested with the client. The use of examples and counter-examples is a good technique to ensure that the client and the specifier understand each other.

The specification is also a contract between the specifier and the implementor. Of course, it is expected that the implementor understands the notation used for the specification. The implementor may not be familiar at all with the client's requirements and his application domain. The natural langage description provided to the client is also essential to the implementor, because it justifies and explains the specification. It allows the implementor to map specification concepts to application domain concepts. The textual description is to a specification what explanations are to formulas in mathematics.

Risks of not Using Specifications

Developing a software system without a specification is a random process. The implementation is doomed to be modified, sometimes forever, because it never precisely matches the client's needs. The goal of a specification is to capture the client's requirements in a concise, clear, unambiguous manner to minimize

---
[1] Hehner E.C.R. (1993) *A Practical Theory of Programming.* Springer-Verlag

the risks of failure in the development process. It is much cheaper to change a specification than to change an implementation.

Additionally, the specification must leave as much freedom as possible to the implementor, in order to find the best implementation in terms of development cost, efficiency, usability, and maintainability. Abstraction is a good mechanism to support implementation freedom. For instance, if a sort function must be specified, the specifier need not to specify that a particular sort algorithm should be used. The implementor is free pick any sorting algorithm like quicksort or bubblesort. Non-determinism is another good mechanism to provide more freedom for the implementation. For instance, one may specify a function that changes a dollar for a set of coins by just stating that the sum of the coins is equal to one dollar. The specification need not to prescribe how the set of coins is selected. During the implementation, an algorithm that minimises the number of coins may be used, or one that gets rid of five-cent coins first, in order to minimize the weight of the coins in the machine (just for the sake of the argument).

Even when the implementation is finished, the specification is very useful. Conducting maintenance without a specification is a risky, expensive business. To modify a program, one must first know what it does.

Validation of a Specification

A fundamental issue is to make sure that the specification "matches" the client's needs. This activity is called *validation*. Note that we use the verb "match" instead a stronger verb like "prove", or "demonstrate", in the definition of the validation concept. By its very nature, a specification cannot be "proved" to match the client's requirements. If such a proof existed, then it would require another description of the requirements. If such a description is available, then *it is* a specification.

A specification is the starting point of the development process. It has the same status as axioms of a mathematical theory. They are assumed to be right. Of course, one can prove that a specification is *consistent* (i.e., that it does not include a contradiction), like one can prove that the axioms of a theory are consistent. But this is a different issue than validation.

Validation consists essentially in stating *properties* about the specification, and in proving that the specification satisfies these properties. Properties describe usage scenarios at various levels of abstraction. They can refer to concrete sequences of events, or they can be general statements about the safety or the liveness of the system.

The more properties are stated, the more the confidence in the specification validity is increased. Properties are like theorems of a theory: they must follow from the specification. In summary, validation is an empirical process; a specification is deemed valid until one finds a desired property that is not satisfied.

Satisfaction of a Specification

It must be possible to demonstrate that the implementation *satisfies* the specification. A first approach is to progressively *refine* the specification until an implementation is reached. If it is possible mathematically to prove that each refinement satisfies the specification, we say that the development process is *formal*. Another approach is to test the implementation. *Test cases* are derived from the specification. The results obtained by running the implementation for these tests cases are compared with the results prescribed by the specification. Such a development process is said to be *informal*. For most practical applications, it is not feasible to exhaustively test a system.

From a theoretical viewpoint, proving the correctness of an implementation is more appropriate than testing it. From a practical viewpoint, testing is easier to achieve. Since Gödel and Turing, we know the strengths and the limitations of formal development processes. For more than thirty years now, computer scientists have investigated the application of mathematics to the development of software systems, with the ultimate goal of developing techniques to prove that an implementation satisfies a specification. Progress has been made, but much remains to be done.

Tools

A semi-formal notation may be supported by tools like editors and syntax checkers. A formal notation, thanks to its formal semantics, may also be supported by interpreters, theorem provers, model checkers, and test case generators. Support for informal notations is limited to general purpose editors using templates for documents.

Structure of the Book

This book is divided in three parts. The first part includes state-based specification methods. In these methods, the description of the system behavior is centered around the notion of state transition. The operations (also called functions) of the system are specified by describing how their execution change the state of the system.

The second part is dedicated to event-based methods. An event is a message that is exchanged between the environment and the system. Event-based methods describe which events can occur and in what order. Some of these methods are related to state-based specifications, as they also describe state transitions. Others use process algebras or traces to describe the possible sequences of events.

The third part includes methods based on three quite different paradigms. The first method uses an algebraic approach. The system is described using sorts, operations and equations. Abstract data types are classical examples of algebraic specifications. The second method is based on higher-order logic and typed lambda calculus. Operations are defined as functions on the system state. The last two are based on Petri nets. A Petri net is a graph with two kinds of vertices: places and transitions. Tokens are assigned to places. The behavior of the system is represented by the movement of tokens between places using transitions.

The Case Study

The next sections reproduce the text of the case study that was submitted to authors and the guidelines for preparing their specifications. The case study seems very simple, the first time through. When reading the various solutions, one quickly finds that its detailed analysis is surprisingly stimulating.

The Text of the Case Study

1. The subject is to invoice orders.
2. To invoice is to change the state of an order (to change it from the state "pending" to "invoiced").
3. On an order, we have one and one only reference to an ordered product of a certain quantity. The quantity can be different to other orders.
4. The same reference can be ordered on several different orders.
5. The state of the order will be changed into "invoiced" if the ordered quantity is either less or equal to the quantity which is in stock according to the reference of the ordered product.
6. You have to consider the two following cases:
   (a) Case 1
       All the ordered references are references in stock. The stock or the set of the orders may vary:

       - due to the entry of new orders or cancelled orders;
       - due to having a new entry of quantities of products in stock at the warehouse.

       But, we do not have to take these entries into account. This means that you will not receive two entry flows (orders, entries in stock). The stock and the set of orders are always given to you in a up-to-date state.
   (b) Case 2
       You do have to take into account the entries of:

       - new orders;
       - cancellations of orders;
       - entries of quantities in the stock.

The Guidelines for Preparing Specifications

Perhaps you will consider that the case study text is incomplete or ambiguous. One goal of this exercise is to know what questions are raised by each method.

You may propose different solutions (expressing consistent requirements) and you will explain how your method(s) have brought you to propose these solutions.

The questions that you had to deal with in order to solve the case study should be stated according to the following guidelines.

- Questions must be on the problem domain. They are directed to the user. They must be specific.
- Questions are better answered by several answers (options); pick one answer to continue the analysis.
- Show what verifications your method has allowed you to do (e.g., detection of inconsistencies in the answers that you have chosen).

Finally, do not extend the domain. For example, do not specify stock management (e.g., when to restock, following what minimum quantity, etc.), do not add new information such as category of customer, category of product, payment modality, bank account, etc.

Warning

This book illustrates some specification methods using a single case study. Although it is an excellent approach, from a pedagogical viewpoint, to provide an overview and a basic comparison of methods, the reader should not conclude that it is sufficient to evaluate and select specification methods. Each method has it strengths and weaknesses. A single case study cannot claim to properly represent all of them.

Wishing to Contribute?

We would like this project to continue to evolve. If you wish to solve this case study using your favorite method, please check the book's web page at

    http://www.dmi.usherb.ca/~spec

Your contribution and comments are welcome. The case study, guidelines, new solutions, comments about solutions, and additional materials about specification methods will be available at this address.

Acknowledgements

This book is part of a long story. In 1994, Henri Habrias proposed to the community of software engineering the Invoicing case study. The first solution, with

SA/RT and *SCCS*, was submitted by Andy Galloway (University of York, U.K.) and distributed to the participants of the École d'été *CEA-EDF-INRIA* in June 1995. Three years later, an International Workshop on Comparing Systems Specification Techniques, titled *"What questions are prompted by one's particular method of specification?"* was co-organized in Nantes by M. Allemand, C. Attiogbé and H. Habrias in March 1998[2].

Marc Frappier visited the Faculté des sciences of the Université de Nantes at IRIN (Institut de Recherches en Informatique de Nantes) in the summer of 1998 and Henri Habrias visited the Département de mathématiques et d'informatique of the Université de Sherbrooke in the fall of 1998 and spring of 1999. During these stays, it has been possible to organise the content of the book and to prepare the final version. The French Ministry of Foreign Affairs supported one of the visits of Henri Habrias to Sherbrooke.

This book was developed and refined in a collaborative effort. Each contributor has reviewed chapters of other contributors. Their mutual suggestions and comments have significantly enriched the final version of this book.

We are grateful to all these persons and institutions.

Sherbrooke and Nantes,   *Marc Frappier*
June 2000   *Henri Habrias*

---

[2] M. Allemand, C. Attiogbé and H. Habrias editors, (Invoice'98) International Workshop on *Comparing Systems Specification Techniques - What Questions Are Prompted By One's Particular Method Of Specification?*, Nantes, France, March 26-27 1998, ISBN 2-906082-29-5

Contents

List of Contributors XXI

Part I State-Based Approaches

1   Z: A Formal Specification Notation
   Jonathan P. Bowen 3

1.1   Overview of the Z Notation 3
      1.1.1   The Process of Producing a Z Specification 3
1.2   Analysis and Specification of Case 1 5
1.3   Analysis and Specification of Case 2 13
1.4   Validation of the Specification 16
1.5   The Natural Language Description of the Specifications 18
1.6   Conclusion 18

2   SAZ: SSADM Version 4 and Z
   Fiona Polack 21

2.1   Overview of the SAZ Method 21
2.2   Analysis and Specification of Case 1 22
      2.2.1   Z Specification 24
2.3   Analysis and Specification of Case 2 27
2.4   Natural Language Description of the Specifications 36
      2.4.1   Case 1 36
      2.4.2   Case 2 36
2.5   Conclusions 37

3   B: A Model-Based Method Using Generalised Substitutions
   Hassan Diab, Marc Frappier 39

3.1   Overview of the B Notation 39
3.2   Analysis and Specification of Case 1 40
      3.2.1   Identifying Operations 40
      3.2.2   Defining the State Space 41

	3.2.3	Defining the Behaviour of the Invoicing Operation	44
	3.2.4	The Product1 Machine	46
3.3	Analysis and Specification of Case 2		49
	3.3.1	Identifying Operations	49
	3.3.2	The Product2 Machine	49
	3.3.3	The Invoicing2 Machine	50
3.4	Validation of the Specification		52
3.5	The Natural Language Description of the Specifications		53
	3.5.1	Case 1	53
	3.5.2	Case 2	53
3.6	Conclusion		54

4 From OMT Diagrams to B Specifications
Philippe Facon, Régine Laleau, Hong Phuong Nguyen 57

4.1	Overview of the Method		57
	4.1.1	The Semi-Formal Specification	57
	4.1.2	The Formal Specification	59
4.2	Specification of Case 1		61
	4.2.1	Object Diagram	61
	4.2.2	Scenarios and State/Transition Diagrams	62
	4.2.3	The Formal Specification	64
4.3	Specification of Case 2		66
	4.3.1	Scenarios and State/Transition Diagrams	67
	4.3.2	The Formal Specification	70
4.4	Validation		74
4.5	The Natural Language Description of the Specifications		75
	4.5.1	Case 1	75
	4.5.2	Case 2	75
4.6	Conclusion		76

Part II Event-Based Approaches

5 Action Systems: A Method Combining State-Based and Event-Based Specification
Jane Sinclair 81

5.1	Overview of Action Systems		81
5.2	Analysis and Specification of Case 1		82
	5.2.1	Modelling the State of the Action System	82
	5.2.2	Defining the Actions	84
	5.2.3	An Action System for Case 1	87
5.3	Analysis and Specification of Case 2		88
	5.3.1	Modelling the State for Case 2	88
	5.3.2	Defining the Actions	89

	5.3.3 An Action System for Case 2	91
5.4	Verification for Action Systems	91
5.5	The Natural Language Description of the Specification	94
	5.5.1 Case 1	94
	5.5.2 Case 2	94
5.6	Conclusion	95

6 Using UML with a Behaviour-Driven Method
Sophie Dupuy, Agnès Front-Conte, Christophe Saint-Marcel 97

6.1	Overview of the UML Notation and of the CSO Method	97
6.2	Case 1	98
	6.2.1 Requirements Capture	98
	6.2.2 Analysis and Design	99
6.3	Case 2	103
	6.3.1 Requirements Capture	103
	6.3.2 Analysis and Design Phase	106
6.4	Natural Language Description of the UML Specifications	111
	6.4.1 Case 1	111
	6.4.2 Case 2	111
6.5	Conclusion	111

7 VHDL: A Hardware Description Language and its Simulation Semantics
Laurence Pierre 113

7.1	Overview of VHDL	113
7.2	Analysis and Specification of Case 1	115
	7.2.1 Identifying Data Structures	115
	7.2.2 Identifying Operations	116
7.3	Analysis and Specification of Case 2	120
7.4	The Natural Language Description of the Specification	128
	7.4.1 Case 1	128
	7.4.2 Case 2	128
7.5	Conclusion	129

8 Estelle: A Formal Description Technique
Eric Lallet, Jean-Luc Raffy 131

8.1	Overview of the FDT Estelle	131
8.2	Analysis and Specification of Case 1	131
	8.2.1 Defining the Architecture of the Specification	132
	8.2.2 Defining the Behaviour	134
8.3	Analysis and Specification of Case 2	137
	8.3.1 Defining the New Architecture	138
	8.3.2 Defining the Behaviour	139
8.4	Validating the Specification	143

8.5	The Natural Language Description of the Specifications	143
	8.5.1 Case 1	143
	8.5.2 Case 2	144
8.6	Conclusion	144

9 SDL: A Language Based on Extended Finite State Machines with Abstract Data Types
P. Poizat 147

9.1	Overview of SDL	147
9.2	Analysis and Specification of Case 1	148
	9.2.1 System Structure	148
	9.2.2 Process Graphs	150
	9.2.3 Sort Definitions	153
	9.2.4 Comments on the First Case Study	157
9.3	Analysis and Specification of Case 2	157
	9.3.1 System Structure	157
	9.3.2 Process Graphs	159
	9.3.3 Sort Definitions	160
9.4	The Natural Language Description of the Specifications	162
	9.4.1 Case 1	162
	9.4.2 Case 2	162
9.5	Conclusion	162

10 (E)-LOTOS: (Enhanced) Language of Temporal Ordering Specification
Kenneth J. Turner, Mihaela Sighireanu 165

10.1	Overview of the LOTOS Notation and Method	165
	10.1.1 The LOTOS and E-LOTOS Languages	165
	10.1.2 Requirements Capture in LOTOS	166
10.2	Analysis and Specification of Case 1	168
	10.2.1 Analysis	168
	10.2.2 Specification	169
10.3	Analysis and Specification of Case 2	170
	10.3.1 Analysis	170
	10.3.2 Specification	174
10.4	Validation and Verification of the LOTOS Specifications	182
	10.4.1 Validation	182
	10.4.2 Verification	183
10.5	Natural Language Description of the Specifications	186
	10.5.1 Case 1	187
	10.5.2 Case 2	187
10.6	Conclusion	187

11 Specifying a Cleanroom Black Box Using JSD
Marc Frappier, Richard St-Denis 191

11.1 Overview of the Method 191
11.2 Analysis and Specification of Case 1 192
    11.2.1 Declaration of Input-Output Space and Entity Types 192
    11.2.2 Definition of Global Constraints 194
    11.2.3 Specification of Input-Output Behaviour 195
11.3 Analysis and Specification of Case 2 195
    11.3.1 Declaration of Input-Output Space and Entity Types 195
    11.3.2 Description of Individual Behaviours of Entities 197
    11.3.3 Definition of Global Constraints 200
    11.3.4 Specification of Input-Output Behaviour 202
11.4 The Natural Language Description of the Specification 203
    11.4.1 Case 1 203
    11.4.2 Case 2 203
11.5 Conclusion 204

Part III Other Formal Approaches

12 Algebraic Specification in CASL
Hubert Baumeister, Didier Bert 209

12.1 Overview of the CASL Notation 209
12.2 Analysis and Specification of Case 1 210
12.3 Analysis and Specification of Case 2 215
12.4 Architectural Specification 221
12.5 The Natural Language Description of the Specification 222
    12.5.1 Case 1 222
    12.5.2 Case 2 223
12.6 Conclusion 223
References 224

13 An Abstract and Constructive Specification in Coq
Philippe Chavin, Jean-François Monin 225

13.1 Introduction to Coq 225
13.2 Terms Analysis 226
    13.2.1 Stock and Orders 226
    13.2.2 Operations 227
    13.2.3 Requirements on Quantities 227
13.3 A Specification for Case 1 228
    13.3.1 Basic Types 228
    13.3.2 State and Operation 230
    13.3.3 Operation "invoice" 230
13.4 A Specification for Case 2 232

		13.4.1 Using General Operations over Sets 232

        13.4.1 Using General Operations over Sets 232
        13.4.2 Reference-Dependent Measure Systems 234
13.5 Experimenting with the Specification 236
        13.5.1 Refining 236
        13.5.2 Running an Example. 238
13.6 Terms Rephrasing 239
13.7 Conclusion. 240

14 Petri Nets: A Graphical Tool for System Modelling and Analysis
Annie Choquet-Geniet, Pascal Richard 241

14.1 Overview of Petri Nets 241
14.2 Analysis and Specification of Case 1 243
        14.2.1 One Order with a Data/Action Approach. 243
        14.2.2 One Order with a Structural Approach 247
        14.2.3 Several Orders 249
14.3 Analysis and Specification of Case 2 252
        14.3.1 Entry Flow in Stocks. 252
        14.3.2 Flows of Orders 253
14.4 Validation of the Specification. 253
14.5 The Natural Language Description of the Specifications 256
        14.5.1 Case 1 256
        14.5.2 Case 2 256
14.6 Conclusion. 256

15 Using Petri Nets and Objects: A Formal yet Expressive Approach
Christophe Sibertin-Blanc 259

15.1   Introduction 259
15.2   A Conceptual Framework for the Representation of Systems 260
15.3   Case 1 262
15.4   The System's Interface 262
15.5   The Components of the System's Structure 262
15.6   The Entities 264
15.7   The Operations 268
15.8   The Actors 269
15.9   The Control Structure 270
15.10 Natural Language Description of the Specifications 275
15.11 Remarks about the Treatment of the Case Study 275

Index 279

List of Contributors

Hubert Baumeister
Institut für Informatik,
Universität München,
Oettingenstr. 67,
D-80538 München,
Germany
baumeist@
informatik.uni-muenchen.de

Didier Bert
IMAG, Laboratoire Logiciels
Systèmes et Réseaux
B.P. 72, 38402
Saint-Martin d'Hères Cedex,
France
Didier.Bert@imag.fr

Jonathan P. Bowen
South Bank University
Centre for Applied Formal Methods
School of Computing,
Information Systems and Mathematics
Borough Road
London SE1 0AA, U.K.
jonathan.bowen@sbu.ac.uk

Philippe Chavin
France Télécom
CNET, DTL/MSV,
2, av. P. Marzin
22307 Lannion Cedex, France
Philippe.Chavin@
cnet.francetelecom.fr

Annie Choquet-Geniet
ENSMA
Laboratory of Applied Computer
Science
Téléport 2, B.P. 109
86960 Futuroscope, France
ageniet@ensma.fr

Hassan Diab
Université de Sherbrooke
Département de mathématiques et
d'informatique
Sherbrooke, Québec, Canada
J1K 2R1
Hassan.Diab@dmi.usherb.ca

Sophie Dupuy
IMAG, Laboratoire Logiciels
Systèmes et Réseaux,
B.P. 72, 38402
Saint-Martin d'Hères Cedex
France
sophie.dupuy@imag.fr

Philippe Facon
CEDRIC-IIE (CNAM)
18 allée Jean Rostand
91025 Évry, France

Agnès Front-Conte
IMAG, Laboratoire Logiciels
Systèmes et Réseaux
B.P. 72, 38402,
Saint-Martin d'Hères Cedex
France
Agnes.Conte@imag.fr

List of Contributors

Andy J. Galloway
High Integrity Systems Engineering
Department of Computer Science
University of York, UK
andyg@cs.york.ac.uk.

Régine Laleau
CEDRIC-IIE (CNAM)
18 allée Jean Rostand
91025 Évry, France
laleau@iie.cnam.fr

Hong Phuong Nguyen
CEDRIC-IIE (CNAM)
18 allée Jean Rostand
91025 Évry, France
phuong@iie.cnam.fr

Marc Frappier
Université de Sherbrooke
Département de mathématiques et
d'informatique
Sherbrooke, Québec, Canada
J1K 2R1
Marc.Frappier@dmi.usherb.ca

Henri Habrias
Université de Nantes
Institut Universitaire de Technologie
Département informatique
and
Institut de Recherches en
Informatique de Nantes
3 rue Ml Joffre, 44041 Nantes
cedex 1, France
henri.habrias@
irin.univ-nantes.fr

Eric Lallet
Institut National des
Télécommunications
9, rue Charles Fourier
91011 Evry cedex, France
eric.lallet@int-evry.fr

Jean-Francois Monin
France Télécom R&D, DTL/MSV
2, av. P. Marzin, 22307
Lannion Cedex, France
JeanFrancois.Monin@
francetelecom.fr

Laurence Pierre
CMI/Université de Provence
Laboratoire d'Informatique de
Marseille
39 rue Joliot-Curie, 13453
Marseille Cedex 13, France
Laurence.Pierre@cmi.univ-mrs.fr

Pascal Poizat
Université de Nantes
Institut de Recherche en
Informatique de Nantes
2, rue de la Houssinière, B.P. 92208
44322, Nantes cedex 3, France
Pascal.Poizat@
irin.univ-nantes.fr

Fiona Polack
University of York,
Department of Computer Science,
YORK YO10 5DD U.K.
fiona@cs.york.ac.uk

Jean-Luc Raffy
Institut National des
Télécommunications
9, rue Charles Fourier
91011 Evry cedex, France
jean-luc.raffy@int-evry.fr

Pascal Richard
ENSMA
Laboratory of Applied Computer
Science
Téléport 2, B.P. 109,
86960 Futuroscope France
richardp@ensma.fr

Richard Saint-Denis
Université de Sherbrooke
Département de mathématiques et
d'informatique
Sherbrooke, Québec, Canada
J1K 2R1
Richard.St-Denis@dmi.usherb.ca

Christophe Saint-Marcel
IMAG, Laboratoire Logiciels
Systèmes et Réseaux
B.P. 72, 38402,
Saint-Martin d'Hères Cedex
France
Christophe.Saint-Marcel@imag.fr

Christophe Sibertin-Blanc
Université Toulouse 1
Place A. France, F-31042
Toulouse Cedex, France
sibertin@univ-tlse1.fr

Mihaela Sighireanu
LIAFA, 2 Place Jussieu
Université de Paris 7
75251 PARIS Cedex 05, France
mihaela.sighireanu@
liafa.jussieu.fr

Jane Sinclair
Department of Computer Science
University of Warwick
Coventry, CV4 7AL, U.K.
jane@dcs.warwick.ac.uk

Kenneth J. Turner
Computing Science and Mathematics
University of Stirling
Stirling, FK9 4LA, Scotland, U.K
kjt@cs.stir.ac.uk

Part I

State-Based Approaches

1 Z: A Formal Specification Notation

Jonathan P. Bowen

1.1 Overview of the Z Notation

Z (pronounced 'zed') is a formal specification notation [9] based on set theory and first order predicate logic. The mathematical notation is supported by a library of operators known as the 'Z toolkit', which is largely formally defined within the Z notation itself [8]. The operators have a large number of algebraic laws which aid in the reasoning about Z specification. As well as the mathematical notation, there is a *'schema'* notation to aid in the structuring of the mathematics for large specification by packaging the mathematical notation into boxes that may be used and combined subsequently.

There are many Z textbooks (e.g., see [1,5,6,10]). A widely used reference book exists [8] and Z is undergoing the lengthy international ISO standardisation process which should help with its acceptance by industry and in the development of tools to support the notation. The theoretical basis of Z is explored in [7] and a range of case studies may be found in [1,4]. [1] includes a comprehensive Z glossary and literature guide as appendices.

1.1.1 The Process of Producing a Z Specification

Z is typically used in a modelling style [2] in which an *abstract state* is included, containing enough information to describe changes in state that may be performed by a number of *operations* on the system. Each of the operations defines a *relation* between a *before* and *after* version of the state. The state may contain *invariants* which are predicates relating the various components in the abstract state which should always apply regardless of the current state of the system.

An *initial state* is defined as a special case of the more general abstract state, with the addition of extra constraining predicates. The description of the system is then modelled by this initial state, followed by an arbitrary interleaving of the operations in any order, only limited by any *preconditions* imposed by individual operations.

Often operations are designed to be *total* (i.e., with a precondition of *true*) so that they can be applied in any situation. This is especially useful in maintenance of the implemented operations (which could typically be procedure calls, for example) since preconditions are not explicitly obvious in a program implementation and a maintainer unaware of such restrictions may be tempted to use the operation in an inappropriate situation.

In the case of Z, a good place to start the specification is by positing a possible abstract state to model the system. Inevitably this will have to be changed in the course of producing the rest of the specification (except in trivial cases) but that is part of the learning process by which knowledge and understanding of the system is gained.

Next some operations which may be performed on the system should be considered. Initially only the result of successful operations which perform the desired result with no problems should be formulated. The abstract state should be modified as required if some important aspect cannot be adequately modelled without it, always checking for the possible effect on other operations.

As the specification evolves, given sets and useful axiomatic or generic definitions can be assumed, then formally defined and added at the beginning of the specification. Errors reports in the case of unsuccessful operations should be considered and added. Some of these will normally be common across several operations in a specification of any size.

In practical specifications, it will be found that parts of the specification are repeated across groups of operations. It is often worthwhile factoring out these parts, presenting and explaining their purpose once, and then using them subsequently. This will considerably reduce the size of most large specifications and make their assimilation easier for the reader.

Total operations are normally formulated typically as a disjunction of the successful and, if required, a number of error cases. An appropriate error indication, normally as some form of output, is normally included depending on the requirements.

Finally (perhaps surprisingly) the initial state should be considered as a special case of the abstract state. Often the contents of much of the state is most easily considered to be empty or to have some fixed value at the start of the life of the system, but may be more loosely specified if the exact value is unimportant.

During the production of the specification, questions will inevitably be raised. These should be discussed within the design team, with other colleagues, or with the customer as appropriate, normally in that order, to resolve the issues. In the next section of this chapter, a Z specification is presented with some of these questions interspersed with the formal Z specification. Informal description of the formal specification is also included. This should be designed to reinforce the concepts presented in the Z specification, especially in relating it to the real world.

In a finished and polished Z specification, the informal annotation should normally be about the same length as the formal description. As a rule of thumb, it is a good idea to attempt to describe each line of predicate in Z schema boxes with a matching sentence of text written in a natural style. Ideally the informal part of the specification should be meaningful on its own, even if the formal part is removed. In fact this could be useful if the description is to be presented to a customer who may be unable to assimilate the Z specification itself.

1.2 Analysis and Specification of Case 1

Most specifications, formal or otherwise, are presented as a *fait accompli* after the specification has been produced, normally with no hint as to how the specification has been produced. There is some guidance on the use of formal methods in general but in the case of specific notations, even most textbooks tend to concentrate on finished specifications rather than the progress of specifications from initial concept (requirements) to completion.

In practice, the *process* of producing the specification can be as important as or even more important than the specification itself. The knowledge gained by the specifier in preparation before consideration of implementation details can be invaluable in resolving errors before the detailed design and subsequent stages, making them much cheaper to correct. In this section we consider typical questions posed during the specification process when using the Z notation for the first case study.

Question 1: What *given sets* are needed for the specification?

Answer: Z, as a typed language, provides the facility of including a number of distinct sets (called '*given sets*' or '*basic types*') for subsequent use in a specification. The sets are potentially infinite unless limited to being finite later in the specification. The set of integers $\mathbb{Z}$ is available in all Z specifications as part of the standard mathematical 'toolkit' library. Other given sets are normally discovered as a Z specification is formulated. Here we define sets of order identifiers and products which can potentially be held in stock:

$[OrderId, Product]$

The exact nature of the elements of these set is unimportant to the specification and is thus not elaborated further. An implementor would chose a specific representation for them in due course.

Question 2: What states can orders have?

Answer: The requirements mention two states, 'pending' and 'invoiced'.

We define a set *OrderState* with just two elements in it to model the states of *pending* and *invoiced* which an order can take as it progresses:

$OrderState ::= pending \mid invoiced$

Here *OrderState* is defined as a given set, but is limited to having two distinct elements, *pending* and *invoiced*, representing different possible states. Further states could be added later if that proves to be necessary.

Question 3: What *abstract state* is needed to model the system?

Answer: In Z, operations normally act on an abstract state, relating a *before state* to an *after state*. We need to model the state products in stock and orders including their invoicing status.

The quantity of each of the products in stock needs to be recorded, so a bag (also known as multiset) can be used to model this in a *vertical schema* called *Stock*:

$$\begin{array}{|l}\text{\textit{Stock}}\\\hline stock : \text{bag}\, Product\\\end{array}$$

This includes a single *state component*, a bag called *stock* drawn from the set of bag *Product*. In Z, as with many programming languages, the ':' in declarations can be read as 'is a member of' like '∈' in predicates. Note that Z is case sensitive and many Z specifications use this in standard ways to help the reader. For example, here lower case names are used for state components and names starting with an upper case letter are used for given sets and schema names.

In the Z toolkit, the set of bags is defined as: bag $X == X \nrightarrow \mathbb{N}_1$, the set of partial functions between some set X and the strictly positive integers (greater than zero). This allows a record of the number of products in stock in the *Stock* schema above. For example, if *nuts* and *bolts* are valid products, then $stock = \{nuts \mapsto 5, bolts \mapsto 6\}$ would indicate that there are 5 *nuts* and 6 *bolts* in stock. $a \mapsto b$ is a graphic *maplet* notation used in Z to indicate the *Cartesian product* pair (a, b).

Question 4: Is it really required that an order be limited to a single type of product and an associated quantity or would a set of these be preferable?

Answer: The informal requirements indicate this, but it might be considered over-restrictive. A user may wish to order several types of product at once and this should be discussed with the customer. Here we assume that the customer decides to allow orders of one *or more* products for extra flexibility, but not empty orders (i.e., an order for no products).

Since *stock* is defined as a bag of products, it is convenient to define an order as a bag of products too. However, whereas the stock may be completely empty, an order must consist of one (or more) products:

$Order == \{order : \text{bag}\, Product \mid order \neq \emptyset\}$

In the above, *Order* is defined using an *abbreviation definition* ('==') and *set comprehension* ('{... | ...}'). Subsequently, any use of *Order* is the equivalent of using the right hand side of this definition directly. This is useful for expressions that are reused a number of times during a specification. The properties of the expression can be introduced in one place informally; the expression can be given a name formally and then used later as required. The constraint predicated after the '|' in the set comprehension above (which can be read as 'such that') normally limits the declaration(s) in some way (here to being non-empty).

The predicate constraint $order \neq \emptyset$ could also have been equivalently written as $\#order > 0$ or $\#order \geq 1$ where '#' indicates the cardinality (size) of a set. If it was decided that only a single product is to be allowed we could write $\#order = 1$. This would allow us to easily change the specification subsequently if the customer changes his/her mind. We could even allow empty orders ($Order ==$ bag $Product$). The rest of the specification can be left the same, whichever of these choices are made.

Continuing with the definition of the abstract model, the status of orders can be modelled as a function from an identifying $OrderId$ to their state (*pending* or *invoiced*). State components $orderStatus$ and $orders$ are packaged into an $OrderInvoices$ schema with appropriate *type* information:

$$
\begin{array}{|l}
\hline
\_OrderInvoices _____ \\
orders : OrderId \nrightarrow Order \\
orderStatus : OrderId \nrightarrow OrderState \\
\hline
\mathrm{dom}\ orders = \mathrm{dom}\ orderStatus \\
\hline
\end{array}
$$

Here, $orderStatus$ and $orders$ are *partial functions* from the set $OrderId$. The functions are partial (i.e., their domains do not necessary cover the whole of the $OrderId$ set in this case) since only valid orders are mapped in this way.

All orders have a status associated with them. This type of general information that must apply at all times (whatever the specific state of the system at any given time) is presented as a state *invariant* predicate in most Z specifications (e.g., dom $orders =$ dom $orderStatus$ above, constraining the domains of both functions to always be the same).

Question 5: Should order identifiers be unique for the entire lifetime of the system?

Answer: We could decide that new identifiers must never have been used previously or that they just need to be unique at any given time. The state specification so far assumes the former, which is easiest. However, if the latter is required, we must augment the state with further information on fresh new references that can be issued at any particular time.

The schemas $Stock$ and $OrderInvoices$ can be combined in a new $State$ schema using *schema inclusion*, together with a further state component $newids$. The inclusion of $Stock$ and $OrderInvoices$ means all the declarations and associated predicates are available.

```
┌─ State ──────────────────────────────────────
│ Stock
│ OrderInvoices
│ newids : ℙ OrderId
│─────────────────────────────────────────────
│ dom orders ∩ newids = ∅
└─────────────────────────────────────────────
```

Question 6: What initial state is required for the system?

Answer: The requirements do not make this clear; if not defined in Z, the system could start in any valid state that satisfies any state invariants. Typically many state components are most usefully initialised to empty sets or some predetermined value. For example:

```
┌─ InitState ──────────────────────────────────
│ State'
│─────────────────────────────────────────────
│ stock' = ∅
│ orders' = ∅
│ newids' = OrderId
└─────────────────────────────────────────────
```

The decoration "'" added to the *State* schema included above percolates through to all the state components declared in the schema ($stock'$, etc.). Note that all the predicates are combined using conjunction by default. $orderStatus' = \emptyset$ is implied by the state invariant dom $orders'$ = dom $orderStatus'$ from the *OrderInvoices'* schema and hence can be omitted. All possible identifiers are available for use initially.

Question 7: Are there any constraints that apply for all operations on the system?

Answer: If so, they may be specified using the 'Δ' convention of Z:

```
┌─ ΔState ─────────────────────────────────────
│ State
│ State'
│─────────────────────────────────────────────
│ newids' = newids \ dom orders'
└─────────────────────────────────────────────
```

Here an undashed *before state* (*State*) and a matching dashed *after state* (*State'*) are included.

If any new identifiers are used for orders (and hence their status) these are no longer available for use by any subsequent operation. Thus they are removed from the set of new identifiers. Any operation including $\Delta State$ need not explicitly consider the value of *newids'* since it will automatically be handled by the predicate in the schema above.

A change of state is specified using the $\Delta State$ schema convention. This defines a 'before' state *State* (which includes the four state component *stock*, *orderStatus*, *orders* and *newids* in this case) and an 'after' state *Invoices'* which includes matching dashed state component (*stock'*, etc.).

Question 8: What operations are required?

Answer: Only a single operation to invoice an order seems to be required since many aspects do not have to be taken into account.

Question 9: What inputs and/or outputs are needed by the operation?

Answer: An input *id?* is required to specify which invoice is to be updated. Note that in Z, a trailing '?' indicates an input and a trailing '!' indicates an output by convention.

Question 10: What *preconditions* apply?

Answer: In Z, preconditions are predicates in operations that apply only to before states and inputs. Preconditions may be calculated by existentially quantifying the after states and outputs and then simplifying the resulting predicate. See later for an example.

For an order to be successfully invoiced, there must be enough stock available to fulfil the order and the status must be pending. These are *preconditions* that must be satisfied to change the order state to *invoiced*.

Question 11: What is the effect of the operation?

Answer: The effect of the operation is a relation between the before state and inputs with the after state and outputs, proving a *postcondition* for the operation. Often, although not always, this can be specified *explicitly* (e.g., in the form $stock' = \ldots$, etc. for all after state components and outputs). Indeed, checking for predicates in this form is a useful check to ensure that no important postconditions have been omitted. The lack of a predicate in this form for a particular after state component or output is not necessarily an indication of an error in the specification, but it is all too easy to omit a predicate of the form $x' = x$ when no change of state is required.

All this information discussed above is included formally in an *InvoiceOrder* operation:

─── *InvoiceOrder* ──────────────────────────
$\Delta State$
$id? : OrderId$
─────────────────────────────
$orders(id?) \sqsubseteq stock$
$orderStatus(id?) = pending$
$stock' = stock \uplus orders(id?)$
$orders' = orders$
$orderStatus' = orderStatus \oplus \{id? \mapsto invoiced\}$
──────────────────────────────────────

$\sqsubseteq$ is the sub-bag relational operator from the Z toolkit. Above this ensures a precondition that their are enough quantities of the required product(s) in stock. For example, $\{nuts \mapsto 3\} \sqsubseteq \{nuts \mapsto 5, bolts \mapsto 6\}$ is *true*.

Another precondition is that the status of the order must be *pending*. If the preconditions are satisfied, the required product quantities are removed from the available stock using the bag difference operator ('$\uplus$', cf. the set difference operator '\' for sets). Here for example, $\{nuts \mapsto 5, bolts \mapsto 6\} \uplus \{nuts \mapsto 3\}$ would result in $\{nuts \mapsto 2, bolts \mapsto 6\}$.

The precondition $id? \in \text{dom } orders$ could be included if an explicit check for $id?$ being a valid existing order identifier is required. This is also equivalent to $id? \in \text{dom } orderStatus$ because of the invariant $\text{dom } orders = \text{dom } orderStatus$. However this precondition is implied by both the preconditions included in the *InvoiceOrder* implicitly since $id?$ is applied to *orders* and *orderStatus* using *function application*; this is only valid if $id?$ (in this case) is in the domain of the function. Here we decide to omit an explicit check for simplicity. However, consideration of this precondition as a separate case could affect the errors conditions returned by the complete operation (see later) and this should be discussed with the customer.

The orders themselves are unaffected by the operation above, as specified by $orders' = orders$. The order status is updated to *invoiced* using the *overriding* operator ('$\oplus$') from the Z toolkit. This operator is commonly used in Z specifications to update a small part of state components that are binary relations (often functions) in Z operation schema. Here the state of the maplet $id? \mapsto pending$ is replaced by a new maplet $id? \mapsto invoiced$, leaving the status of all other orders unchanged.

Question 12: What about error conditions?

Answer: Normally successful operations, where the preconditions are satisfied and the operation does what is required, are considered first in Z. The precondition can be calculated and the error condition(s) must have a precondition which handle the negation of this to eventually produce a *total operation* with a precondition of *true* (i.e., it can be invoked safely at any time) by combining the successful and error cases using disjunction.

Question 13: Are *error reports* required?

Answer: Nothing is said in the requirements, but most customers would wish to know if an operation was successful or not once it has been undertaken. They will probably wish to know the nature of the error as will if more than one error is possible in a particular operation. Thus we define a set of possible reports from operations:

$Report ::= OK \mid order\_not\_pending \mid not\_enough\_stock \mid no\_more\_ids$

If further error reports prove necessary (e.g., if the system is upgraded later), they could be added to *Report* above as required subsequently. Above we define all error reports used in this chapter.

For successful operations, a suitable report is normally required to inform the user. Since this is a standard feature of successful operations, this can be separated out in a separate schema production an output report $rep!$:

$\begin{array}{|l}\hline \text{\_Success_____} \\ rep! : Report \\ \hline rep! = OK \\ \hline \end{array}$

Question 14: What if the order state is not pending?

Answer: For error cases where the precondition does not hold, it is normal to assume the state is not to change. We define an error schema with a precondition that is the negation of one of the preconditions in the *InvoiceOrder* schema:

$\begin{array}{|l}\hline \text{\_InvoiceError_____} \\ \Xi State \\ id? : OrderId \\ rep! : Report \\ \hline orderStatus(id?) \neq pending \\ rep! = order\_not\_pending \\ \hline \end{array}$

$\Xi State$ ensures that all the dashed state components in the after state are the same as the matching undashed state components in the before state; in this case, $stock' = stock \wedge \ldots$ Thus, the entire state afterwards is the same as the state before in the case of the error above.

Question 15: What if not enough stock is available for the order?

Answer: Here we return an alternative error report so the user can detect which error has occurred:

$\begin{array}{|l}\hline \text{\_StockError_____} \\ \Xi State \\ id? : OrderId \\ rep! : Report \\ \hline \neg\ orders(id?) \sqsubseteq stock \\ rep! = not\_enough\_stock \\ \hline \end{array}$

Question 16: Should either error take priority if they both occur?

Answer: If so, an extra predicate giving the negation of the other error's precondition will be needed in one or other error schema above. If not, perhaps because the customer has no preference, this can be left non-deterministic. The decision can then be made by the implementor, depending on which is easiest, most efficient, etc., in the final design. It is good practice to leave design decisions to after the specification stage if they are not important at this point to give the design team as much freedom as possible in the implementation.

An error schema covering the case of $id? \notin \text{dom } orders$ explicitly (i.e., the specified $id?$ is not a valid order in the system) could also be added if required by the customer, but we have omitted this case here for brevity. Instead one or other of the two errors that are included may be returned (non-deterministically) in this case.

A total operation for ordering where the precondition is *true* can now be specified:

$InvoiceOrderOp ==$
$\quad (InvoiceOrder \wedge Success) \vee InvoiceError \vee StockError$

The above is a *horizontal schema* definition for a new schema $InvoiceOrderOp$ in terms of a number of existing schemas. These are combined using schema operators, namely schema conjunction ('$\wedge$') and disjunction ('$\vee$'), based on the matching logical connectives. Both operators merge the state components of the schemas involved. Any components with the same name must be type-compatible (and are normally declared in an identical manner to avoid confusion). The predicates in the schemas involved are combined using logical conjunction or disjunction respectively.

Schema conjunction is normally used when building up a larger specification from smaller specification parts. Schema disjunction is normally used when specifying choice between two or more alternatives, typically successful and error operations. Normally any preconditions are disjoint to avoid any unexpected consequences. In a total operation, the disjunction of all the preconditions of the schema being combined is *true*.

If we do not have to take new orders, cancellations and addition to the stock into account, no other operations are required. However the precondition of the $InvoiceOrder$ operation schema is such that the invoice must already be *pending* and there must be enough stock available to fulfil the order. Other operations are needed to make these true. Here we could assume that an arbitrary operation $\Delta State$ can be invoked at any time before $InvoiceOrderOp$ operations.

In Z, exactly which schemas represent the abstract state, initial state and allowed operations is normally left informal and is just indicated in the accompanying text. There is no syntactic feature to distinguish these in Z, although some tools (e.g., the ZANS animator) have hidden directives to indicate these if required. In this particular example, the allowed operations is an area that would certainly need further discussion with the customer to avoid any misunderstanding.

1.3 Analysis and Specification of Case 2

Question 17: What extra operations are needed?

Answer: Assuming that Case 2 is an extension of Case 1, three further operations are indicated from the requirements to handle new orders, cancellation of orders and entries of quantities in the stock. However, these are not elaborated further.

Question 18: What inputs/outputs, preconditions and postconditions need to be included for an operation to handle new orders?

Answer: An order must be provided as an input and a valid fresh identifier is output by the operation. A new order leaves the stock unchanged but updates the orders and their status appropriately.

$$
\begin{array}{|l}
\hline
\_NewOrder _____ \\
\Delta State \\
order? : Order \\
id! : OrderId \\
\hline
id! \in newids \\
stock' = stock \\
orders' = orders \cup \{id! \mapsto order?\} \\
orderStatus' = orderStatus \cup \{id! \mapsto pending\} \\
\hline
\end{array}
$$

Note that $id!$ is not explicitly set and can be any convenient new identifier. Here we assume that the status of the new order is *pending*; this should be discussed with the customer to check that this is what is actually required.

Question 19: When cancelling an order, is information concerning the order to be retained by the system?

Answer: We could either remove all information associated with the order from the system completely, or retain this information for possible future use. Here we assume that the information is no longer required, which is the simplest option, but this should be discussed with the customer. Perhaps some sort of auditing will be required of the system, including cancelled orders.

Question 20: What inputs/outputs, preconditions and postconditions are required for an operation to handle cancellations of orders?

Answer: Cancelling an order completely removes an existing order (determined by a valid order identifier input $id?$) from the system:

$$
\begin{array}{|l}
\hline
\textit{CancelOrder} \\
\Delta State \\
id?: OrderId \\
\hline
orderStatus(id?) = pending \\
stock' = stock \\
orders' = \{id?\} \mathbin{\lhd\!\!\!-} orders \\
orderStatus' = \{id?\} \mathbin{\lhd\!\!\!-} orderStatus \\
\hline
\end{array}
$$

The Z toolkit domain anti-restriction operator '$\mathbin{\lhd\!\!\!-}$' used above removes part of a relation (often a function) where the domain overlaps with a specified set. In the above example, a single element is removed in each case. We have assumed that the status of the order to be cancelled is *pending* as opposed to *invoiced* since this avoids problems of re-adding stock; this should be discussed with the customer. As for the *InvoiceOrder* operation previously, $id? \in \text{dom } orders$ is implied.

Note that cancelled order identifiers can in fact be inferred as $OrderId \setminus (newsids \cup \text{dom } orders)$ given the operation above. This could be useful if further requirements are added in the future.

Question 21: Is the finiteness of stock quantities (or any other state component for that matter) important?

Answer: Here natural numbers have been used for stock quantities and these are potentially infinite and hence of unbounded size in any corresponding implementation. Practical implementations will require some limit on the maximum size of stock, often determined by the system's computer architecture. If this is to be modelled in the specification, additional preconditions and error schemas will be required. In the specification below we assume no such requirements, but finiteness of state components is something that should always be discussed with the customer in practice.

Question 22: What inputs/outputs, preconditions and postconditions are required for an operation to handle entries of quantities in the stock?

Answer: Entering new stock can be effected using bag union:

$$
\begin{array}{|l}
\hline
\textit{EnterStock} \\
\Delta State \\
newstock?: \text{bag } Product \\
\hline
stock' = stock \uplus newstock? \\
orders' = orders \\
orderStatus' = orderStatus \\
\hline
\end{array}
$$

The bag union operator ('$\uplus$') takes two bags and forms a new bag consisting of the sums of matching elements in these two bags (or just the elements in cases where there is no match). For example, $\{nuts \mapsto 5, bolts \mapsto 6\} \uplus \{nuts \mapsto 3, washers \mapsto 1\}$ would result in $\{nuts \mapsto 8, bolts \mapsto 6, washers \mapsto 1\}$.

Here we assume that there is no limit on the amount of stock that can be held; in practice there may be a limit; this should be discussed with the customer and added as a precondition if appropriate.

Question 23: Are error reports required and to what level of detail?

Answer: Most customers will want operations to report errors and take appropriate action in these cases (typically although not always leaving the system state unchanged). The error report could simply be some status value or further information could be useful. Details of error handling are often omitted or glossed over in requirements documents, but should be discussed in detail with the customer before implementation. Producing a Z specification and calculating preconditions of successful operation is a good way to determine what errors are relevant to each operation. In Case 2, the following additional error reports are needed.

In the *NewOrder* operation $id! \in newids$ implies that $newids \neq \emptyset$. This is an example of an *implicit precondition* (i.e., a precondition that is not explicitly stated). Such preconditions can be found by formally calculating the precondition. This involves existentially quantifying the after states and outputs:

$\exists State'; id! : OrderId \bullet$
$\quad newids' = newids \setminus \mathrm{dom}\, orders' \land$
$\quad id! \in newids \land$
$\quad stock' = stock \land$
$\quad orders' = orders \cup \{id! \mapsto order?\} \land$
$\quad orderStatus' = orderStatus \cup \{id! \mapsto pending\}$

The *one-point rule* allows existentially quantified variables that occur once in the form '$x = \ldots$' to be eliminated, giving:

$\exists id! : OrderId \bullet id! \in newids$

Since for an element to be a member of a set, the set must be non-empty, this simplifies to:

$newids \neq \emptyset$

Because of this implicit precondition, the (perhaps unlikely) event of running out of new identifiers needs to be handled:

―― *IdError* ――――――――――――――――――
$\Xi State$
$rep! : Report$
――――――――――
$newids = \emptyset$
$rep! = no\_more\_ids$

Notice that the value of *id*! is not explicitly defined in the case of an error and thus could take on any value.

The total operations with appropriate reports can now be specified:

$NewOrderOp == (NewOrder \land Success) \lor IdError$

$CancelOrderOp == (CancelOrder \land Success) \lor InvoiceError$

$EnterStockOp == (EnterStock \land Success)$

Question 24: Are further operations such as status operations required?

Answer: It is often useful to have operations which return part of the state while leaving the system state unchanged. Once an abstract state for the modelling of the system has been formulated, this can be inspected and potentially useful status operations can be suggested to the customer. In this case, the state components comprise of *orderStatus*, *stock* and *orders* and information on any of these could be returned.

1.4 Validation of the Specification

There are a number of checks that are worth performing on a Z specification once a draft has been formulated to reduce the number of errors it contains. For example:

- Check that the change of state for all components of the abstract state has been considered in every operation. It is easy to forget some parts of the state, in which case the meaning of the specification is that the after state for that component is totally unrelated to the before state and thus may take on any arbitrary value in an implementation. This is rarely what the customer wants in practice.

- Check that preconditions of successful and error parts of operations are disjoint in general. Otherwise there may be incompatibilities or potentially even a *false* specification otherwise.

- Check that preconditions of total operations are *true*. If they are not, there some cases that are not specified and which may be problematic in the implementation or subsequent maintenance.

- Check the specification type-checks using a mechanical type-checker. If the specification is not type-correct it is meaningless in a formal sense, although of course it can still impart some useful information to a human reader. There are a number of both free (e.g., ZTC) and commercial (e.g., CADiZ, Formaliser and fUZZ) Z type-checkers now available, so there is no excuse not to type-check all but the most trivial Z specifications. The Z text presented in this chapter has been type-checked using the fUZZ and ZTC tools.

- Attempt validation proofs to check the specification behaves as expected. If provable, these help in confirming the correct understanding and intuition of the specification; if they turn out to be false this may indicate a problem in the specification, or at least in the understanding of it. Mechanical tool support for proofs in Z, such as Z/EVES, is available, but takes a significant amount of skill to use effectively.
- Animate the specification (e.g., using the ZANS animator associated with the ZTC type-checker). This can be useful to check the specification acts as expected, but will typically only work for 'explicit' and finite cases where the after state and output are defined explicitly and deterministically in terms of the before state and inputs. Normally a specification will need some adaptation to allow it to be animated. Nevertheless, this may prove to be a useful exercise in the removal of errors from the original specification. Indeed, ZANS reports whether operations are *explicit* (i.e., all the after state components and outputs are deterministically defined in terms of the before state components and inputs) and this is itself useful information for checking a specification.

  An alternative approach is to rapid-prototype the specification in a high-level programming paradigm, such as a logic or functional programming language. Prolog is a popular choice for rapid-prototyping Z specifications.

Note that a Z specification cannot be *verified* formally in general since there is (normally) no other mathematical description to verify it against. Typically requirements used to produce a formal specification are informal (e.g., natural language, diagrams, etc.), and this is certainly true in this case.

However it is possible to *validate* a Z specification by posing challenge hypotheses that are believed (and hoped) to be true for the intuition of the developer. Proving these to be true increases the confidence in the correctness of the specification (i.e., that the specification is what is required).

Checks on the consistency of the specification can also be formally undertaken as proofs. For example, the existence of an initial state for the entire system, or a post-state for each operation, can be checked. In general it is considered desirable in Z to specify total operations where the precondition is *true* (as demonstrated earlier in this chapter). The precondition for each operation can be formally calculated to check this (as done earlier for the *NewOrder* operation in Section 1.3).

Animation (attempting to execute the specification directly) or rapid-prototyping (producing an executable version of the specification with minimal development using a very high-level programming language, e.g., in the form of a logic program or a functional program) are additional approaches that help in the validation of the specification.

1.5 The Natural Language Description of the Specifications

The Z-style of specification dictates that the natural language description should accompany the formal Z text. This is what has been done in Sections 1.2 and 1.3 although extra didactic material has also been included.

Typically the informal description is of approximately the same length as the formal description, and certainly this is a good guideline to follow. It is a good aim to describe the system being specified in a form such that removal of the formal text would still render an understandable informal document. Often it is found that producing a formal Z document results in a better, clearer, less ambiguous informal description of the system as well (e.g., for inclusion in a manual or for presentation to a customer).

1.6 Conclusion

Z is mainly used at the specification level. Some data and operation refinement is possible in Z but at some point a jump to code must be made, typically informally. A program is considered correct with respect to a Z specification operation if it can be run in more situations (the precondition is more relaxed) or if it is more deterministic (the postcondition is more strict). However, many Z operations already have a precondition of *true* (i.e., the operation is 'total' and can be used in any situation) and are often 'explicit' (i.e., the operation is deterministic). In the operations specified in this chapter, total operations have been provided. Most of the operations are explicit apart from the allocation of identifiers for new orders.

If an operation is invoked in a state where it is not defined, then anything can happen. It is typically not desirable, and is the reason why total operations are normally specified.

If significant formal development is required, it is normally better to use a notation designed for this, such as B. However, many systems can cost-effectively benefit from formal specification alone, to help in avoiding the introduction of errors at the specification stage. In this case, Z is a very appropriate general purpose formal specification to use. Normally, formal *development* is much more expensive than formal *specification* and may only be worthwhile in very high-integrity systems [3].

The Z specification in this chapter was originally produced in less than a day. Problems, inconsistencies and misunderstandings have been resolved by the author alone on an ad hoc basis. A number of specific questions have been raised explicitly and possible different specifications presented. The next step in practice would be to discuss these with the customer to solve the issues; however this has not yet been done. Thus the case study specification as presented is a specification in the course of construction and perhaps has added interest for that reason.

For further on-line information on Z maintained by the author, see:

http://archive.comlab.ox.ac.uk/z.html

References

1. Bowen J.P. (1996) Formal Specification and Documentation Using Z: A Case Study Approach. International Thomson Computer Press, London
2. Bowen J.P., Hinchey M.G. (1997) Formal models and the specification process. In: Tucker, Jr. A.B. (Ed.) The Computer Science and Engineering Handbook. CRC Press, chapter 107, 2302–2322.
3. Bowen J.P., Hinchey M.G. (1999) High-Integrity System Specification and Design. Formal Approaches to Computing and Information Technology series (FACIT). Springer-Verlag, London
4. Hayes I.J. (Ed.) (1993) Specification Case Studies 2nd edition. Prentice Hall International Series in Computer Science, London
5. Jacky J. (1997) The Way of Z: Practical Programming with Formal Methods. Cambridge University Press, Cambridge
6. Potter B.F., Sinclair J.E., Till D. (1996) An Introduction to Formal Specification and Z, 2nd edition. Prentice Hall International Series in Computer Science, London
7. Spivey J.M. (1988) Understanding Z: A Specification Language and its Formal Semantics. Volume 3, Cambridge Tracts in Theoretical Computer Science. Cambridge University Press, Cambridge
8. Spivey J.M. (1992) The Z Notation: A Reference Manual, 2nd edition. Prentice Hall International Series in Computer Science, London
9. Wing J.M. (1990) A specifier's introduction to formal methods. IEEE Computer, 23(9):8–24. Also in [3], 167–199
10. Woodcock J.C.P., Davies J. (1996) Using Z: Specification, Proof and Refinement. Prentice Hall International Series in Computer Science, London

2 SAZ: SSADM Version 4 and Z

Fiona Polack

2.1 Overview of the SAZ Method

SAZ [4,6] is an integrated method developed at the University of York[1]. The method takes a diagram-and-text specification and develops a formal description of (Z) state and operations. SAZ was originally developed [7] for use with SSADM version 4, and has been shown to raise issues which are not traditionally apparent in systems analysis and design [5].

SAZ and SSADM. SSADM version 4 [2,3] and its subsequent variants form the UK *de facto* standard for information systems development. The method is best suited to complex, multi-analyst projects. However, the philosophy of SSADM version 4 is adaptation, and it is thus possible to apply selected parts of the method to much smaller information systems, such as these case studies. SSADM version 4 provides a development structure, and suggested diagram-and-text techniques.

SAZ uses SSADM Requirements Specification (RS). This is derived from a Requirements Analysis (RA which extracts and clarifies requirements using high-level data and functional models. RS specifies an abstract system to meet the requirements using data, dynamic and functional models. SSADM includes minimal cross-checking among its models; constraints (dynamic and static) are not routinely recorded.

The first task of the developer is to determine which parts of the method are appropriate for a project. The RA techniques used on the case studies comprise an entity-relationship diagram with simple documentation and a logical data flow diagram (DFD). Using the SSADM RS techniques, the data model is then validated against the scope of the system. The data flow diagram is reworked to *function definitions*. These, rather than the DFDs, are the specification of system processing. Function definitions are text descriptions of the processing required of the system, and are derived by identifying system events and tracing their effects through the DFD. SSADM advises that the results are referred to

---

[1] The project, which was carried out at the Department of Computer Science, University of York, 1990-94, was supported by the UK Science and Engineering Research Council under grants GR/F98529 and GR/J81655.

client users, who may combine, divide or replicate the functions. The RS also considers the dynamics of each entity, using entity life histories (ELHs).

The case studies use the notations suggested (but not mandated) by SSADM version 4. The specifications are developed sequentially through the chapter.

SAZ and Z. This chapter uses a conventional Z approach[2] and Z notations defined in the draft standard [8]. Data types (for attribute domains) are defined as Z given sets, enumerated types and schemas. Schemas define the types of entities, sets of instances, and relationships. Z processing is defined on the combined state schema. Z specifications of SSADM function definitions are completed using schema calculus [9].

2.2 Analysis and Specification of Case 1

The SSADM **RA** is expressed as a high level data model and a data flow model.

Question 1: What entities and relationships can be identified?

Answer: The case study refers to orders and quantities ordered from stock. These are modelled as order and product entities. It is assumed that orders have customers. Each instance of product must be related to one or more instances of order, whilst each instance of order must be related to exactly one product.

Question 2: How are customer and order instances related?

Answer: Customers could be either tightly bound to orders or allowed to exist independently. The former is assumed here.

These features are modelled in Figure 2.1. In the diagram, boxes represent entity types; lines represent relationships between the entities. The diagram states that an instance of order must be related to one customer and one product; an instance of customer must be related to one or more orders; an instance of product may be related to some orders.

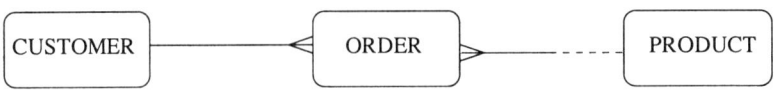

Fig. 2.1. SSADM-style Logical Data Model

---

[2] SAZ Z style has varied over the years. The Z in this case study is close to the original SAZ approach [7], which is less elegant than later work. Presentation follows the style of [1]. The Z in this chapter has been type-checked and set using the CADiZ tool, available by ftp, see http://www-users.cs.york.ac.uk/˜ian/cadiz/.

Question 3: What information does the system hold on these entities?
Answer: It is stated that orders are for quantities of a product, and that products have a stock level. No other data is within the scope of the system.

Question 4: How is it known that an order has been invoiced?
Answer: It is stated that the status of orders changes from *pending* to *invoiced*.

The SSADM data dictionary which accompanies the data model would comprise dozens of forms, at too low a level of abstraction. Here, the attributes of each entity in Figure 2.1 are summarised as a simple table:

ORDER	quantity ; status
PRODUCT	stock level

Question 5: What processes, data stores and external entities exist?
Answer: There is only an order-processing process. This interacts with stored orders and stock levels. Although external entities must be involved in triggering this processing, these are outside the case study scope.

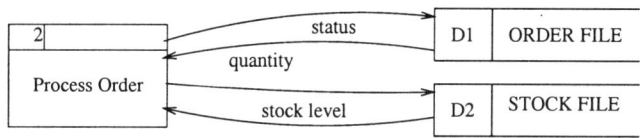

Fig. 2.2. DFD using SSADM logical DFD notations

Figure 2.2 shows the single process, *Process Order*. The arrows are data flows to and from the data stores, *Order File* and *Stock File*. Additional documentation is not included, since the explanation is the case study text.

In SSADM RA, data stores on DFDs correspond to one or more entities from the data model. This is a non-rigorous matching, in which some entities, or attributes may be present in more than one data store. Here, the order file comprises the order and customer entities; the stock file is the product entity.

The **RS** comprises a data model and a SSADM function definition. There is no significant dynamic component to the system.

Extending the Data Model. Using SSADM's approach, relational identifiers are added to the data model created in the RA.

Question 6: Are there any unique identifiers inherent in the system?
Answer: None is described.

Conventionally, identifiers are either an existing (set of) attribute(s) which must have a unique value for any tuple, or an attribute added to act as a surrogate key. The latter is used, since the data specification is abstract, and there are no grounds for assessing the properties of potential tuples. The surrogate attributes are named with the entity name followed by *Id*.

Function Definitions. There is one function definition, corresponding to the process in Figure 2.2.

Question 7: Are all orders processed as soon as they are received?
Answer: Yes. The set of orders is always up-to-date.

Question 8: How are orders validated and processed?
Answer: Implicitly, the order must be for an existing product. The detail of the processing algorithm is not relevant at this level of abstraction. This is represented as an atomic (i.e., indivisible) process which, when there is sufficient stock, reduces the quantity in stock and sets the status of the order to *invoiced*.

Question 9: What happens to any partially met orders?
Answer: An order is met either in full or not at all. An order which cannot be met is explicitly still *pending*.

The SSADM-style function definition is expressed as follows.

Function Definition 1: Process Order
Order processing involves checking the stock level of the ordered product. The order status is set to *invoiced* if it can be met from stock and to *pending* otherwise. The stock level is reduced by the ordered amount.

2.2.1 Z Specification

The Z State in SAZ defines data types, entity types, entity sets, and then the full state including relationship representations.

Question 10: What are the domains (sets of permitted values) of the quantity and stock level attributes?
Answer: The domains need to be numeric.

The most general solution would be to use real numbers which could represent volumes of a product. However, the less-general integer (whole number) type is used here, since this is the only built-in type in Z. It is assumed that stock level is at least 0 (i.e., the domain is natural numbers), that quantity at least 1, and that the domains have the same upper limit.

The Z defines domains by defining two subsets of natural numbers. This captures the required minima and imposes an arbitrary upper limit, *MAX*.

$MAX : \mathbb{N}_1$
$STOCK\_LEVEL == 0 \mathinner{.\,.} MAX$
$QUANTITY == 1 \mathinner{.\,.} MAX$

The domain of the *status* attribute is defined explicitly by enumeration:

$STATUS ::= pending \mid invoiced$

The entity identifiers (Question 6) are defined as Z given sets since their details are irrelevant at this level of specification.

$[CUSTOMER\_ID, ORDER\_ID, PRODUCT\_ID]$

The set of customers is simply a set of identifiers.

$CUSTOMER\_SET == [customers : \mathbb{F}\ CUSTOMER\_ID]$

The other entity type definitions use Z schemas to declare the attributes and domains, and then define sets of instances using partial functions from identifiers to the entity type[3].

$ORDER == [quantity : QUANTITY;\ status : STATUS]$

$ORDER\_SET == [orders : ORDER\_ID \nrightarrow ORDER]$

$PRODUCT == [stockLevel : STOCK\_LEVEL]$

$PRODUCT\_SET == [products : PRODUCT\_ID \nrightarrow PRODUCT]$

Question 11: Can a customer place more than one order for the same product?

Answer: The case study is not explicit about customers. The SSADM data model is not capable of expressing such structural constraints. The options are that multiple orders for the same product are permitted or multiple orders are not permitted. The former is selected here since it is a more abstract solution.

The complete state schema includes the three entity set definitions, and adds Z declarations expressing the relationships in Figure 2.1. The predicates express each entity's participation in the relationships: mandatory relationships are represented by equality; optional relationships by set inclusion.

―― STATE ――――――――――――――――――――――――――
$CUSTOMER\_SET;\ ORDER\_SET;\ PRODUCT\_SET$
$orderCustomerRel : ORDER\_ID \nrightarrow CUSTOMER\_ID$
$orderProductRel : ORDER\_ID \nrightarrow PRODUCT\_ID$
―――――――――――――――――――――――――――――――
$\text{dom}\ orderCustomerRel = \text{dom}\ orderProductRel = \text{dom}\ orders$
$\text{ran}\ orderCustomerRel = customers$
$\text{ran}\ orderProductRel \subseteq \text{dom}\ products$
―――――――――――――――――――――――――――――――

---

[3] These are presented in horizontal format to save space.

The Z processing. models the semantics of the SSADM function definition, above (see Question 8). There is no consideration of how orders arrive.

Following common Z practice, SAZ defines the processing schemas and corresponding error schemas. These do not update the state, but output explanatory messages. Conventional Z style uses an output message for each possible outcome. The following message type is defined here.

$PROCESS\_MESSAGE ::= stockTooLow \mid alreadyProcessed \mid orderNotThere \mid unknownProcessError \mid processedOK$

The processing input is an order identifier, and its output is the appropriate message. The predicates specify the operation preconditions (Question 8), that the order exists, that it is in the *pending* state, and that there is sufficient stock of the ordered product. The operation postcondition, also expressed as a predicate, updates the state of the order and the level of stock for the ordered product. Other state elements are unchanged.

```
┌─ PROCESS_ORDER ─────────────────────────────────────
│ ΔSTATE; Ξ CUSTOMER_SET
│ ordId? : ORDER_ID
│ processingMessage! : PROCESS_MESSAGE
├─────────────────────────────────────────────────────
│ ordId? ∈ dom orders ∧ (orders ordId?).status = pending
│ (products(orderProductRel ordId?)).stockLevel ≥
│     (orders ordId?).quantity
│ (orders' ordId?).status = invoiced
│ (products(orderProductRel' ordId?)).stockLevel =
│     (products(orderProductRel ordId?)).stockLevel −
│     (orders' ordId?).quantity
│ dom products' = dom products
│ orderProductRel' = orderProductRel
│ orderCustomerRel' = orderCustomerRel
│ processingMessage! = processedOK
└─────────────────────────────────────────────────────
```

The Z error schema specifies that the state does not change. Its predicates comprise the negations of the precondition predicates in the above schema, each of which returns an appropriate error message.

$$\begin{array}{|l}
\text{\underline{}} PROCESS\_ORDER\_ERR \text{\underline{}} \\
\Xi STATE \\
ordId? : ORDER\_ID \\
processingMessage! : PROCESS\_MESSAGE \\
\hline
processingMessage! = \\
\quad (\text{if } ordId? \notin \text{dom } orders \text{ then } orderNotThere \\
\quad \text{else}(\text{if}(orders\ ordId?).status \neq pending \\
\qquad \text{then } alreadyProcessed \\
\quad \text{else}(\text{if}(products(orderProductRel\ ordId?)).stockLevel < \\
\qquad (orders\ ordId?).quantity \text{ then } stockTooLow \\
\quad \text{else } unknownProcessError)))
\end{array}$$

The specification is completed using a schema calculus disjunction.

$ProcessFunction == PROCESS\_ORDER \vee PROCESS\_ORDER\_ERR$

2.3 Analysis and Specification of Case 2

The case study defines a single state space. Thus, the data model and Z state are not changed for Case 2.

RA Modifications. The processing, and thus the DFD (Figure 2.3), must express the receipt and cancellation of orders and the arrival of new stock. The notation is as for Figure 2.2, except that data store D1 appears twice, to facilitate drawing. The duplication is indicated by the added bar at the left of the data store boxes.

The SSADM DFD notation does not allow hanging data flows. Data flowing in and out of the system requires terminal external entities (ellipses). Since the case study has no information on the interaction of the system and its environment, these are given arbitrary identifiers.

Question 12: What happens when stock is received?

Answer: As a result of receipt of stock, the status of one or more orders for the product may be changed to *invoiced*. This requires *pending* orders for this product to be re-processed. The case study gives no information about how this occurs, and at this level of abstraction, none is assumed.

RS Modifications. The function definitions extend that presented for Case 1. The RS incorporates system dynamics for each entity in Figure 2.1, expressed in text (for Customer and Product) or as an entity life history (ELH, Figure 2.4).

Question 13: How does the client envisage the processing being allocated to SSADM function definitions, in order to support the users' roles?

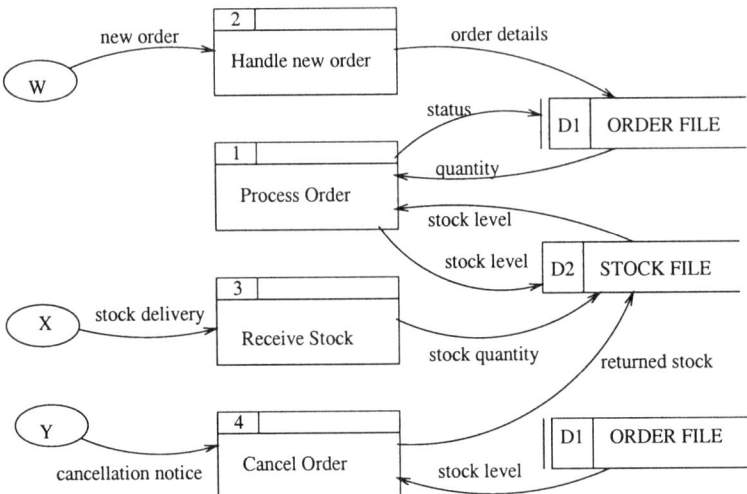

Fig. 2.3. Extended DFD, SSADM logical DFD notations

Answer: The case study provides no information on the client's business. Options are to keep separate order receipt, order processing, order cancellation and stock receipt, or to give some combined function definitions. Here, order processing is combined with each of the other three separate function definitions.

Function Definition 1: Receive Order
Order is entered in the system (DFD process 2). It is processed immediately. If it can be met from stock (quantity $\leq$ stock), its status is set to *invoiced* and the level of stock reduced by the ordered amount; otherwise it is set to *pending* (DFD process 1).

Question 14: When can an order be cancelled?

Answer: The case study provides no information. Options are to restrict cancellation to *pending* orders, to impose some cut-off, or to permit any order to be cancelled. The latter is chosen since this is the most general solution.

Question 15: What happens when an order is cancelled?

Answer: The case study provides no information. Options, given that it has been decided to accept cancellations at any stage, are to delete or retain the record of the cancelled order. The latter would require an attribute to indicate that an order had been cancelled. The former option is chosen here. If an order is in the *invoiced* state, then the amount of stock assigned to it is added to the stock for that product. The system treats this in the same way as the receipt of new stock (see Question 12).

> **Function Definition 2: Cancel Order**
> An order is cancelled and any stock allocated to it is reinstated to the product (DFD process 4). Any *pending* order which can be met from any returned stock has its status set to *invoiced* (DFD process 1). This is repeated until the stock or the *pending* orders for that product are exhausted. The cancelled order is deleted.

> **Function Definition 3: Receive Stock**
> When stock is received for a product known to the system, the amount of stock received is added to the product's current stock level (DFD process 3). Any pending order which can be met is processed (DFD process 1). This is repeated until the stock or the *pending* orders for that product are exhausted.

Dynamic Model. The set of events affecting the system is incomplete.

Question 16: How are products created and deleted?

Answer: The set of known products could be the set of products ever ordered, a set of products defined by the company, or a set of products currently in stock. Here it is assumed that there is a set of products defined by the company. The events announcing the introduction or removal of a product are outside the case study scope. It is assumed that deliveries of stock (and orders) are accepted only for known products.

Between the notification of creation and deletion, the dynamics of a product is a continuous cycle of stock changes.

Question 17: How are customers created and deleted?

Answer: Every order must have a customer, so an order for an unknown customer might either be rejected or trigger creation of a new customer instance. The latter is chosen here. No other way of creating a customer instance is specified. The deletion of a customer might occur on request or when the last order for that customer is deleted. Deletion on request could entail removal of linked order records, or require that all orders for that customer had already been deleted. Here, the specification assumes that the customer is deleted when their last order is deleted.

The dynamics of customer are simply a creation event and a deletion event.

The order dynamics are expressed in an ELH. This notation is hard to use well, and thus hard to validate. Cross-referencing to other models is implicit. However, the permitted processing sequences are critical to the success of the specification. The event effects are the leaf (larger text) boxes, read left-to-right. The children of a node (box) may be in sequence (unannotated), groups of options (each with *o* in one corner), or repeated zero or more times (each with * in one corner).

The expressed dynamics complement the function definitions, and are derived from Questions 8, 9, 14, and 16.

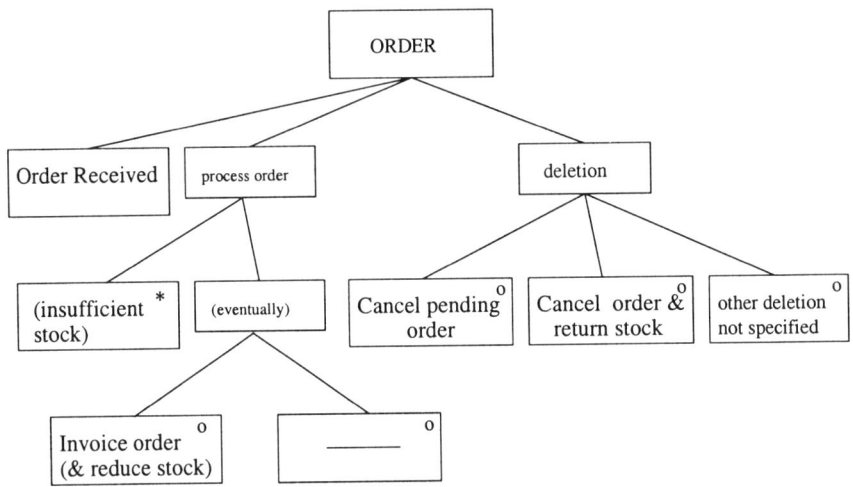

Fig. 2.4. Creation part of the Entity Life History of Order

The reading of Figure 2.4 is that an order instance is created by an event called here *Order Received*. It is then processed. The first processing event may occur zero, one or many times because there is *insufficient stock*. Eventually, the iterations cease. There are two possible event effects which cause this. The first, presumed to be consequent on the receipt of stock, is *Invoice order*, with its side effect *reduce stock*. The alternative is a null event, a diagrammatic ruse to model the fact that a pending order may be susceptible to other events without being invoiced.

The final set of effects on an order instance are due to *deletion* events. Two effects are modelled here, and others may exist. These are options, indicating that the effect of deletion is determined by the status of the order instance. The deletion of a pending order is different to that of an order to which stock has been assigned.

A full interpretation of the effects of events on the system requires that the ELH is read in parallel with the function definitions derived by the RS, above. Thus, function definition 1 explains (implicitly) that the effect labelled *(insufficient stock)* sets or retains the order status, *pending*, whilst that headed *Invoice order...* occurs if an order can be met, and sets the order status to *invoiced*). Details of deletion effects are in function definition 2, above.

The Z Processing. Each SSADM function definition results in a schema calculus expression, which is constructed from schemas specifying the relevant processing for each part of the state.

The **receipt of an order** (function definition 1) is specified in four parts. The first defines the elements common to the receipt of all orders. The specification requires an output message of the type,

$ORDER\_MESSAGE ::= unknownProductOrdered \mid orderIdExists \mid$
$\quad unknownOrderError \mid orderProcessed \mid orderPending$

The inputs are identifiers of an order, a customer and a product and an instance of order. The product identifier must already exist, but the order identifier must not. The remaining predicates formalise the text of function definition 1.

```
┌─ ENTER_ORDER_COMMON ──────────────────────────────────────
│ ΔSTATE
│ custId? : CUSTOMER_ID
│ prodId? : PRODUCT_ID
│ newOrdId? : ORDER_ID
│ newOrd? : ORDER
│ ordMessage! : ORDER_MESSAGE
│ ─────────────────────────────────────────────────────────
│ prodId? ∈ dom products
│ newOrdId? ∉ dom orders
│ customers' =
│     if custId? ∈ customers then customers else customers ∪ {custId?}
│ orders' = orders ∪ {(newOrdId? ↦ newOrd?)}
│ orderCustomerRel' = orderCustomerRel ∪ {(newOrdId? ↦ custId?)}
│ orderProductRel' = orderProductRel ∪ {(newOrdId? ↦ prodId?)}
```

The additional processing of a pending order simply adds it to the state:

```
┌─ ENTER_PENDING ────────────────────────────────────────────
│ ENTER_ORDER_COMMON
│ ─────────────────────────────────────────────────────────
│ newOrd?.quantity > (products prodId?).stockLevel ⇒
│     newOrd?.status = pending
│ products' = products
│ ordMessage! = orderPending
```

For an order which can be met from stock, the definition is as follows.

```
┌─ ENTER_INVOICED ───────────────────────────────────────────
│ ENTER_ORDER_COMMON
│ ─────────────────────────────────────────────────────────
│ newOrd?.quantity ≤ (products prodId?).stockLevel ⇒
│     newOrd?.status = invoiced
│ {prodId?} ⊲ products' = {prodId?} ⊲ products
│ (products' prodId?).stockLevel =
│     (products(prodId?)).stockLevel − newOrd?.quantity
│ ordMessage! = orderProcessed
```

The error schema negates the outstanding preconditions from each schema.

```
┌─ ENTER_ERR ─────────────────────────────────────────
│ ΞSTATE
│ newOrdId? : ORDER_ID
│ prodId? : PRODUCT_ID
│ orderMessage! : ORDER_MESSAGE
│ ────────────────────────────────────────────────
│ orderMessage! = if prodId? ∉ dom products
│                 then unknownProductOrdered
│                 else if newOrdId? ∈ dom orders
│                      then orderIdExists
│                      else unknownOrderError
└─────────────────────────────────────────────────────
```

The full definition is a schema calculus disjunction, as before.

receiveOrderFunction ==
    ENTER_PENDING ∨ *ENTER_INVOICED* ∨ *ENTER_ERR*

The Z definition of the **cancellation of an order** (function definition 2) expresses the *cascade delete* required to enforce the mandatory relationships in Figure 2.1 (see Question 2). The full specification is split in to logical components, and again requires a message type:

CANCEL_MESSAGE ::= *cancelledPending* | *cancelledInvoiced* |
    orderNotFound

The input is an order identifier, which must exist in the set of known orders.

```
┌─ CANCEL_ORDER_COMMON ───────────────────────────────
│ ΔSTATE
│ ordId? : ORDER_ID
│ cancelMessage! : CANCEL_MESSAGE
│ ────────────────────────────────────────────────
│ ordId? ∈ dom orders
│ orders' = {ordId?} ⩤ orders
│ orderProductRel' = {ordId?} ⩤ orderProductRel
│ orderCustomerRel' = {ordId?} ⩤ orderCustomerRel
│ customers' = (if {ordId?} ⩤ orderCustomerRel = ∅
│               then customers \ {orderCustomerRel ordId?} else customers)
└─────────────────────────────────────────────────────
```

Cancellation of pending orders is a simple deletion. Its additional predicates are *(orders ordId?).status = pending*, *products' = products*, and *cancelMessage! = cancelledPending*. When an invoiced order is cancelled, its stock is returned. The schema outputs the product identifier for later use. [4]

---

[4] Details of *CANCEL_ORDER_PENDING* and *CANCEL_ORDER_ERROR* schemas are not shown.

2 SAZ: SSADM Version 4 and Z   33

$$
\begin{array}{|l}
\_\textit{CANCEL\_ORDER\_INVOICED} _____ \\
\textit{CANCEL\_ORDER\_COMMON} \\
\textit{prodId}! : \textit{PRODUCT\_ID} \\
\hline
(\textit{orders ordId}?).\textit{status} = \textit{invoiced} \\
(\textit{products}(\textit{orderProductRel ordId}?)).\textit{stockLevel} + \\
\quad (\textit{orders ordId}?).\textit{quantity} \leq \textit{MAX} \\
\{(\textit{orderProductRel ordId}?)\} \vartriangleleft \textit{products}' = \\
\quad \{(\textit{orderProductRel ordId}?)\} \vartriangleleft \textit{products} \\
(\textit{products}'(\textit{orderProductRel ordId}?)).\textit{stockLevel} = \\
\quad (\textit{products}(\textit{orderProductRel ordId}?)).\textit{stockLevel} + \\
\quad\quad (\textit{orders ordId}?).\textit{quantity} \\
\textit{prodId}! = (\textit{orderProductRel ordId}?) \\
\textit{cancelMessage}! = \textit{cancelledInvoiced}
\end{array}
$$

Cancellation of an order releases stock, which can be used to re-process orders. This is specified in two parts, and requires a further output message type:

$IP\_MESSAGE ::= furtherOrdsProcessed \mid noFurtherOrdsProcessed$

A summation operator is defined as a function from a set of numbers to a single number; the details are not relevant at this level of abstraction:

$sumOf : \mathbb{F}\,\mathbb{N}_1 \to \mathbb{N}_1$

The re-processing first selects a set of *pending* orders which could be met from the product stock. This is an arbitrary set such that no further order could be met. This level of abstraction is not concerned with optimising or otherwise rationalising the set of orders selected (Question 12).

$$
\begin{array}{|l}
\_\textit{SELECT\_INVOICEABLE\_ORDERS} _____ \\
\Delta \textit{STATE} \\
\textit{prodId}?, \textit{prodId}! : \textit{PRODUCT\_ID} \\
\textit{invoiceableSet}! : \mathbb{F}\ \textit{ORDER\_ID} \\
\hline
\textit{invoiceableSet}! = \\
\quad \{os : \textit{orderProductRel}^{\sim}(\!|\ \{\textit{prodId}?\}\ |\!) \mid \\
\quad\quad (\textit{orders os}).\textit{status} = \textit{pending} \land \\
\quad\quad sumOf\{\textit{ord} : \textit{orders}(\!|\ \{os\}\ |\!) \bullet \textit{ord.quantity}\} \leq \\
\quad\quad\quad (\textit{products prodId}?).\textit{stockLevel}\} \\
\textit{prodId}! = \textit{prodId}?
\end{array}
$$

The selection predicate produces a set of invoiceable orders which correspond to the product identifier. This uses the relational image of the product identifier over the relationship function, *orderProductRel* $^{\sim}(\!|\ (\{prodId?\})\ |\!)$. All members of the set have *pending* status and the sum of quantities of the included orders is less than the stock level of the product.

The selected set of orders is input to the second part of the definition. Unless the set is empty (i.e., there are no invoiceable orders), the status of each order is set to *invoiced* and the stock level of the product reduced by the sum of the ordered quantities.

```
┌─ INVOICE_PENDING_ORDERS ─────────────────────────────────┐
│ ΔSTATE                                                    │
│ prodId? : PRODUCT_ID                                      │
│ invoiceableSet? : 𝔽 ORDER_ID                              │
│ ipMessage! : IP_MESSAGE                                   │
├───────────────────────────────────────────────────────────┤
│ orderCustomerRel' = orderCustomerRel                      │
│ orderProductRel' = orderProductRel                        │
│ customers' = customers                                    │
│ invoiceableSet? ≠ ∅ ⇒                                     │
│     (∀ os : invoiceableSet? •                             │
│         (orders' os).status = invoiced ∧                  │
│         invoiceableSet? ⩤ orders' = invoiceableSet? ⩤ orders) ∧ │
│     (products' prodId?).stockLevel = (products prodId?).stockLevel − │
│         sumOf{ord : orders⦇ invoiceableSet? ⦈ • ord.quantity} ∧ │
│     ({prodId?} ⩤ products' = {prodId?} ⩤ products ∧       │
│     ipMessage! = furtherOrdsProcessed)                    │
│ invoiceableSet? = ∅ ⇒ orders' = orders ∧                  │
│     products' = products ∧                                │
│     ipMessage! = noFurtherOrdsProcessed                   │
└───────────────────────────────────────────────────────────┘
```

The predicates of this schema define the after state of products and orders. The predicates specifying the unchanged parts of the system use domain subtraction to extract the unchanged order and product instances, for example $\{prodId?\} ⩤ products'$.

The formal definition of function definition 2 is expressed in two steps, using schema calculus pipes, $\gg$, which link the output of the first schema to the inputs of the second.

$WHOLE\_INVOICE\_PENDING\_ORDERS ==$
  $SELECT\_INVOICEABLE\_ORDERS$
  $\gg$
  $INVOICE\_PENDING\_ORDERS$

$cancellationFunction ==$
  $CANCEL\_ORDER\_PENDING \lor$
  $CANCEL\_ORDER\_ERROR \lor$
  $(CANCEL\_ORDER\_INVOICED \gg$
     $WHOLE\_INVOICE\_PENDING\_ORDERS)$

The Z specification of function definition 3, **handle stock receipt** requires a further message type:

$STOCK\_MESSAGE ::= productNotInCatalogue \mid tooMuchStock \mid$
$\quad stockDeliveryOK \mid unknownDeliveryError$

The schema outputs the product identifier, *prodId!*, to facilitate subsequent order processing. The predicates check that the upper limit of the stock level domain wont be exceeded, add the new stock amount, and leave all other parts of the state explicitly unchanged.

―― $RECEIVE\_STOCK$ ――――――――――――――
$\Delta STATE$
$prodId?, prodId! : PRODUCT\_ID$
$amount? : \mathbb{N}_1$
$stockMessage! : STOCK\_MESSAGE$
――――――――――――――――――――――
$prodId? \in \text{dom } products$
$(products\ prodId?).stockLevel + amount? \leq MAX$
$(products'\ prodId?).stockLevel =$
$\quad (products\ prodId?).stockLevel + amount?$
$customers' = customers \land orders' = orders$
$orderProductRel' = orderProductRel$
$orderCustomerRel' = orderCustomerRel$
$stockMessage! = stockDeliveryOK$

The error schema is again a simple negation of preconditions:

―― $RECEIVE\_STOCK\_ERR$ ――――――――――――
$\Xi STATE$
$prodId? : PRODUCT\_ID$
$amount? : \mathbb{N}_1$
$stockMessage! : STOCK\_MESSAGE$
――――――――――――――――――――――
$stockMessage! =$
$\quad \text{if } prodId? \notin \text{dom } products$
$\quad\quad \text{then } productNotInCatalogue$
$\quad \text{else if } (products\ prodId?).stockLevel + amount? > MAX$
$\quad\quad \text{then } tooMuchStock$
$\quad \text{else } unknownDeliveryError$

The full definition uses the schema composite defined for cancellation:

$stockReceiptFunction ==$
$\quad (RECEIVE\_STOCK \gg$
$\quad\quad WHOLE\_INVOICE\_PENDING\_ORDERS) \lor$
$\quad RECEIVE\_STOCK\_ERR$

2.4 Natural Language Description of the Specifications

2.4.1 Case 1

The system has a data structure comprising customers, orders and products. An order must relate to a customer and a product. Only products exist independently in the system.

Customer details are not defined at this level. Orders have status (pending or invoiced) and quantity (a whole number between 1 and some arbitrary upper limit), whilst products have stock level (a whole number between 0 and some arbitrary upper limit).

There is one process in the system. This compares the quantity attribute of a *pending* order to the stock level of the related product. If the order can be met, then the status is set to *invoiced* and the stock level is reduced by the ordered quantity. No other state elements are changed. A message reports the success of the process. The process fails if the order is not in the system, it is not in the *pending* state, or there is not enough stock for the product. The failed process outputs an explanatory message but makes no change to the system state.

2.4.2 Case 2

The data structure is the same as for Case 1.

The system processing comprises three function definitions, the receipt of an order, the cancellation of an order, and the receipt of stock.

The receipt of an order adds the order instance, and its links to a customer and a product instance, to the system state, on the conditions that the order identifier does not already exist in the system and the ordered product is known to the system. An order from a customer not known to the system causes the creation of a new customer instance. The processing of an order is an integral part of its receipt. This compares the ordered quantity to the stock level of the ordered product. If the order can be met, then the status is set to *invoiced* and the stock level is reduced by the ordered quantity. Otherwise the status is set to *pending* and the product state is unchanged. Explanatory messages are output.

The cancellation of an order and the receipt of stock use a common sub-process which selects an arbitrary set of *pending* orders which could be met from the stock level of the relevant product. If there are some such orders, those in the selected set have their status set to *invoiced*; the product stock level is reduced by the sum of the ordered quantities of the selected orders.

Cancellation of orders can occur at any time. This removes the order instance and its relationships. Any order in the system can be cancelled. If the order is the only one for its customer, then the customer instance is removed, otherwise the state of customer is unchanged. If the order to be cancelled is in the *pending* state, no other changes occur. If it is in the *invoiced* state, then the stock for the related product is increased by the ordered quantity and the common sub-process is triggered. Messages are output indicating what the process achieved.

When stock is received for a known product, the received quantity is added to the stock level of the product, on condition that domain maximum is not exceeded. The common sub-process is triggered. Messages are output indicating what the process achieved.

In all the function definitions, the specification explicitly does not update the state whenever the processing is invalid (i.e., the operation preconditions are not met by the system and/or the process inputs). Each failure outputs an explanatory message.

2.5 Conclusions

The SAZ method is applicable to abstract system specification. Lower level design or implementation issues such as the sequencing of components within atomic processes or selection algorithms are not in the scope of the method. The analysis and specification of the invoicing case study using SAZ demonstrates the complementarity of the formal and structured notations. SAZ provides a more complete specification than either of its components, and a more coherent method than exists for the Z notation.

SAZ addresses the problem of ill-defined model overlap, characteristic of all structured methods, by representing the models in one (Z) notation. The processing is expressed (and type-checked) in terms of the formal system state, and the complete specification could be subjected to formal proofs of consistency.

In SAZ, each model (data model, functional model, dynamic model, Z model) is a view of the system providing its own insights about the system. SAZ can thus exploit the complementary strengths of the techniques. However, the lack of formally-demonstrated equivalences among the models introduces a new case of the general failure of structured methods to adequately consider model overlap.

Model and process documentation is a common failing of development methods. SAZ addresses the weak SSADM model documentation, using Z to clarify data domains, constraints and operation details at an appropriate level of abstraction. However, none of the component techniques includes rigorous documentation of inherent assumptions. These include presumptions in the definition of the *SumOf* operator in the Z processing (Case 2), the sources and sinks of data crossing the system boundary in the DFDs (Cases 1 and 2), and the uniqueness requirement on entity identifiers.

References

1. Barden R., Stepney S., Cooper D. (1994) *Z In Practice*. BCS Practitioner Series. Prentice-Hall, New York
2. CCTA (1990) *SSADM Version 4 Reference Manual*. NCC Blackwell Ltd, Oxford
3. Goodland M., Slater C. (1995) *SSADM Version 4. A Practical Approach*. McGraw-Hill, London
4. Mander K.C., Polack F. (1995) Rigorous specification using structured systems analysis and Z. *Information and Software Technology*, 37(5):285–291

5. Parker H.E.D., Polack F., Mander K.C. (1995) Trial of SAZ : Reflections on the use of an integrated specification method. In H. Habrias, editor, *Z Twenty Years On: What Is Its Future?, Nantes, France, October 1995*. IRIN, University of Nantes
6. Polack F., Whiston M., Mander K.C. (1993) The SAZ project : Integrating SSADM and Z. In J.C.P. Woodcock and P.G. Larsen, editors, *FME'93 : Industrial Strength Formal Methods at Odense, Denmark, April 1993*, volume 670 of *LNCS*, pages 541–557. Springer-Verlag, Heidelberg
7. Polack F., Whiston M., Mander K.C. (1994) The SAZ method version 1.1. Technical Report YCS207, University of York
8. Toyn I. (1999) Z notation – final committee draft. Technical report, ISO, Project No JTC1.33.45, Available from http://www-users.cs.york.ac.uk/~ian/zstan/.
9. Woodcock J.C.P. (1989) Structuring specifications in Z. *Software Engineering Journal*, 4(1):51–65

3 B: A Model-Based Method Using Generalised Substitutions

Hassan Diab and Marc Frappier

3.1 Overview of the B Notation

The B notation [1] was developed by Jean-Raymond Abrial. It supports a large segment of the development life cycle, from specification to implementation. The B notation is formal: it has an axiomatic semantics based on the weakest-precondition calculus of Dijkstra [6]. Abrial has significantly extended the initial set of Diskstra's guarded commands, proposing a complete specification and design notation scalable to large system development. Some of these extensions are inspired from the work of the programming research group at Oxford (*e.g.*, [7]). The B notation is closely related to the Z notation and the VDM notation (Abrial was a strong contributor to the development of Z).

The basic building block of B specifications is the notion of an *abstract machine*. Such a construct serves to encapsulate suitable (set-theoretic) *state variables*, the values of which must always satisfy its *invariant* (stated as a predicate). The behavioural aspects are specified in terms of an *initialisation*, and a set of *operations* that may be used to access or modify this abstract state.

One distinctive characteristic of the B method is that every such specification is validated by means of (automatically generated) *proof obligations*. At the level of an abstract machine the main proofs ensure that its initialisation *establishes* the specified invariant, and that this is then *preserved* by any calls to its associated operations (see Section 3.4).

Both the initialisation and each individual operation are defined using *generalised substitutions*. Such substitutions are similar to conventional 'assignment statements', but with a well-defined (mathematical) semantics. They identify which variables are modified, without mentioning those that are not. The generalisation proposed by Abrial allows the definition of non-deterministic specifications, guarded specifications and *miraculous* specifications. For some initial state, a miraculous specification may terminate in a state which satisfy any predicate, including **false**. Obviously, a miraculous specification is not implementable.

Large machines are constructed using smaller machines through various machine access relations. A machine may *include*, *use*, *see*, *import* or *extend* other machines. Each access relation imposes constraints on the access, from the referencing machine, to the various parts of the referenced machine. Encapsulation is supported by allowing the modification of the state variables only through the operations of a machine; on the other hand, a state variable may be read by the referencing machines in some of the access relations. Other details on the B notation will be provided as the case study specifications are presented.

There are two commercially available case tools that support the B notation: Atelier B [8] and the B tool [5]. They both provide syntax checkers, theorem provers and document management facilities. For this case study, we used Atelier B.

3.2 Analysis and Specification of Case 1

There are several ways of tackling a specification problem with the B notation. In this chapter, we start by identifying the operations required from the system according to the user requirements; operations provide the inputs, the outputs and the relationship between. Alternative approaches [1] begin with the identification of the state variables and their invariant.

3.2.1 Identifying Operations

The first question one should ask to conduct the analysis is:

Question 1: What operations are required from the system?

Answer: The only operation required is **invoice_orders**.

The next question is:

Question 2: What are the input parameters of this operation?

Answer: The user requirements provides that orders are invoiced according to the state of the stock. There are two options:

1. invoice all pending orders;
2. invoice a subset of the pending orders.

We select option 2. Therefore, a set of orders is an input parameter of the operation.

This choice raises another question:

Question 3: In what sequence should the orders of this set be processed?

Answer: The processing sequence is important, because it may affect the ability to invoice a particular order. For instance, assume that two orders reference the same product and that there is enough stock for only one of them. Depending on the sequence in which these orders are processed, one order will be invoiced and the other will remain in the state pending, since there is not enough stock left after invoicing the first order. There are three options:

1. nondeterministically select a sequence in the set of orders;

2. accept as input a sequence of orders instead of a set of orders;
3. accept as input a single order.

We select option 3, because of its simplicity. Hence, we assume that the operation takes one order in parameter instead of a set of orders; the user has to invoke the operation once for each order, thereby specifying his preferred sequence of processing for orders.

Note that it is possible in B to specify nondeterministic operations; hence, either option in the answer above can be chosen. However, specifying the invoicing of a sequence of orders is more difficult (significantly) than specifying the invoicing of a single order. This fact may seem surprising, because a natural reflex would be to specify the invoicing of a sequence of orders by a loop over the sequence elements and invoicing them one by one. But, loop statements and sequential composition (";") are not allowed at the specification level in B. They are only allowed in implementations.

Question 4: How does the user specify the order?

Answer: There are two options:

1. submit as input a complete order with all its product references;
2. submit as input the order number.

We select option 2 since it is the most practical solution from a user perspective.

Question 5: How does the user specify the stock?

Answer: We assume that the stock is not an input parameter. Rather, the operation uses the current status of the stock, which means that the stock is accessed through state variables.

Question 6: Does the operation have output parameters?

Answer: We assume that the operation has a single output, a response code, indicating if the order was successfully invoiced.

3.2.2 Defining the State Space

Before proceeding with the definition of the operation body, we must define the state space of the specification. We mentioned previously that the main building block of a B specification is the machine construct. The next decision to take is to determine how many machines are required. This is an internal issue which does not involve the user. For the sake of reusability and maintainability, it is desirable to define highly cohesive machines. An appropriate solution is to create two machines, *Product1* and *Invoicing1*. We first provide the definition of the *Invoicing1* machine. The first clause provides the machine name.

MACHINE

Invoicing1

The next clause defines the sets which are used as types for state variables and operation parameters. We may ask the following questions to the user.

Question 7: What are the possible values for the order number, the product number, the ordered quantity, the order status and the output message?

Answer: The user requirements are not specific about the type of these elements. We choose to defer the definition of a type for an order number and a product number. We assume that the ordered quantity is a natural number. An order status is either *Order_pending* or *Order_invoiced*. An output message is either *Updated* or *Not_updated*.

In B, we may defer the actual definition of types to implementation. In the SETS clause given in the sequel, we define the possible values for the status of an order and the output messages. The specification of the possible values for order are deferred to implementation. The **INVARIANT** clause will assign a type to each state variable.

Question 8: How many products does an order reference?

Answer: The user requirements are rather ambiguous about this issue. For the following statement of the user requirements

> "On an order, we have one and only one reference to an ordered product of a certain quantity. The quantity can be different to other orders.",

we see two interpretations:

1. an order contains exactly one product reference;
2. an order may contain several product references, but each product is referenced only once per order.

We select option 2. In the sequel, the word *item* denotes the reference of a product on an order.

The next clause defines the sets of machine *Invoicing1*.

SETS

   ORDER;
   STATUS = { *Order_pending*, *Order_invoiced* };
   RESPONSE = { *Updated*, *Not_updated* }

The set *ORDER* contains the set of valid order numbers. The definition of the elements of set *ORDER* is deferred to the implementation of this machine. The other sets, *STATUS* and *RESPONSE*, are defined by enumeration. The former represents the possible values for the status of an order while the latter represents possible outputs for operation **invoice_order**. The sets of a **SETS** clause are assumed to be finite and non-empty.

The next clause, **INCLUDES**, provides that machine *Invoicing1* has direct read access to the state variables of machine *Product1*, and that it may invoke *Product1* operations to modify *Product1* state variables. The definition of machine *Product1* is given in Section 3.2.4.

INCLUDES

   Product1

The include relationship is transitive for variables: if some machine M includes machine *Invoicing1*, it can access state variables of *Product1*. The include relationship is *not* transitive for operations. Clause **PROMOTES** *op_name* may be used in machine *Invoicing1* to state that operation *op_name* from machine *Product1* is also an operation of machine *Invoicing1*.

The state of machine *Invoicing1* is defined using four variables given in the **VARIABLES** clause. Each variable is given a type in the **INVARIANT** clause. It represents a possible formalisation of the answers to Question 7 and Question 8.

VARIABLES

   order, status, item, ordered_qty

INVARIANT

$$order \subseteq ORDER \land$$
$$status \in order \rightarrow STATUS \land$$
$$item \in order \leftrightarrow product \land$$
$$ordered\_qty \in item \rightarrow \mathbf{NAT}$$

Variable *order* contains the set of order numbers currently in the system. It is a subset of set *ORDER* (the set of all valid order numbers, as mentioned earlier). Variable *status* is a total function ($\rightarrow$) from *order* to *STATUS*; it provides the status of an order. Variable *item* is a relation ($\leftrightarrow$) between *order* and *product*. Variable *product* is defined in machine *Product1*, which will be described in Section 3.2.4. Variable *ordered_qty* provide the ordered quantity of an item.

If the reader is accustomed to the formal notation for relational database specification, he might find the following alternative state space definition more natural.

VARIABLES

order, item

INVARIANT

$order \subseteq ORDER \times STATUS \land$
$item \subseteq ORDER \times PRODUCT \times \mathbf{NAT}$

These definitions provide that *order* and *item* are relations. In B, one must use projection functions **prj**$_1$ or **prj**$_2$ to access a particular *coordinate* (*i.e.,* an *attribute* in relational database terminology) of a tuple of a Cartesian product. That makes specifications less explicit, thus harder to read and understand. Moreover, the integrity constraints that the order number is unique (primary key) and that a couple order number and product is also unique are already catered for in the first definition. Consequently, the first definition of the state space is preferred.

The **INITIALISATION** clause defines the initial state of the *Invoicing1* machine.

INITIALISATION

$order := \emptyset \ ||$
$status := \emptyset \ ||$
$item := \emptyset \ ||$
$ordered\_qty := \emptyset$

Each variable is assigned a value using an *elementary substitution*. An elementary substitution is of the form $v := t$, where v is a state variable or an operation output parameter, and t is a term. An elementary substitution behaves like an assignment statement: after the execution, the new value of v is t; the other variables of the machine are not modified; the state variables in t refer to the value before the execution. In this case, we have chosen to initialise each variable to empty. In B, a function is represented by a set of pairs (*i.e.,* a deterministic binary relation). The operation "||" denotes the simultaneous execution of all the elementary substitutions.

3.2.3 Defining the Behaviour of the Invoicing Operation

We may now define the body of operation **invoice_order**. The following questions are raised.

Question 9: What are the necessary conditions to invoice an order?

Answer: According to the user requirements, the system can invoice an order if:

1. its status is pending;

2. it contains at least one product reference;
3. there is enough stock for each product reference of the order.

Question 10: What is the result of the operation if the previous conditions are satisfied?

Answer: According to the user requirements, we have:

1. the status is set to invoiced;
2. the items of the order are removed from the stock.

In addition, we assume that the output message "*Updated*" is issued.

Question 11: What is the result of the operation if the previous conditions are not satisfied?

Answer: We assume that:

1. the system state is unchanged;
2. the output message "*Not_updated*" is issued.

We provide below the specification of the operation according to these answers.

OPERATIONS

$response \longleftarrow$ **invoice_order**$(oo) \;\hat{=}$

    PRE
        $oo \in ORDER$
    THEN
      IF
        $status(oo) = Order\_pending \land$
        $oo \in \mathbf{dom}(item) \land$
        $\forall pp.(\; pp \in product \;\; \land \;\; (oo \mapsto pp) \in item$
            $\Rightarrow$
            $ordered\_qty(oo \mapsto pp) \leq quantity\_in\_stock(pp))$
      THEN
        $\mathbf{status}(oo) := Order\_invoiced \;\|$
        decrease_stock(
            $\lambda\, pp.(\; pp \in product \;\; \land \;\; (oo \mapsto pp) \in item$
                $|$
            $ordered\_qty(oo \mapsto pp))) \;\|$
        $response := Updated$
      ELSE
        $response := Not\_updated$
      END
    END

The operation has an input parameter, *oo*, and an output parameter, *response*. Parameter *response* is set to *Updated* if the order was successfully invoiced, otherwise it is set to *Not_updated*.

To write a complex operation that modifies several variables, elementary substitutions are combined using compound substitutions. The main substitution of operation **invoice_order** is a *precondition* substitution of the form **PRE** p **THEN** S **END**, where p is a predicate and S is a substitution. This construct means that the substitution (corresponding to S) is only well-defined when p holds – which gives rise to a (static) proof obligation in the context of each separate call (as opposed to a 'run-time' test). A minimal precondition for an operation must specify at least the 'types' of its input parameters, if any, but as shown in the sequel, additional constraints may be introduced as well.

The **THEN** part of the precondition substitution is expressed as a *conditional* substitution of the form **IF** p **THEN** S_1 **ELSE** S_2 **END**, where p is a predicate, and S_1 and S_2 are substitutions. Such a construct has the same meaning as in conventional programming language. The condition of the **IF** contains three conjuncts which refer to the three conditions raised in the answer of Question 9. Two variables of machine *Product1* are referenced: *product*, which denotes the set of product numbers currently in the system; *quantity_in_stock*, which denotes the number of product units in inventory for a product number.

The **THEN** part of the **IF** contains a multiple substitution of the form $S \| T$. Substitutions S and T are executed simultaneously. Note that the first elementary substitution is of the form $f(xx) := t$; it is an abbreviation of the substitution $f := f \mathbin{\triangleleft\!\!-} \{(xx, t)\}$, where $\mathbin{\triangleleft\!\!-}$ is the override operation for relations (recall that a function is represented by a deterministic binary relation). Operator $\mathbin{\triangleleft\!\!-}$ is defined as follows using operators $\triangleleft$ (domain restriction), $\triangleleft\!\!\!-$ (domain subtraction), and $\mapsto$ (pair construction). Let r and s be relations and A be a set; we have

$$A \triangleleft r \triangleq \{x, y \mid x \mapsto y \in r \land x \in A\}$$

$$A \triangleleft\!\!\!- r \triangleq (\mathbf{dom}(r) - A) \triangleleft r$$

$$r \mathbin{\triangleleft\!\!-} s \triangleq (\mathbf{dom}(s) \triangleleft\!\!\!- r) \cup s \ .$$

The next substitution of the **THEN** clause is a call to operation **decrease_stock** of machine *Product1*. This operation accepts one parameter, a partial function f from *product* to **NAT**, and reduces the stock of $f(pp)$ units for each product pp in the domain of f. The argument provided in the operation call is a function defined using a lambda abstraction $\lambda x.(p \mid e)$. It denotes a function f whose domain is the set of x such that p holds and the image of x is given by expression e.

3.2.4 The Product1 Machine

The *Invoicing1* machine includes the *Product1* machine. Its definition is given below.

MACHINE

Product1

SETS

PRODUCT

VARIABLES

product, quantity_in_stock

INVARIANT

$product \subseteq PRODUCT \land$
$quantity\_in\_stock \in product \rightarrow \mathbf{NAT}$

INITIALISATION

$product := \varnothing \;\|$
$quantity\_in\_stock := \varnothing$

The *Product1* machine would be better encapsulated if we had defined an operation to access the quantity in stock. However, it would be useless in this case to define such an operation, because the B notation does not allow a call to an operation in the predicate accessing the quantity in stock in operation **invoice_order**. The encapsulation mechanism of B may seem weaker than those typically found in an object-oriented programming language, where it is possible to prevent an external access to class variables. However, encapsulation is fostered at a different level of abstraction in B. A machine may be refined and implemented using machines with completely different state variables, as long as they preserve the signature of the operations and their observable behaviour. A machine M is refined by a machine N, noted $M \sqsubseteq N$, if and only if, for any sequence of operation calls where machine M terminates, machine N also terminates and delivers a result that machine M can deliver. Hence, machine N refines machine M by possibly extending the set of call sequences where M terminates and by possibly reducing the nondeterminacy of M.

Machine *Product1* has only one operation, **decrease_stock**, which is invoked from machine *Invoicing1* when an order is invoiced, or when product units are removed from the inventory.

OPERATIONS

decrease_stock($prod\_qty$) $\triangleq$

   PRE
   $prod\_qty \in product \nrightarrow \mathbf{NAT} \land$
   $\lambda\ xx.(\ xx \in \mathbf{dom}(prod\_qty)\ |\ quantity\_in\_stock(xx) - prod\_qty(xx))$
   $\in product \nrightarrow \mathbf{NAT}$
   THEN
   $quantity\_in\_stock := quantity\_in\_stock \Leftarrow$
   $\lambda\ xx.(\ xx \in \mathbf{dom}(prod\_qty)\ |\ quantity\_in\_stock(xx) - prod\_qty(xx))$
   END

Operation **decrease_stock** has one input parameter, $prod\_qty$. The first conjunct of the precondition provides that this parameter is a partial function ($\nrightarrow$) from $product$ to the set of natural numbers. For each product pp in the domain of function $prod\_qty$, the operation must reduce the quantity in stock by $prod\_qty(pp)$ units. The override of the quantity in stock is carried out with a function defined by a lambda abstraction.

To preserve the invariant of machine *Product1*, which provides that the quantity in stock is a natural number, we must verify in the precondition of **decrease_stock** that there are enough units in inventory for each product in the domain of function $prod\_qty$. When an operation defined using a **PRE** p **THEN** S **END** is called, it is the responsibility of the caller to ensure that the operation is invoked in a state where p is satisfied. Otherwise, the operation call *may* abort (it *may* terminate because the implementation of an operation is allowed to weaken the precondition defined in the abstract machine). To prove that an operation op preserves the invariant, it is also necessary to prove that the precondition of each operation called by op is satisfied.

Note that we could have specified this conjunct in an **IF** substitution within the **THEN** part of the **PRE** substitution. In that case, the substitution would terminate normally without modifying the inventory if there was not enough stock. It would then be natural to add an output parameter to the operation indicating if the inventory has been successfully modified, like we did for operation **invoice_order**.

Several specification styles may be used in B. A typical B specification is structured into 'layers' of machines. An interface layer defines the interaction with the environment using input-output operations. This layer reads inputs from the environment, validates them, calls appropriate operations of machines from an object layer to compute the responses (outputs) and to update the state of the objects, and writes the responses to the environment.

Our specification of the invoicing case study does not include an interface layer. We only specify machines of the object layer. Moreover, our specifications are incomplete, as they do not contain all the operations that would be expected for a complete system. For instance, we have omitted an operation to add a product to the set of products (variable *product*). The next chapter also presents a B specification, which is derived from an OMT object model. Its object layer is more structured than the one present in this chapter.

3.3 Analysis and Specification of Case 2

Case 2 is an extension of Case 1. We have defined new machines, *Product2* and *Invoicing2*, which have the same state space (state variables and invariant) as the machines in Case 1, but we have added to these machines operations to increase stock and to manage orders. In the sequel, we identify the operations and provide their specifications.

3.3.1 Identifying Operations

Question 12: What are the operations required?

Answer: Considering the user requirements of Case 2, we have identified the following operations in addition to the operations of Case 1:

- **increase_stock**, which is the inverse of the **decrease_stock** operation; it takes a set of items and increases the quantity in stock for these items;
- **create_order**, which creates an order;
- **add_item**, which adds an item to an order;
- **cancel_order** and **cancel_item**, which are the inverse of the previous two operations. We assume that these operations only modify pending orders; invoiced orders cannot be modified.

No other operation is needed, considering the given requirements. Note that there is no operation to create a new product or to delete a product from the stock.

3.3.2 The Product2 Machine

Operation **decrease_stock** is the same as in machine *Product1*; hence we omit its definition. Operation **increase_stock** is similar to **decrease_stock**. Its definition is given below.

$\textbf{increase\_stock}(prod\_qty) \triangleq$

    PRE
        $prod\_qty \in product \nrightarrow \textbf{NAT} \land$
        $\lambda\ xx.(\ xx \in \textbf{dom}(prod\_qty)\ |\ quantity\_in\_stock(xx) + prod\_qty(xx))$
          $\in product \nrightarrow \textbf{NAT}$
    THEN
        $quantity\_in\_stock := quantity\_in\_stock \Leftarrow$
          $\lambda\ xx.(\ xx \in \textbf{dom}(prod\_qty)\ |$
            $quantity\_in\_stock(xx) + prod\_qty(xx))$
    END

3.3.3 The Invoicing2 Machine

Operation **invoice_order** is the same as in *Invoicing1*; we omit its specification. Operation **create_order** uses a nondeterministic substitution, the unbounded choice (clause **ANY-WHERE-THEN-END**), to pick a value for local variable oo that satisfies the condition $oo \in ORDER - order$. This order number is then used to create a new order whose status is pending. The definition of this operation is given below.

OPERATIONS

$response \leftarrow$ **create_order** $\triangleq$

  IF
    $order \neq ORDER$
  THEN
    ANY oo **WHERE**
      $oo \in ORDER - order$
    THEN
      $order := order \cup \{\ oo\ \}\ ||$
      status$(oo) := Order\_pending\ ||$
      $response := Updated$
    END
  ELSE
    $response := Not\_updated$
  END

The next operation adds an item to an order. It updates the state if and only if the order status is pending and if the product of the item is not already referenced on the order. Its definition is very similar to operation **create_order**.

$response \leftarrow$ **add_item**$(oo, pp, qq) \triangleq$

  PRE
    $oo \in ORDER \wedge$
    $pp \in PRODUCT \wedge$
    $qq \in$ **NAT**
  THEN
    IF
      $oo \in order \wedge$
      $status(oo) = Order\_pending \wedge$
      $pp \in product \wedge$
      $(oo,pp) \notin item$
    THEN
      $item := item \cup \{oo \mapsto pp\}\ ||$
      ordered_qty$(oo \mapsto pp) := qq\ ||$

```
            response := Updated
        ELSE
            response := Not_updated
        END
    END
```

The next operation, **cancel_order**, removes a pending order from the set of orders. It must update all variables related, by the invariant, to the set *order* and the relation *item*.

$response \leftarrow$ **cancel_order**$(oo) \triangleq$

    PRE
        $oo \in ORDER$
    THEN
        IF
            $oo \in order \land$
            $status(oo) = Order\_pending$
        THEN
            $order := order - \{oo\}\ ||$
            $item := \{oo\} \lhd\!\!\!- item\ ||$
            $ordered\_qty := (\{oo\} \lhd\!\!\!- item) \lhd\!\!\!- ordered\_qty\ ||$
            $status := \{oo\} \lhd\!\!\!- status\ ||$
            $response := Updated$
        ELSE
            $response := Not\_updated$
        END
    END

Operation **cancel_item** is very similar to operation **cancel_order**.

$response \leftarrow$ **cancel_item**$(oo, pp) \triangleq$

    PRE
        $oo \in ORDER\ \land$
        $pp \in PRODUCT$
    THEN
        IF
            $oo \in order\ \land$
            $status(oo) = Order\_pending\ \land$
            $pp \in product\ \land$
            $(oo,pp) \in item$
        THEN
            $item := item - \{oo \mapsto pp\}\ ||$
            $ordered\_qty := \{oo \mapsto pp\} \lhd\!\!\!- ordered\_qty\ ||$
            $response := Updated$

        ELSE
            $response := Not\_updated$
        END
    END

3.4 Validation of the Specification

We have mentioned previously that operations must preserve the invariant. The B method defines proof obligations for each operation and for initialisation substitutions. Discharging these proof obligations provides a form of specification validation. As an example, the following predicate is part of a proof obligation (a simplified version) for operation **create_order**.

(1) $order \subseteq ORDER \land$
(2) $order \neq ORDER \land oo \in ORDER \land oo \notin order$
        $\Rightarrow$
(3) $order \cup \{oo\} \subseteq ORDER$

This predicate provides that when the invariant holds (1) and when the conditions of the **PRE** and **ANY** clauses hold (2), the substitution applied to the invariant must also hold (3). In other words, after adding oo to $order$, $order$ must still be a subset of $ORDER$.

We have used Atelier B to generate all the proof obligations and to conduct the proofs. Its theorem prover has automatically discharged all proof obligations except one – which was very easy to prove in interactive mode. Interactive proofs may represent a fair challenge. When the prover fails to find a proof, one must determine whether there is something wrong in the specification or if the prover is simply unable to find a proof. When the specification seems correct, one must build a proof in interactive mode. This task requires a good knowledge of the proof rules used by the prover and the different ways of applying them. It is sometimes necessary to rewrite specifications in a different manner to obtain proof obligations which are easier to discharge with the theorem prover. Difficult proof obligations are usually good hints that the specification needs to be rewritten in a simpler manner.

Table 3.1 provides a summary of the proof obligation statistics.

We have found one defect in our specification with the theorem prover. In the precondition of operation **increase_stock**, we had forgotten to check that, for each product, the number of product units plus the quantity in stock did not exceed **MAXINT**. We found several defects with the type checker of Atelier B. Before using the prover, we conducted several inspections and walkthroughs of the specification which allowed us to find various defects.

Table 3.1. Proof obligation statistics

Machine	Proof Obligations	Automatic Proofs	Interactive Proofs
Product1	5	5	0
Invoicing1	7	7	0
Product2	7	7	0
Invoicing2	22	21	1
Total	41	40	1

3.5 The Natural Language Description of the Specifications

3.5.1 Case 1

An order has a number, a status, and items. The status may be *Order_pending* or *Order_invoiced*. An item is reference to a product in an order. Each item has an ordered quantity given by a natural number. Among the items of a given order, there must not be two references to the same product. The stock consists of a set of products. A quantity in stock, given as a natural number, is associated to each product.

The system provides an operation, **invoice_order**, which accepts an order number as input, and produces an information message as output. This operation behaves as follows. If the order status is *Order_pending*, if it has at least one item, and if, for each item, the ordered quantity is greater or equal to the quantity in stock, then the order status is changed to *Order_invoiced*, the quantity in stock for each product referenced in an item is decreased by the ordered quantity, and the information message is set to *Updated*; otherwise, the order and the stock are left unchanged, and the information message is set to *Not_updated*.

To invoice a set of orders, the user must invoke operation **invoice_order** once for each order, in the sequence he prefers. There is no concurrency in the system: it is assumed that operations are invoked in sequence.

3.5.2 Case 2

It is an extension of Case 1. The definitions of orders and stock are the same as in Case 1. New operations are provided. Operation **create_order** creates an order with an empty set of items. The order must not *exist* in the system, that is, it has never been created, or it has been created then deleted. Operation **add_item** adds an item to an order. The product reference must not exist in the order. Operation **cancel_order** and **cancel_item** are the inverses of operations **create_order** and **add_item**, respectively. These last three operations update the system state only if the order status is *Order_pending*; invoiced orders cannot be modified.

3.6 Conclusion

The elicitation of the invoicing user requirements using B lead us to a more precise statement of the expected system functions. We had to specify the inputs, the outputs, the state space and the relation between them. The fact that we have used a formal language does not prevent us from creating incorrect description of the user requirements; it only allows us to make precise statements which can then be systematically validated to determine if they are appropriate.

Mathematics provided a common language for resolving arguments and discussions between the authors during the validation. This is a significant improvement over classical informal methods like structured analysis [9] or object-oriented analysis [3]. The precise semantics of the B notation and its powerful data abstractions like sets, functions and relations allowed us to identify exactly what information the system could convey and the exact behaviour of the operations transforming this information. Using mathematics and the B notation helped dispel ambiguities and misunderstandings in matching the user requirements with the specification. The B notation, as described in [1], does not allow to model concurrency or dynamic constraints. We refer the reader to [4] for a treatment of concurrency and [2] for the specification of dynamic constraints.

Readability is one of the weaknesses of a formal notation like B. It comprises a large array of symbols, some of them which are not common in ordinary mathematics. Moreover, the "structure" of a state space is not as easy to grasp in a B specification as it is in a graphical notation like an entity-relationship (E-R) model. For instance, consider an order and an item. In an E-R model, they would be represented as two entities with a relationship between them. The attributes would be listed on each entity. The same information in a B specification is given in a flat list of predicates. It takes more time to get a good mental representation of the information structure in a B specification than with a graphical E-R model.

Acknowledgements

The authors would like to thank Henri Habrias and Pierre Levasseur for useful suggestions on improvements to the specification.

References

1. Abrial J.-R. (1996) *The B-Book*. Cambridge University Press
2. Abrial J.R., Mussat L. (1998) Introducing Dynamic Constraints in B, in Bert D. (Ed.) *B'99: Recent Advances in the Development and Use of the B Method*. LNCS 1393, Springer-Verlag, 83–128.
3. Booch. G. (1994) *Object-Oriented Analysis and Design with Applications*. 2nd edition, Benjamin-Cummings

4. Butler M., Waldén M. (1996) Distributed System Development in B, in Habrias H. (Ed). *First Conference on the B Method.* Institut de Recherche en Informatique de Nantes, Nantes, France, 155–168.
5. B-Core Limited: Oxford, United Kingdom, http://www.b-core.com
6. Dijkstra E.W. (1976) *A Discipline of Programming.* Prentice Hall
7. Morgan C. (1990) *Programming from Specifications.* Prentice Hall
8. Stéria Méditerranée: Aix-en-Provence, France, http://www.atelierb.societe.com
9. Yourdon E. (1989) *Modern structured analysis.* Yourdon Press

4 From OMT Diagrams to B Specifications

Philippe Facon, Régine Laleau, and Hong Phuong Nguyen

4.1 Overview of the Method

To specify the proposed case study, we first use semi-formal notations (object diagram, state/transition diagram, ...) which give an initial graphical overview of the information system. Then, by applying diverse rules [4,5], we derive a partial B formal specification [1]. Finally, this specification is completed by the body of the operations and the invariants corresponding to integrity constraints which couldn't be graphically expressed.

4.1.1 The Semi-Formal Specification

For the static aspect, we use object diagrams defined by OMT [6] associated with some notations of MERISE [7]. The dynamic aspect is expressed using OMT state/transition diagrams and scenarios. We will begin by presenting the basic diagram concepts used in this study.

Object Diagrams. The *entity* concept is used to structure the knowledge about objects: an entity assembles the objects sharing common characteristics (attributes and methods). An object represents an instance of an entity. An *attribute* is defined by its name and has a type that determines the set of its possible values.

Links between objects may be defined. In our model, a link concerns exactly two objects and may have attributes. A type of link is called an *association*. For a given association, a link is completely identified by the two objects it connects. An association is characterised by its name and cardinality constraints with values *1,1* or *1,n* or *0,1* or *0,n*. (minimum and maximum numbers of links for each object). We have chosen the graphical notation of the method MERISE since it seems to be the most intuitive.

It is not possible to express the whole semantics of the static part of an application only with graphical notations. Therefore *integrity constraints* may be defined in natural language, that usefully complete the object diagrams.

Scenarios and State/Transition Diagrams. A state/transition diagram is a graph whose nodes are states and whose directed arcs are transitions labelled by event names. It is defined in order to describe the dynamic behaviour of each object of an entity. Definitions of the basic concepts of state/transition diagrams are given following [6]. Nevertheless, we have extended some of them in order to clarify their use.

An *event* is a one-way transmission of information from one object to another. Events may have parameters (graphically represented in parentheses after the event name). A *state* is an abstraction of the value of some attributes and links of an object. A state specifies the response of the object to input events.

A *transition* allows an object to pass from a receiving state to a target state when an event occurs. A transition may be subjected to a *condition*: an event may trigger a transition only if its condition is satisfied. Such a condition is a Boolean function. It is graphically represented in brackets. An *action* associated with an event is executed when this event occurs and the possible condition is true.

We assume that an event may only appear if the condition on the transition is true. This means the user has to verify the condition before transmitting the event. The alternative is to take into account in the state/transition diagrams all the possible cases (with regard to error handling) and ensure that for each event there is only one transition whose condition is satisfied. The disadvantage is that diagrams become quickly unreadable.

A *state/transition diagram* relates events and states and concerns a single entity. All the transitions leaving a state must correspond either to different events or, if there are several transitions associated with the same event, each transition must be guarded by a condition and all the conditions must be disjoint. Thus it is a deterministic system. We consider there is no possible parallelism in the event handling.

All the objects of an entity share the same state/transition diagram. Thus, each event is implicitly parameterised by the object subjected to the transition (called the *current object* of the state/transition diagram and written o by convention). The following conventions are used in state/transition diagrams. Events are written in italics, actions in simple characters. When the name of an event and the name of the associated action are the same, they are merged and written in bold on the transition.

The objects of a system interact by *exchanging events*. An object may perform the action of sending an event to another object when a transition is triggered. This is represented by a dashed line arrow from a transition to the entity of the received object. The arrow is labelled by this object and the event name.

Actions are applied on a single object. In object terminology, they correspond to instance operations. An entity operation has to choose the object (or the set of objects) to process according to a criterion before its execution. Then, state/transition diagrams are not sufficient. We introduce a new notion: *diagram associated to the entity administrator*.

The entity administrator is a special object which has neither attributes nor association links. It has an overall vision allowing it to manage all the entity objects. Its role is to select the object (or the objects) on which an action will be executed according to a criterion. Its diagram must be able first to describe the fact that it is in a state where it may always receive events, then select the object(s) and return to its original state in order to receive new events. This situation is described by a self- transition.

The selection supplies either an object or a set of objects (belonging to the same entity) corresponding to criteria. In these two cases, the administrator has to send an event to the state/transition diagram of the selected object(s) to signify the action to be processed and the change of state of the object(s). This emission is represented by the concept "events exchange", that is, a dashed line arrow towards the object entity name, labelled * in the case of a set of selected objects. Recall that there is no event parallelism, thus events are sent sequentially but in an unspecified order. The criterion selection of the objects is expressed by a clause on the arrow. The chosen objects have to be in the initial state of the transition triggered by the event in order that the change of state be possible.

An *event trace diagram* is composed of a sequence of events, as well as the sender object and receiver object of each event. In this diagram, each entity is represented by a vertical line and each event by an horizontal arrow from the sender object to the receiver object. We have extended this diagram by adding another vertical line. This line is devoted to a special object called "Exterior" in order to express all the events coming from outside the system, called *input events*. There are two kinds of input event: random event (for each user demand) and temporal event (for example every evening, ...).

An event trace diagram is a set of scenarios. We consider that a *scenario* is a sequence of events that occurs during one particular execution of the system and that is started by a triggering input event followed by a sequence of internal events, with, at the end, the possibility of sending output events.

4.1.2 The Formal Specification

In B, large machines are constructed using smaller machines through various access links. A machine Ma may *use* another machine Mb: the variables of Mb can be used but not modified in Ma. A machine Ma may *include* another machine Mb: the variables of Mb can be used or modified in Ma but only by using the operations of Mb.

The B machines are obtained in three steps:

Object Diagram Translation[4]. A machine is associated to each entity. Each entity is modelled by the set of all the possible objects and a variable representing the set of existing objects. Each attribute is modelled by a relation between the set of existing objects and the attribute type. This machine contains also the basic operations (create, delete, change of attribute values, ...). Each association is modelled by a variable which is a relation between two sets of existing objects. The machine which contains the association variable is determined according to association characteristics. Roughly speaking, if operations are defined on an association, a new machine is created, otherwise the association variable is defined in one of the two entity machines. Finally, a machine Interface is defined which groups together all the machines using *Includes*.

Scenario and State/Transition Diagram Translation [5]. There are three phases. The first phase replaces natural language annotations on state/transition diagrams (in conditions, selection criteria of administrator diagrams, É) with B notations. These notations use the B expressions generated in step a. In particular, actions on transitions are replaced by basic operations.

The second phase generates B operation skeletons. Each state is specified by a predicate and each scenario is translated into a B operation that formally specifies the effect on the system data of the input event associated to the scenario. We have defined translation rules depending on the type of scenario, which allows us to generate the global structure of the operation. Its body consists of calls to basic operations that correspond to the actions described in state/transition diagrams. The state/transition diagrams also help us to identify the parameters and pre-conditions (condition on the transition, and typing of current object and parameters). Furthermore, they help to determine the additional proof obligations on the generated operations.

The last one concerns the allocation of the generated operations to the machines obtained at the first step. Since these operations are interface for users, they are put in the machine Interface.

Completing the Obtained Machines with Operation Bodies and Invariants Corresponding to Integrity Constraints which Cannot be Graphically Expressed. Figure 4.1 illustrates the structure of a B specification generated from OMT diagrams. The basic operations concerning each entity and each association are first specified separately from the machine itself (1). Due to B technical constraints, two operations of a machine Mb cannot be called in parallel in an operation of a machine Ma which includes Mb. So, we have to pre-compose some of these operations to form one elementary operation before introducing it in a machine entity (2). Operation bodies of the machine Interface are composed of different elementary operation calls (3).

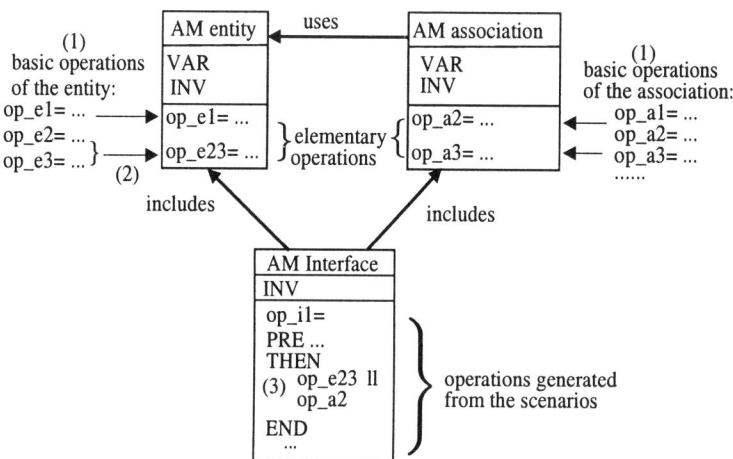

Fig. 4.1. The general structure of a B specification

4.2 Specification of Case 1

4.2.1 Object Diagram

In order to build the object diagram, the first question that is raised is:

Question 1: What are the entities, association, attributes required from the system?

Answer: We consider the following sentences of the case study:

1. "On an order, we consider one and only one reference to an ordered product of a certain quantity. The quantity may be different to other orders". So we define:

   - two entities Order and Product;
   - an association Reference between these two entities with the cardinality constraint (1,1) for Order;
   - an attribute Ordered_Qty. As the cardinality constraint for Order is (1,1), this attribute is defined in Order rather than in the association Reference.

2. "The same reference may be ordered on several different orders": the cardinality constraint between Product and Reference is (0,n).

3. "... if the ordered quantity is either less or equal to the quantity which is in stock according to the reference of the ordered product": we define an attribute Stock_Qty for Product, that gives the quantity in stock for each product.

Question 2: What are the types of the attributes?

Answer: No precision is given in the case study text. We assume that an order quantity and a stock quantity are natural numbers.

Thus we obtain the partial object diagram (partial because it may be extended during the dynamic analysis), illustrated in Figure 4.2.

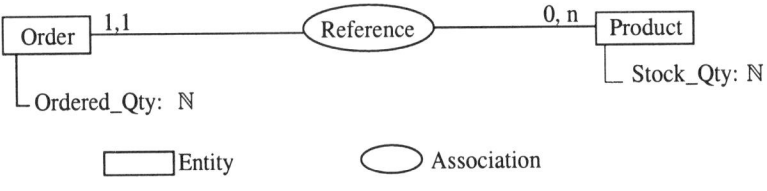

Fig. 4.2. The partial object diagram of Case 1

4.2.2 Scenarios and State/Transition Diagrams

First we need to identify the different scenarios.

Question 3: What are the input events that may occur in the system?
Answer: The only input event is invoicing orders.

Question 4: What are the parameters of this event?
Answer: No details are given in the case study text, two options may be considered:

1. invoice a set of pending orders;
2. invoice one order.

We select Option 2 (in Case 2, we will choose Option 1). Thus an invoice is an implicit parameter of the event invoicing.

Question 5: How this order is chosen?
Answer: Again, two options may be considered:

1. the order is determined by the system (for example according to its receipt date);
2. the order is chosen by the user.

We select Option 2; thus invoicing is a random event.

Question 6: What are the effects of the event on the system data?
Answer: According to the user requirements, we have:

- the corresponding order is invoiced;
- the quantity in stock of the ordered product is reduced, so an internal event Change_Qty is defined from Order to Product.

Figure 4.3 illustrates the event trace diagram, which is composed of only one scenario.

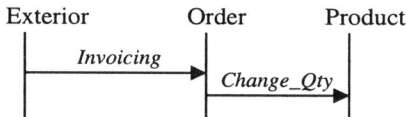

Fig. 4.3. The event trace diagram of Case 1

Question 7: Is it possible to invoice any order?
Answer: The state of an invoicing order must be "pending".

Question 8: What are the conditions required to trigger the transition associated to the event invoicing?
Answer: The only condition that must be satisfied to trigger the transition is that there is enough stock for the ordered product.

Figure 4.4 provides the state/transition diagrams of Order and Product.

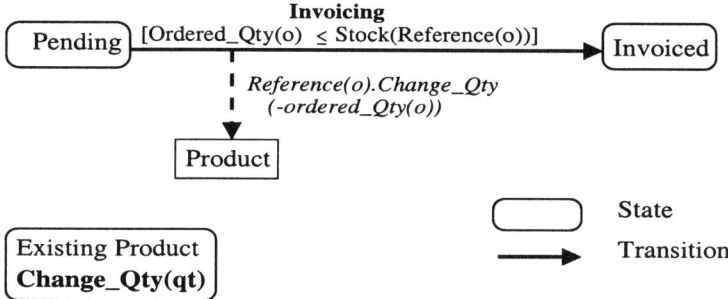

Fig. 4.4. The state/transition diagrams of Case 1

Recall that state/transition diagrams are first annotated with natural language expressions that are then replaced by B notations. But in this chapter, for lack of space, they are written directly in the B notation. This assumes that the static part of the machines presented in Section 4.2.3 has already been obtained by translation of the object diagram following the rules given in Section 4.1.2.

4.2.3 The Formal Specification

By applying the rules described in Section 4.1.2, we obtain (with the convention: clauses not automatically generated are in italics):

Steps a and b.

- An abstract machine Product for the entity Product which comprises the set of existing products and the variable representing the attribute Stock_Qty.

MACHINE	Product
SETS	PRODUCTS
VARIABLES	Products, Stock_Qty
INVARIANT	Products $\subseteq$ PRODUCTS $\wedge$ Stock_Qty $\in$ Products $\rightarrow$ NAT
INITIALISATION	*Products, Stock_Qty := $\emptyset, \emptyset$*

- An abstract machine Order1 for the entity Order which comprises the set of existing orders, the variable representing the attribute Ordered_Qty. In order to determine in which machine the association Reference is defined, the following question is raised:

Question 9: Is it possible to change the reference of an order?

Answer: We assume it is not possible. So the variable which represents the association is defined in the machine Order1.

A *Uses* link from Order1 to Product is created in order to define this variable. In order to represent the states Pending and Invoiced of the Order state/transition diagram, a new attribute Or_State is introduced to the entity Order.

MACHINE	Order1
USES	Product
SETS	ORDERS ; STATE = {pending, invoiced}
VARIABLES	Orders, Or_State, Reference, Ordered_Qty
INVARIANT	Orders $\subseteq$ ORDERS $\land$ Or_State $\in$ Orders $\to$ STATE $\land$ Reference $\in$ Orders $\to$ Products $\land$ Ordered_Qty $\in$ Orders $\to$ NAT
INITIALISATION	$Orders, Or\_State, Reference, Ordered\_Qty :=$ $\emptyset, \emptyset, \emptyset, \emptyset$

Question 10: What are the basic operations (that is creation, deletion, update of attributes) of the machines Product and Order1?

Answer: In Product, we consider only the basic operation Change_Qty. The other operations (as create or delete a product) are not required in the case study.

```
Change_Qty(pd, qt ) =
PRE    pd ∈ Products ∧
       qt ∈ INTEGER ∧
       Stock_Qty(pd) + qt ≤ MAXINT
THEN   Stock_Qty(pd) := Stock_Qty(pd) + qt
END
```

Note that the third conjunct of the precondition was added during the proof phase.

For the same reasons, in Order1, we consider only the basic operation Change_State concerning the change of state of an order.

```
Change_State(or,new_state) =
PRE    or ∈ Orders ∧ new_state ∈ STATE
THEN   Or_State(or) := new_state
END
```

- A machine Interface_1, which includes these two machines and contains the operation Invoicing corresponding to the scenario of Case 1.

```
MACHINE        Interface_1
INCLUDES       Product, Order1
DEFINITIONS    Pending_Order_Set == Or_State⁻¹[{pending}] ;
OPERATIONS
  Invoicing(or) = ...
END
```

Pending_Order_Set is the predicate which defines the state Pending.

Figure 4.5 provides the specification architecture.

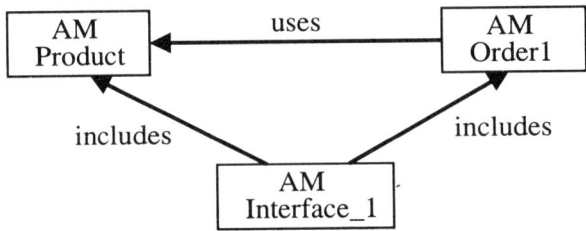

Fig. 4.5. The specification architecture

Step c.

Question 11: What is the body of the operation Invoicing?

Answer: It consists of two operation calls: one is Change_Qty in order to modify the quantity in stock of the ordered product and the second is Change_State in order to set the status of the invoicing order to "invoiced".

```
Invoicing(or) =
  PRE    or ∈ Pending_Order_Set ∧
         Ordered_Qty(or) ≤ Stock_Qty(Reference(or))
  THEN   Change_State(or,invoiced)||
         Change_Qty(Reference(or),-Ordered_Qty(or))
  END
```

The precondition incorporates the predicate of the source state and the condition of the transition related to the event Invoicing.

4.3 Specification of Case 2

The object diagram is the same for the two cases.

4.3.1 Scenarios and State/Transition Diagrams

Question 12: What are the input events?

Answer: According to the requirements, we have defined three random events:
- Create_Or which triggers the creation of a new order for a given product and a given quantity.
- Add_Stock which triggers a stock increase for a given product.
- Cancel an order. We assume that it is possible to cancel an order either of its states: if it is in the Pending state, the event Cancel_Pending_Or triggers only the deletion of the order, otherwise the event Cancel_Invoiced_Or triggers in addition the increase of the quantity in stock of the product referenced by the cancelled order. This increase corresponds to the quantity previously ordered.

Question 13: When is an order invoiced?

Answer: Several options are possible:
1. as in Case 1, when the user decides it;
2. when the order is created if there is enough stock for the ordered product. Furthermore the quantity in stock is decreased;
3. each time there is a stock increase, a set of pending orders may be automatically invoiced.

We select the last two options since the first one has been considered in Case 1.

Note that the second option corresponds to the event Create_Or. Its effect is to invoice an order if possible, otherwise the order is in Pending state. The third option means that the events Add_Stock and Cancel_Invoiced_Or may lead to invoice pending orders. This raises another question:

Question 14: What pending orders are chosen in order to be invoiced?

Answer: We assume that a maximal set of pending orders will be invoiced. Maximal means that if another order were added to the set, it could not be met from stock. Note that several maximal sets are possible. At this level of design, we do not need to specify the chosen set.

Figure 4.6 illustrates the event trace diagram of Case 2.

The scenario corresponding to the event Add_Stock requires further comments. When it arrives at the relevant product, it may raise the event Choose_Orders, in the Order Administrator, that selects a maximal set of orders to be invoiced and triggers the event Change_State on each order in this set. Change_Qty events are triggered for the relevant products.

Figure 4.7 illustrates the state/transition diagram of Order. The transition from Pending to Invoiced may be read as follows: a pending order can become invoiced when an event Change_State occurs. However this event can be raised only if the condition (Ordered_Qty(o)$\leq$Stock_Qty(Reference(o))) is true. In this

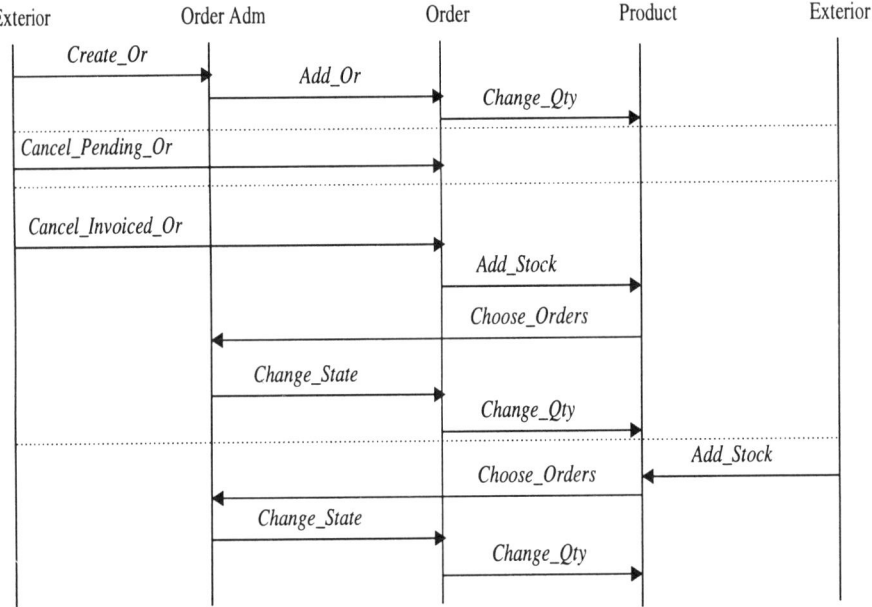

Fig. 4.6. The event trace diagram of Case 2

case the basic operation Change_State in the class Order is called and the event Change_Qty is sent to the relevant product.

Figure 4.8 provides the state/transition diagram of the Order Administrator. The event Choose_Orders triggers an action which corresponds to an entity operation because the set of orders to invoice is not yet determined. Thus, we have to define a diagram associated with the administrator of the entity Order which will choose a set of orders satisfying the following three criteria:

- the orders are in the Pending state;
- the sum of ordered quantity of the orders in this set is either less than the quantity in stock of the referenced product;
- it is a maximal set.

The last two conditions are expressed in the "Let" clause in Figure 4.8. The action on this set invoices each order, changing its state and reducing the quantity in stock of the referenced product. Figure 4.9 provides the state/transition diagram of Product.

Remarks.

- In order to simplify the diagrams we have omitted the type of the event parameters in the different conditions.

4 From OMT Diagrams to B Specifications   69

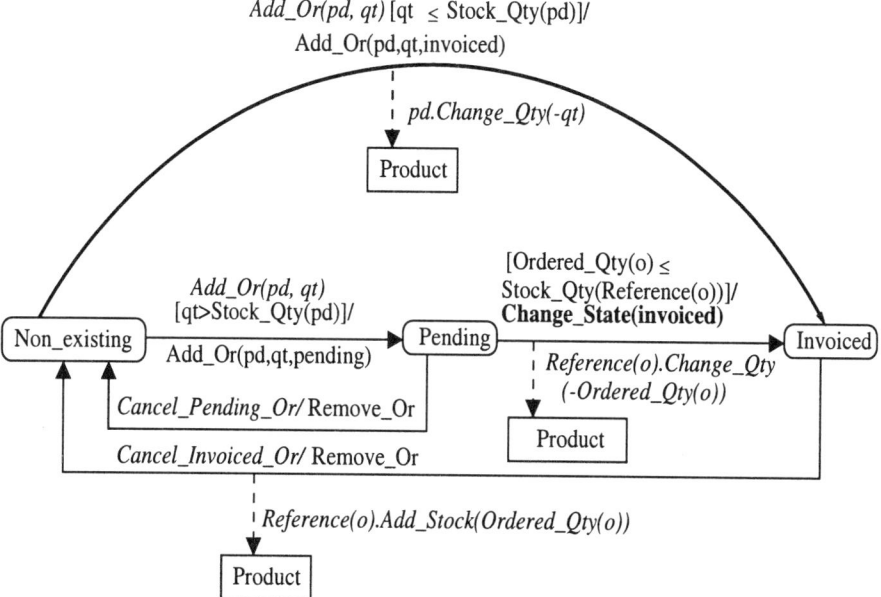

Fig. 4.7. The state/transition diagram of Order

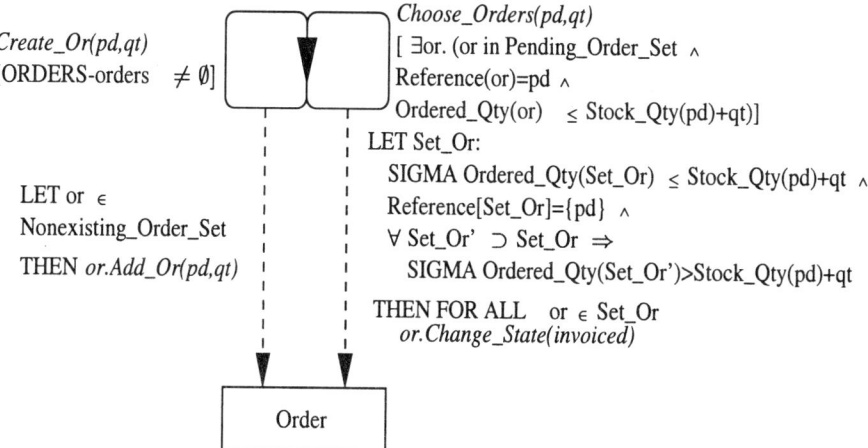

Fig. 4.8. The state/transition diagram of the Order Administrator

- Note that the chosen strategy (automatic invoicing of a maximal set of pending orders for each stock quantity augmentation) may be statically expressed by the following integrity constraint (which cannot be graphically expressed). IC1: There is no pending order for which there is sufficient stock.

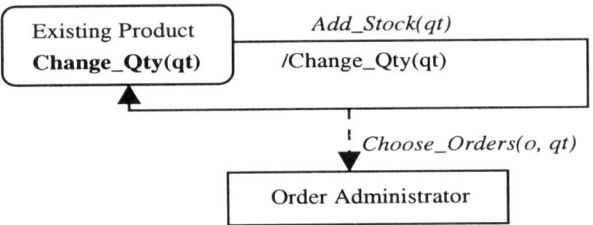

Fig. 4.9. The state/transition diagram of Product

4.3.2 The Formal Specification

- The architecture of the specification is the same as for the first case study.
- The machine Product is unchanged.
- The machine Order2 has the same static part as Order1 and contains basic operations (add to, delete from or change the state of a set of orders).

Add_Or(or, pd, qt, state) =
PRE $or \in ORDERS - Orders \land$
          $pd \in Products \land$
          $qt \in NAT \land$
          $state \in STATE$
THEN $Orders := Orders \cup \{or\}$ ||
         $Reference := Reference \cup \{or \mapsto pd\}$ ||
         $Ordered\_Qty := Ordered\_Qty \cup \{or \mapsto qt\}$ ||
         $Or\_State := Or\_State \cup \{or \mapsto state\}$
END

Remove_Or(or) =
PRE $or \in Orders$
THEN $Orders := Orders - \{or\}$ ||
         $Or\_State := \{or\} \triangleleft Or\_State$ ||
         $Reference := \{or\} \triangleleft Reference$ ||
         $Ordered\_Qty := \{or\} \triangleleft Ordered\_Qty$
END

Change_State(Or, new_state) =
PRE $Or \subseteq Orders \land$
          $new\_state \in STATE$
THEN $Or\_State := Or\_State \mathbin{<+} Or \times \{new\_state\}$
END

It also contains an operation pre-composed from basic operations. Indeed Interface_2 has an operation which corresponds to the effect in the scenario associated with the triggering input event Cancel_Invoiced_Or. This operation cancels an invoiced order. Then the quantity in stock of the relevant product is increased so that the invoicing of pending orders may be done. We note that the two basic operations: Remove_Or and Change_State of the machine Order2 would be called in the operation Cancel_Invoiced_Or, which is not possible in B. In order to solve this problem, we need to pre-compose these two basic operations into a new operation: Remove_Change_State.

Remove_Change_State(or, Or, new_state) =
PRE $or \in Orders \land$
 $Or \subseteq Orders \land$
 $new\_state \in STATE$
THEN $Or\_State := (\{or\} \triangleleft Or\_State) <+ Or \times \{new\_state\} \parallel$
 $Orders := Orders - \{or\} \parallel$
 $Reference := \{or\} \triangleleft Reference \parallel$
 $Ordered\_Qty := \{or\} \triangleleft Ordered\_Qty$
END

- The machine Interface_2 contains the operations associated with the four input events of the event trace diagram of Case 2. Note that the integrity constraint IC1 has been translated by an invariant.

$\forall or. \ (or \in Pending\_Order\_Set \Rightarrow$
$\qquad Ordered\_Qty(or) > Stock\_Qty(Reference(or)))$

The following three definitions correspond to the predicate of the different states of the State/Transition diagram of Order.

Nonexisting_Order_Set $== ORDERS - Orders$;

/*the set of pending orders */
Pending_Order_Set $== Or\_State^{-1}[\{pending\}];$

/*the set of invoiced orders */
Invoiced_Order_Set $== Or\_State^{-1}[\{invoiced\}];$

In order to make the operations more readable, we have introduced new definitions.

Order_Product_Set(pd) $== Reference^{-1}[\{pd\}];$
/*the set of orders concerning the product pd */

May_Be_Invoiced(pd,qt) corresponds to the condition of the transition Choose_Orders in the State/Transition diagram of Order administrator.

> **May_Be_Invoiced(pd, qt)** ==
> $\quad \exists cc.(cc \in (Pending\_Order\_Set \cap Order\_Product\_Set(pd)) \wedge$
> $\quad\quad Ordered\_Qty(cc) \leq qt)$;
> /* the product pd may be invoiced for a quantity in stock qt */

The last two ones correspond to the selection criteria of the same transition.

> **Cond_To_Invoice(Or, pd, qt)** ==
> $\quad Or \subseteq Pending\_Order\_Set \wedge$
> $\quad Or \neq \emptyset \wedge$
> $\quad Or \subseteq Order\_Product\_Set(pd) \wedge$
> $\quad SIGMA(xx).(xx \in Or|Ordered\_Qty(xx)) \leq qt$
> /* Or is a set of orders which may be invoiced
>   for the product pd in quantity qt */
>
> **Max_To_Invoice(Or, pd, qt)** ==
> $\quad Cond\_To\_Invoice(Or, pd, qt) \wedge$
> $\quad \forall Or2.(Or2 \subseteq Pending\_Order\_Set \wedge Or \subset Or2$
> $\quad\quad \Rightarrow$
> $\quad\quad not(Cond\_To\_Invoice(Or2, pd, qt)))$
> /* Or is a maximum set which may be invoiced */

Let us detail how we obtain an operation (for example Create_Or):

- its parameters are those of the input event Create_Or in the Order administrator diagram;
- its precondition is the condition of the transition triggered by this event;
- the construction "Let or ..." is translated into the ANY substitution in B;
- the "IF ... THEN ... END" substitution corresponds to the two possible transitions associated with the event Add_Or in the Order diagram, according to the condition "qt≤Stock_Qty(pd)";
- the body of the conditional substitution consists of calls to the basic operations mentioned on the transitions.

> **Create_Or(pd, qt)** =
> **PRE** Nonexisting_Order_Set $\neq \emptyset \wedge$
> $\quad\quad$ pd $\in$ Products $\wedge$
> $\quad\quad$ qt $\in$ NAT
> **THEN ANY** or **WHERE** or $\in$ Nonexisting_Order_Set
> $\quad\quad$ **THEN IF** qt $\leq$ Stock_Qty(pd)
> $\quad\quad\quad\quad$ **THEN** Add_Or(or, pd, qt, invoiced) ||
> $\quad\quad\quad\quad\quad\quad$ Change_Qty(pd, - qt)
> $\quad\quad\quad\quad$ **ELSE** Add_Or(or, pd, qt, pending)
> $\quad\quad\quad\quad$ **END**
> $\quad\quad$ **END**
> **END**

Cancel_Pending_Or(or) =
PRE   or ∈ Pending_Order_Set
THEN Remove_Or(or)
END

Cancel_Invoiced_Or(or) =
PRE   or ∈ Invoiced_Order_Set ∧
         $Stock\_Qty(Reference(or)) + Ordered\_Qty(or) \leq MAXINT$
THEN
    IF $May\_Be\_Invoiced(Reference(or),$
        $Stock\_Qty(Reference(or)) + Ordered\_Qty(or))$
    THEN
        ANY *Or* **WHERE**
          $Max\_To\_Invoice(Or, Reference(or),$
            $Stock\_Qty(Reference(or)) + Ordered\_Qty(or))$
        THEN
            $Remove\_Change\_State(or, Or, invoiced) \parallel$
            $Change\_Qty(Reference(or), Ordered\_Qty(or) -$
              $SIGMA(xx).(xx \in Or | Ordered\_Qty(xx)))$
        END
    ELSE
        $Remove\_Or(or) \parallel$
        $Change\_Qty(Reference(or), Ordered\_Qty(or))$
    END
END

```
Add_Stock(pd, qt) =
PRE   pd ∈ Products ∧
      qt ∈ NAT ∧
      Stock_Qty(pd) + qt ≤ MAXINT
THEN
/* for each stock augmentation, a maximal set of pending orders is invoiced*/
      IF May_Be_Invoiced(pd, Stock_Qty(pd) + qt)
      THEN
            ANY Or WHERE
                  Max_To_Invoice(Or, pd, Stock_Qty(pd) + qt)
            THEN
                  Change_State(Or, invoiced) ||
                  Change_Qty(pd, qt−
                        SIGMA(xx).(xx ∈ Or|Ordered_Qty(xx)))
            END
      ELSE
            Change_Qty(pd, qt)
      END
END
```

4.4 Validation

In order to check the consistency between the operations and the data of a machine, the B method defines proof obligations. Furthermore, we generate a new proof for each operation corresponding to a scenario, that is for each operation of the machine Interface_2. This proof allows us to check that this operation establishes the predicate(s) of the target state(s) of the scenario. It is defined according to the type of the scenario.

For a scenario corresponding to only one transition, if OP is the associated operation, S its corresponding substitution, P its precondition, I the invariant and Pred the predicate of the target state, we obtain: $(P \wedge I) \Rightarrow [S] (I \wedge Pred)$. Note that this could be obtained by viewing a scenario as a refinement of an operation "PRE P THEN X:Pred" where X stands for the modified state variables.

These abstract machines have been proved using Atelier B from Digilog [3]. Table 4.1 presents for each machine:

- generated proof obligations;
- proofs automatically achieved by the tool;
- proofs that have been manually proven by using the interactive mode of the tool;
- the last column shows that all the interactive proofs have been solved.

We have examined why some proof obligations have not been automatically solved by the tool. Some are related to the specific invariant of the Interface_2

Table 4.1. Summary of the proofs

Machine	Proof Obligations	Automatic Proofs	Interactive Proofs	% Proved
Product	5	5 (100 %)	0 (0 %)	100 %
Order_2	24	21 (87 %)	3 (13 %)	100 %
Interface_2	38	28 (74 %)	10 (26 %)	100 %
Total	67	54 (81 %)	13 (19 %)	100 %

machine (corresponding to the constraint IC1); others are related to the override operator (<+) applied to a set of orders in Order2; finally some correspond to a lack of rules in the prover (specially for the SIGMA operator).

4.5 The Natural Language Description of the Specifications

4.5.1 Case 1

An order has only one product reference, an ordered quantity which is a natural number and a status which specifies if it is a pending or an invoiced order. A product may be ordered by several orders. For each product a quantity in stock is defined, it is a natural number.

There is one input event Invoicing which takes an order as input. It can occur only if there is enough stock for the ordered product and if the order status is Pending. This event triggers an operation whose effects are: change the order status to Invoiced and decrease the quantity in stock of the relevant product by the ordered quantity.

4.5.2 Case 2

The definitions of order and product are the same as in Case 1. The following input events are defined:

- Create an order: the event may occur only if the product exists in the system and if the system can accept new orders. It triggers an operation which creates a new order for a given product and a given quantity. If there is enough stock for the relevant product, then the order status is Invoiced and the quantity in stock is decreased. Otherwise, the order status is Pending.
- Cancel an order. We assume that it is possible to cancel an order in either state: if it is in Pending state, the event Cancel_Pending_Or triggers only the deletion of the order, otherwise the event Cancel_Invoiced_Or triggers in addition the increase of the quantity in stock of the product referenced by the cancelled order. This increase corresponds to the quantity previously ordered.

- Increase the quantity in stock for a given product.

Furthermore we have chosen the following option: each time there is a stock increase, a maximal set of pending orders may be automatically invoiced if there is enough stock. Maximal means that if another order were added to the set, it could not be met from stock. Note that several maximal sets are possible. At this level of design, we do not need to specify the chosen set.

4.6 Conclusion

The use of graphical notations allowed us to obtain very quickly a first intuitive overview of the two studies. However, some properties are not formalisable in this way, for instance the invoicing strategy. Moreover, such graphical notations lead sometimes to over-specification (for example defining an execution order between actions on a transition). Thus there is often at the same time under- and over-specification.

From this first view, the derivation of a B formal specification has raised new questions. The direct writing of a B specification would perhaps have raised the same questions, but without that intuitive view, useful for end-users. Thus, the OMT - B combination appears to be fruitful, by accumulating the advantages of both methods.

However, this combination raises several problems, specially for the dynamic aspects:

- the state-transition diagrams are assumed to be used at all stages, from specification to detailed design. Now, by their operational aspect, they are more adapted to the design than to the specification step. It is certainly not satisfactory to start from a design formalism to derive a specification. Thus, we have used scenarios as much as state/transition diagrams: the former are considered as secondary in OMT, but they are more specification oriented than the latter.
- the semantics of state/transition diagrams is not always clear: for instance is it possible to have an event when no condition is true? (And if it is, how is such an event handled?). In this chapter, we have assumed that such a case is not possible: the diagrams provide preconditions (thus proof obligations) to the events. But another possible interpretation would consider the diagrams as being incomplete (not giving the error cases).
- last, there is no notation in OMT to precisely describe set of objects. Thus it is difficult to express for example that an event is sent to all objects belonging to a certain set. For that, we have been obliged to introduce a new kind of diagrams, that is, administrator diagrams.

Nevertheless, the state/transition diagrams would be essential again in the design (refinement) phase, not developed here. Then, our formalisation would allow us to study rigorously the consistency between the different OMT models:

for instance the consistency between scenarios and state/transition diagrams would be expressed by refinement proof obligations.

Furthermore, in a system, two kinds of properties may be modelled:

- operational (or functional) properties that describe a system in a "passive" way by giving its data (or entities) and the global operations that act upon them;
- behavioural properties such as temporal properties (how long does it take to invoice an order?), liveness properties (a pending order must become invoiced) or concurrency control, that is managing simultaneous events (new orders, stock entries... that simultaneously occur in the system).

In B, the first set of properties may be directly verified thanks to the B model itself. Conversely, behavioural properties are more difficult to verify, even if they could be expressed in B but in a somehow artificial manner. Note that "dynamic invariants" [2] proposed by J.R. Abrial attack some of these problems.

References

[1] Abrial J.R. (1996) The B-Book, Cambridge University Press.
[2] Abrial J.-R., Mussat L. (1998) Introducing Dynamic Constraints in B. In: 2nd International B Conference, Montpellier, France, April 1998. Springer-Verlag, LNCS Vol. 1393, 83-128.
[3] DIGILOG groupe STERIA (1996) Atelier_B Reference Manual. DIGILOG, BP 16000, 13791 Aix-en-Provence Cedex 3 France.
[4] Facon P., Laleau R., Nguyen H. P. (1996) Mapping Object Conceptual Diagrams into B Specifications. In: Proceedings of the Methods Integration Workshop, Leeds, United Kingdom, March 1996, Springer-Verlag, EWiCS.
[5] Nguyen H.P. (1998) Dérivation de spécifications formelles B à partir de spécifications semi-formelles. PHD thesis, CEDRIC laboratory, Paris, France.
[6] Rumbaugh J., Blaha M., Premerlani W., Eddy F., Lorensen W. (1991) Object-Oriented Modelling and Design. Prentice Hall, New Jersey.
[7] Tardieu H., Rochfeld A., Colletti R. (1983) La méthode Merise - Tome 1 : Principe et outils. Les Éditions d'Organisation, Paris, France.

Part II

Event-Based Approaches

5 Action Systems: A Method Combining State-Based and Event-Based Specification

Jane Sinclair

5.1 Overview of Action Systems

Action systems [1] combine a definition of system state with an explicit description of how and when state-modifying events may occur. This example follows the work of Morgan [7] and Butler [2], in which these two aspects are given equal importance. Action systems describe both the succession of events in a system and the way in which system state changes. However, they are not tied to any one particular state-description notation and may be thought of as providing a framework which can, if required, be combined with other approaches. For example, the Z notation [10] offers significant advantages in the way state descriptions can be structured. This can be put to use within an action system as demonstrated below. The additional aspect of supporting event description and refinement means that features of event-based notations such as CSP [5] can be exploited for action systems too.

An action system consists of a *state*, an *initialisation* and a set *of labelled actions*. The state is a collection of variables, with an optional predicate (called an *invariant*) relating them. The values of state variables may be altered by the initialisation and by each action of the system. An action consists of a *guard* and a *command*. The guard is a predicate describing the states in which the action may be executed. The command describes how the state changes when the action is executed. One way to represent a command is using a statement from Dijkstra's Guarded Command Language [4] (which uses simple assignment, sequencing, alternation and iteration) but other notations may also be used. The invariant provides an additional implicit constraint on the initialisation and all actions.

Execution of an action system proceeds by first performing the initialisation. The guards of all actions are then evaluated and actions whose guard is true are said to be *enabled*. The environment is offered the choice between all actions currently enabled. When one is chosen, the corresponding command is executed and the guards of all actions are then re-evaluated. This procedure is continued. If no action is enabled the system is said to be *deadlocked*. If an action aborts (for example, with a non-terminating loop), the action system *diverges*, that is, it behaves unpredictably.

One way to view the execution of an action system is in terms of its state, considering the way the values of state variables change as execution proceeds.

Another aspect concerns the possible sequences of actions which may occur. In referring to these, it is convenient to make use of *labels*. A label is an identifier, each action being associated with a label unique within the system. For example, if an action system has actions labelled a and b with the guard of each of these being *true*, then both actions are always enabled. Thus, after initialisation, any sequences involving a's and b's will be possible for the system. These sequences are referred to as *traces* of the system.

When an action system executes, several actions may be enabled at any point. The choice of which one should be selected is governed by the environment. For example, there may be a human user making decisions at each stage. Alternatively, there may be an interface with other components, which can themselves be specified using action systems. When action systems execute in parallel, commonly labelled actions occur together, providing communication channels between the separate action systems. Thus, action systems can provide a state-based approach to the development of distributed systems. Definitions and examples of parallel composition and refinement are given by Butler [2].

5.2 Analysis and Specification of Case 1

Case 1 of the requirements addresses the invoicing of orders. For an action system, both the state of the system and the required actions must be identified. Either may be addressed first. Once the actions have been decided upon, each one can be specified in detail by providing a guard and a command. Here, the state is considered first, with Z notation [10] used where appropriate. At the end of the section, the individual parts of the specification will be brought together and the action system for Case 1 will be presented.

5.2.1 Modelling the State of the Action System

The state variables must be identified. In addition, we have chosen a notation which provides information on the *type* of each variable (that is, the set of values over which it may range), so we must also consider how these should be defined.

Question 1: What are the state variables?

Answer: The orders are obviously important and will be updated when invoicing occurs. The stock should also be represented.

Question 2: What factors are important in defining types for these variables?

Answer: Relevant to an order are: the status, the product referred to, the quantity ordered. Also, since there can be many orders, we need a means of distinguishing between them. An order number can be used for this purpose. Each order should have a unique order number. For stock, there are products, each associated with a current stock level. These are all considered in detail below.

There is no need to provide any details about products, so we can simply regard them as being drawn from the set, $PRODUCT$, which represents the set of all possible products. In Z this is formally specified as:

$[PRODUCT]$

The status is a little different: it can take one of only two possible values. The following definition creates the type $STATUS$ with precisely these two elements:

$STATUS ::= pending \mid invoiced$

The amount of an order, and the level of stock too, can both be represented as non-negative integers, that is, as elements of $\mathbb{N}$. For simplicity, we also assume that invoice numbers are drawn from $\mathbb{N}$. These basic building blocks can be used to construct suitable types for the state variables. A question arises:

Question 3: The requirements are ambiguous as to how many products may be referenced by a single order. How should they be interpreted?

Answer: It is assumed that each order references a single product.

As with many other aspects of specification, the way in which orders are defined is to some extent a matter of specification style. Of the four components of an order identified above, the order number is distinguished by being uniquely associated with an order. In view of this, we choose to specify $Order$, whose members each have a status, a product and an amount. Order numbers are then assigned via a function (see below). One way to define $Order$ is as a Z schema, which specifies that any order has these three named components.

$$\begin{array}{|l}\hline Order \\ \hline status : STATUS \\ product : PRODUCT \\ quantity : \mathbb{N} \\ \hline \end{array}$$

If o is an order, declared $o : Order$, then its individual components may be referred to as $o.status$, $o.product$ and $o.quantity$. Multiple orders can be represented by defining a function which associates an order number with an order. An existing order can be accessed by applying the function to the order number. Considering the domain of the function raises a further question:

Question 4: Can any number of orders be accommodated?

Answer: It is assumed that there will be some finite capacity.

This will allow us to explore the case where capacity is reached. We introduce *maxorders* for the maximum number of orders which can be held:

$\mid maxorders : \mathbb{N}$

The state variable which we have been working towards defining is the collection of orders. This can now be given as:

$orders : 1 \mathinner{.\,.} maxorders \nrightarrow Order$

Each order in the system is associated with a unique order number drawn from the range $1 \mathinner{.\,.} maxorders$. The function used is *partial*, that is, not every number in that range need currently be in use. The *domain* of the function (written dom *orders*) gives the set of order numbers currently in use.

We now move on to consideration of the stock. It needs to be represented since invoicing can occur only when there is sufficient stock.

Question 5: Little guidance is given in the requirements about the nature of stock. Is the updating of stock to be included at this stage? Are all possible products known from the outset? Will it be possible for new products to be deleted and added?

Answer: Stock is decreased when an order is invoiced: this will be represented. No other stock-changing activity is included in Case 1. The requirements make no reference at all to dealing with products. An arbitrary choice must be made. Here it is assumed that certain (but not necessarily all) products are known to the system. This would give scope for dealing with new and old products and unrecognised product identifiers - although this is beyond the current requirements.

Another partial function is used to represent the stock.

$stock : PRODUCT \nrightarrow \mathbb{N}$

Each product known to the system is associated with a number representing the stock level of that product. The set of products known to the system is referred to as dom *stock*. Having decided upon the state variables *orders* and *stock*, it is appropriate to consider the relationship between them.

Question 6: Is an invariant needed?

Answer: Firstly, it is worth noting that the type information already given tells us quite a lot about these variables and must certainly be respected throughout the specification. Considering the relationship between *stock* and *orders*, there is a possible connection in terms of products. That is, we might wish to allow only those orders which have a known product number. However, we choose to allow orders with unknown product numbers. This will have implications for the definition of actions later on. Having made this decision, no invariant is needed.

5.2.2 Defining the Actions

The initialisation and actions of the action system are now considered.

Question 7: What are the initial values of the state variables?

Answer: The requirements say that the stock and orders will be "given in an up-to-date state". We cannot say precisely what values they will each have, but they must be of the correct type.

The following initialisation reflects this answer by setting the values to be some (unspecified) member of the correct type:

$orders :\in 1 .. maxorders \twoheadrightarrow Order$
$stock :\in PRODUCT \twoheadrightarrow \mathbb{N}$

The symbol $:\in$ represents assignment of a value chosen from the set on the right hand side. This is *nondeterministic choice*, that is, it is made internally with no reference to the environment. When executed, this selects non-predetermined values for *orders* and *stock*. Given more precise requirements, the nondeterminism could be resolved (that is, the choice narrowed down) accordingly.

Question 8: What actions are required?

Answer: The only action needed in this case is one to invoice orders.

Question 9: What are the inputs to the invoice action?

Answer: The answer to this depends on the way in which orders to be invoiced are to be chosen. Some possible ways to do this are:

- an order number is supplied as an input;
- a set of order numbers is supplied as an input;
- a pending order is automatically chosen and invoiced;
- all pending orders are automatically invoiced.

The last two cases again represent nondeterministic choices of the action system. The first approach is chosen here.

We write $o? : \mathbb{N}$ to represent the input order number. Note that $orders\ o?$ gives the order associated with $o?$. The status, for example, may be referenced by: $(orders\ o?).status$. For clarity, the following shorthand will be used:

Expression	**Shorthand**	**Refers to**
$(orders\ o?).status$	$status_{o?}$	status of order with number $o?$
$(orders\ o?).product$	$product_{o?}$	product of order with number $o?$
$(orders\ o?).quantity$	$quantity_{o?}$	quantity of order with number $o?$

Question 10: When will the invoiced action be enabled?

Answer: The answer to this question dictates the interface between the action system and its environment. There are several possibilities:
- the environment is allowed to choose the action at any point - but if invoicing is not possible for some reason, an *error case* may be appropriate.

- the environment is offered the invoiced action only when certain conditions are met (such as there being some orders whose status is currently *pending*).

Here, we choose the first possibility.

Question 11: Under what circumstances can an order (identified by $o?$) be successfully invoiced?

Answer: The following conditions must all be met.

$o? \in \operatorname{dom} orders$	• the order number is known
$status_{o?} = pending$	• the order has status pending
$product_{o?} \in \operatorname{dom} stock$	• the ordered product is known
$quantity_{o?} \leq (stock\ product_{o?})$	• there is sufficient stock

Question 12: What should the invoice action do in this case?

Answer: It should change the status of the order to *invoiced* and decrement the stock count.

To decrement the stock value for the product on the invoice we write:

$stock\ product_{o?} := (stock\ product_{o?}) - quantity_{o?}$

After this assignment, the product number we are interested in maps to a new stock value calculated by subtracting the ordered quantity from the old value. An assignment to change the status of the order may be specified:

$status_{o?} := invoiced$

Question 13: What should happen if the "successful case" conditions are not met? Should there be some response from the action system?

Answer: The requirements say nothing about this. A sensible option seems to be to leave the state unchanged. Responses indicating error (or indeed success) are also useful. An action system does not have to provide output, but in this case we choose to do so. For Case 1, we distinguish simply between the case where all the conditions of Question 11 are met and the case in which they are not. That is, only one error message is used.

Since action systems provide the opportunity to consider the interface between the action system and its environment we ask:

Question 14: How and when should responses be delivered?

Answer: Even in a very simple case such as this, choices can be made concerning the way output is handled. Two possibilities are given.
- An output is given immediately by the invoicing action. In this case, the output is an indivisible part of the invoice action - that is, the output must occur before execution of the action system can proceed.

- The output activity is made into a separate action, allowing it to be split from the activity of updating state variables. This would allow, for example, for the buffering of outputs.

Here, the second option is chosen: the response will be given by a separate action (although buffering is not modelled here).

To do this, an additional state variable, *resp*, can be introduced to record the outcome of the invoice action. This can be used to trigger the output action, which we label *response*. When *resp* contains a reply waiting for output, *response* can be enabled. The situation of no reply waiting could be represented by some special value (*Nil*, say) for *resp*. A type for the reply is defined:

$Reply ::= Ok \mid Error \mid Nil$

The action *response* can then be defined as having output $r!$: *Reply* and guard $resp \neq Nil$. The command part should set the output $r!$ to the current waiting value, and update *resp* to show that this output is no longer waiting. This is given by the following simultaneous assignment:

$resp, r! := Nil, resp$

The decision to include a response means that the answers to some previous questions have to be revised. The initialisation would now include:

$resp := Nil$

since no response is waiting initially. The *invoice* action will set *resp* to either *Ok* or *Error* as appropriate. Finally, if the *invoice* action were allowed to occur repeatedly without the output being dealt with, then *resp* would be overwritten. This can be prevented by allowing *invoice* to be offered only when *resp* has value *Nil*. The effect of this is discussed further below.

5.2.3 An Action System for Case 1

All the parts for constructing the specification have now been introduced and explained. This is brought together in Figure 5.1 as an action system which is given the name *Case* 1. The additional syntactic features used in this definition are as follows. The keywords **var** and **init** are used to introduce the description of system state and initialisation as discussed above. The keyword **action** precedes each action, and is immediately followed by the label for that action. The keyword **in** indicates that input is required for this action as defined by the variables following the keyword. A similar convention is used for **out**. The action definition follows the symbol, $:-$, and is given in the format:

$guard \longrightarrow command$

Following the model of execution described above, immediately after initialisation, only *invoice* is enabled. Execution of *invoice* results in *response* being enabled. Thus, *invoice* alternates with *response* in traces of the system. Buffering using a sequence of waiting responses would provide a more flexible interface.

$$Case1 \cong \left(\begin{array}{l} \textbf{var}\ \ orders : 1 \mathinner{\ldotp\ldotp} maxorders \twoheadrightarrow Order; \\ \qquad stock : PRODUCT \twoheadrightarrow \mathbb{N}; \\ \qquad resp : Reply \\ \textbf{init}\ \ orders :\in 1 \mathinner{\ldotp\ldotp} maxorders \twoheadrightarrow Order; \\ \qquad stock :\in PRODUCT \twoheadrightarrow \mathbb{N}; \\ \qquad resp := Nil \\ \textbf{action}\ invoice\ \textbf{in}\ o? : \mathbb{N}\ : - \\ \qquad resp = Nil \longrightarrow \\ \qquad\qquad \textbf{if}\ o? \in \text{dom}\ orders \wedge \\ \qquad\qquad\qquad status_{o?} = pending \wedge \\ \qquad\qquad\qquad quantity_{o?} \leq (stock\ product_{o?}) \\ \qquad\qquad \textbf{then}\ status_{o?} := invoiced; \\ \qquad\qquad\qquad (stock\ product_{o?}) := (stock\ product_{o?}) - quantity_{o?}; \\ \qquad\qquad\qquad resp := Ok \\ \qquad\qquad \textbf{else}\ resp := Error \\ \textbf{action}\ response\ \textbf{out}\ r! : Reply\ : - \\ \qquad resp \neq Nil \longrightarrow resp, r! := Nil, resp \end{array} \right)$$

Fig. 5.1. Action system specification of the Invoice Case Study: Case 1

5.3 Analysis and Specification of Case 2

All our efforts in Case 1 can be put to good use in Case 2. The changes in requirements ask for additional features concerning stock control and management of orders. In this section the additional features are identified and specified.

5.3.1 Modelling the State for Case 2

Question 15: Should the state be any different from that in Case 1?

Answer: No, the same variables are needed. Although we are required to perform some additional tasks, the state as already defined can support this.

To add a little extra interest, we consider how the specification should be modified if required to give separate error messages indicating which of the several unsuccessful cases has arisen. To do this, the type *Reply* is defined to include the necessary error cases.

$Reply ::=\ OrderBookFull\ |\ StockAdded\ |\ InsufficientStock\ |\ AlreadyInvoiced$
$\qquad\quad |\ AddedOrder \langle\!\langle 1 \mathinner{\ldotp\ldotp} maxorders \rangle\!\rangle\ |\ InvalidOrder\ |\ Cancelled\ |\ Invoiced$

The only new syntax here concerns the case of adding a new order: the reply, *AddedOrder*, will also include the order number of the new order.

5.3.2 Defining the Actions

Question 16: What additional actions are required?

Answer: Case 2 should add orders, cancel orders, and add stock.

Each action will be considered in turn before bringing the whole action system together. As in Case 1, the approach will be to allow each action to be selected at any point as long as no output is waiting, so the guard in each case will be: $resp = Nil$. In defining the command part of an action, the more general **if ... fi** format for choice is used. This allows a number of alternative branches to be specified, as shown below. Branches are separated by the box symbol, □.

Adding an order

Question 17: When an order is added, how is its order number assigned?

Answer: It would be possible either to allow the order number to be given as an input or to allow the action system to choose a number from those currently unused. The latter option is chosen here.

The *addorder* action is defined in Figure 5.2. To add a new order requires alteration to the *orders* state component only. The product and quantity for the new order will need to be supplied, and these are given as inputs. The command part of the action has two branches corresponding to the two possible cases: either there is room for a new order to be added or there is not (with # giving the cardinality of the set). In the latter case the response indicates that no more orders can be taken. In the former, an unused order number, o, is selected using the nondeterministic choice described above. The expression $(1 .. maxorders) \setminus (\text{dom } orders)$ gives the set of all possible order numbers minus the set of those currently in use. The **local** construct allows o to be defined and referred to as a local variable within the command. With o selected, the new order can be added with status *pending*. The term $(\mu\ ord : Order\ |\ ...)$ constructs a value of type *Order* by giving a value for each of its components. The *maplet* notation, written $o \mapsto ...$ indicates that a mapping of o to the given order is the new addition to the *orders* function.

Adding stock

To add stock, only the *stock* function is altered. This is defined in Figure 5.3. If required, a limit could be placed on the maximum levels of stock allowed.

Cancelling an order

The action to be taken when an order is cancelled is not clearly stated in the requirements, but it would seem to depend on the status of the order. If the order is still pending it can simply be removed. If it has already been invoiced the situation is more complicated.

action *addorder* **in** $p? : PRODUCT;\ n? : \mathbb{N}\ :\ -$
   $resp = Nil \longrightarrow$
      if $\#(\text{dom } orders) < maxorders \longrightarrow$
         (**local** $o :\in (1\mathrel{..} maxorders) \setminus (\text{dom } orders)$ **in**
            $orders := orders \cup \{o \mapsto (\mu\ ord : Order \mid ord.status = pending\ \wedge$
            $\qquad\qquad\qquad\qquad\qquad\qquad\qquad\qquad\qquad ord.product = p?\ \wedge$
            $\qquad\qquad\qquad\qquad\qquad\qquad\qquad\qquad\qquad ord.quantity = n?)\};$
            $resp := AddedOrder(o)$
)
      $\square\ \neg\ (\#(\text{dom } orders) < maxorders) \longrightarrow$
         $resp := OrderBookFull$
      fi

Fig. 5.2. The action *addorder*

action *addstock* **in** $p? : PRODUCT;\ n? : \mathbb{N}\ :\ -$
   $resp = Nil \longrightarrow$
      $(stock\ p?) := (stock\ p?) + n?;$
      $resp := StockAdded$

Fig. 5.3. The action *addstock*

Question 18: What happens when cancelling an order - particularly if it has already been invoiced?

Answer: In the absence of further guidelines, an arbitrary decision is made to allow invoiced orders to be cancelled. The stock is replaced. This might be seen as modelling the return of unwanted goods. An alternative would be to allow cancellation of pending orders only.

The action *cancelorder* with input order number o is specified in Figure 5.4. Here, there are three alternatives in the command. If the order number is unknown, a response is assigned to indicate this. For a known order number, the cases depend on whether the order status is *pending* or *invoiced*, with the specification in each case according with the answer to the previous question. The notation $\{x\} \triangleleft f$ denotes the resulting function when x is removed from the domain of f.

Removing stock

Question 19: Should removal of stock be represented as a separate action?

Answer: Removal of stock is associated only with the invoicing of orders, so here it is incorporated with the *invoiceorder* action. It would also be possible to have a separate removal action which could form part of the interface.

action *cancelorder* **in** $o? : \mathbb{N} : -$
$\quad resp = Nil \longrightarrow$
$\quad\quad$ **if** $o? \notin \text{dom } orders \longrightarrow$
$\quad\quad\quad resp := InvalidOrder$

$\quad\quad \square\ (o? \in \text{dom } orders) \wedge status_{o?} = pending \longrightarrow$
$\quad\quad\quad orders := \{o?\} \lhd orders;$
$\quad\quad\quad resp := Cancelled$

$\quad\quad \square\ (o? \in \text{dom } orders) \wedge status_{o?} = invoiced \longrightarrow$
$\quad\quad\quad orders := \{o?\} \lhd orders;$
$\quad\quad\quad resp := Cancelled;$
$\quad\quad\quad (stock\ product_{o?}) := (stock\ product_{o?}) + quantity_{o?}$
$\quad$ **fi**

Fig. 5.4. The action *cancelorder*

Invoicing an order

The action to invoice an order requires the input of an order number. The order must have status *pending* and there must be sufficient stock available to cover the amount required. The action *invoiceorder* is described in Figure 5.5.

Question 20: Further questions concerning orders are raised. Should an order number represent a particular order once and for all time? Should each order identifier be completely fresh? Should there be some distinction between current orders and old orders?

Answer: Here, if an order is cancelled then the index may be reused. There is no other way that an order "leaves" the system.

5.3.3 An Action System for Case 2

The actions named in the action system are those defined in Figures 5.2 to 5.5. Before bringing the actions together in an action system (Figure 5.6), one question remains:

Question 21: How should Case 2 be initialised?

Answer: It is assumed that *stock* and *orders* are initially empty, written, $\emptyset$.

5.4 Verification for Action Systems

The use of action systems allows verification of properties concerning the system state and of properties more usually associated with event-based approaches. A semantic basis for such proof can be provided by defining the *weakest precondition* (wp) for actions and sequences of actions. The wp for a statement s to

action *invoiceorder* **in** $o?: \mathbb{N} \ : \ -$
  $resp = Nil \longrightarrow$
    if $o? \notin \text{dom } orders \longrightarrow$
      $resp := InvalidOrder$

    $\square \ (o? \in \text{dom } orders) \land (status_{o?} \neq pending) \longrightarrow$
      $resp := AlreadyInvoiced$

    $\square \ (o? \in \text{dom } orders) \land (status_{o?} = pending) \land$
      $((stock \ product_{o?}) < quantity_{o?}) \longrightarrow$
      $resp := InsufficientStock$

    $\square \ (o? \in \text{dom } orders) \land (status_{o?} = pending) \land$
      $((stock \ product_{o?}) \geq quantity_{o?}) \longrightarrow$
      $(stock \ product_{o?}) := (stock \ product_{o?}) - quantity_{o?};$
      $status_{o?} := invoiced;$
      $resp := Invoiced$
    fi

Fig. 5.5. The action *invoiceorder*

$$Case2 \ \widehat{=} \ \begin{pmatrix} \textbf{var } orders : 1..maxorders \nrightarrow Order; \\ \quad stock : PRODUCT \nrightarrow \mathbb{N}; \\ \quad resp : Reply \\ \textbf{init } orders, stock, resp := \emptyset, \emptyset, Nil \\ \textbf{action } addorder \textbf{ in } p?: PRODUCT; \ n?: \mathbb{N} \\ \textbf{action } cancelorder \textbf{ in } o?: \mathbb{N} \\ \textbf{action } addstock \textbf{ in } p?: PRODUCT; \ n?: \mathbb{N} \\ \textbf{action } invoiceorder \textbf{ in } o?: \mathbb{N} \\ \textbf{action } response \textbf{ out } r!: Reply \ : - \\ \quad resp \neq Nil \longrightarrow resp, r! := Nil, resp \end{pmatrix}$$

Fig. 5.6. Action system specification of the Invoice Case Study: Case 2

establish a condition p is defined as the predicate describing the set of all states from which execution of statement s is guaranteed to terminate in a state satisfying p. For wp definitions, the reader is referred elsewhere [4,7]. To show that, for example, a specification establishes and maintains invariant I we can verify:

$wp(init, I) = true$ "*init* establishes I"
$I \Rightarrow wp(a, I)$ for each action a "if I is true before a then I is true after a"

This same approach can be used to prove that some general property holds for a specification. For example, to show that the limit of *maxorders* is not exceeded, the above conditions should be proved with I being: $\#orders \leq maxorders$. Other properties concerning change of state may also be verified. For instance, to show that the invoice action has no effect on the orders unless the status of the requested order is pending, we need to prove that for any input value o:

$$wp(invoiceorder.o, orders' \neq orders) \Rightarrow status\ o = pending$$

where *invoiceorder.o* represents the input action with input value o, and *orders'* is the state of orders after the action has occurred.

Another area in which verification may be of use concerns the sequences of actions which may occur and the interface between the action system and its environment. It can be verified whether certain sequences of actions are possible traces of the system since a sequence s of actions is a trace if and only if execution of the initialisation followed by execution of each element of s in turn is guaranteed to terminate. This is again formalised using the wp definitions. We would find, for example, that an invoicing action cannot be immediately followed by another, that is:

$$\langle invoiceorder.o1, invoiceorder.o2 \rangle$$

is not a possible trace. However, for certain values of $o1$ the following is a trace:

$$\langle invoiceorder.o1, response.InvalidOrder \rangle$$

As in CSP, not only traces, but also *failures* and *divergences* may be defined. A failure is a trace, t, together with a set, S, of actions, where execution of t can lead to a state in which no action from S is enabled. A divergence is a trace which aborts. This allows a finer distinction between action systems than traces alone, since some action systems may have equivalent traces but different failures and divergences. Among the useful properties which can be verified for an action system is freedom from deadlock. This involves a proof that, no matter what trace has occurred, it is not possible for all actions to be denied to the environment. If G is defined to be the disjunction of all guards of the action system, then the action system is deadlock-free if G is invariant for the system.

Another aspect of verification for action systems is that of proving refinement. Refinement conditions for action systems are given by Woodcock and Morgan [9] and Butler [2]. An action system can be refined to a parallel composition of several subsystems. This corresponds to the development of the system to a distributed implementation. It is quite likely that a system for updating orders and stock levels could be accessed by a number of users acting concurrently. It is also possible that the system itself may be distributed. These situations can be represented by parallel composition of action systems, with refinement verified against a top level specification. With an action system representation it is possible to refine a top level specification like those given here to a description of the system as the parallel composition of two or more separate subsystems which act in parallel. For example, here we might separate out the invoicing system and the stock control system. Certain operations could occur together, for example orders could be placed in the system at the same time as stock was updated. Other actions, for example, two which update the stock, must still be consecutive rather than concurrent. Parallel composition for action systems allows communication to occur through shared actions. This additional communication can be hidden within the system to leave an external interface equivalent to the original.

Action systems provide a way of specifying and verifying many aspects of a system. However, the effort required for proof in anything but the smallest system is considerable. Research on machine-based support continues.

5.5 The Natural Language Description of the Specification

5.5.1 Case 1

Orders are identified by order number. There is a limit, *maxorders*, on the maximum number of orders that can be dealt with at any one time. Each order is for a specified amount of a single product and has a status of either *pending* or *invoiced*. The current stock level of each known product is recorded.

Initially, orders and stock are assumed to have some (unspecified) appropriate value. An action is required to *invoice* orders. This will be offered when no output is enabled and requires an order number as input. If the input order number is known, the status of the order is *pending*, and there is sufficient stock, then the order is invoiced. This involves setting its status to *invoiced* and decreasing the current stock level of the ordered product by the amount stated on the order. A reply indicates success. If one or more of the three conditions is not met, an error message is generated and both the order and the stock will remain unchanged.

The *response* action is enabled when a reply is waiting. The reply is output and a *Nil* value used to indicate that no further output is now waiting. When the action system is executed, the initialisation is first performed. After that, execution of the *invoice* action alternates with the *response* action.

5.5.2 Case 2

This extends Case 1 by adding actions to add and cancel orders and to add stock. It also supplies a richer range of responses. The description of orders and stock levels is the same as in Case 1. To add an order, details of the product and quantity ordered are supplied as inputs. A currently unused order number is assigned by the system. If the maximum number of orders has already been reached, an error message is generated and the order is not added. Cancelling an order may be carried out irrespective of the status of the order. If the order has already been invoiced, the stock is returned. The order is deleted and the order number may later be reused. Stock may be added for any product. There is no limit to the amount of stock that can be held. Execution is similar to Case 1, with the *response* action alternating with other actions in the system.

5.6 Conclusion

Action systems provide a notation for describing the interaction of events in a state-based system. During the development process, questions will naturally arise concerning both *what* the operations are required to do and *when* they can occur, highlighting any ambiguity in the requirements in both these aspects. It is a very useful combination for the invoice case study since, although description of the state seems fundamental, the interface and the interaction of events is important too. This becomes even more apparent if a distributed implementation is required. The action system notation, which gives equal importance to describing both state and actions, is well-suited to this task.

Although action systems have a precise formal semantics [7,2], there is no need to be prescriptive in the notation used. Here, it was shown that Z schemas can be slotted into the action system framework. This can allow users to work with their own favourite state-description notation and helps with structuring the description of system state and also of actions. Any notation which can be given a weakest precondition semantics (as outlined in Section 4) is acceptable.

In common with other formal notations, action systems provide a basis for verification and refinement of the system. Both state-based properties (such as invariant properties) and event-based properties (such as freedom from deadlock) can be expressed and verified, as can steps of refinement. A single action system may be refined to a distributed implementation of subsystems working in parallel [2].

A disadvantage of the approach is that, currently, proofs are done by hand and can be difficult. Support for verification is under investigation and, although this could be a useful aid, it is unrealistic to suppose that the task will become a completely straightforward one. Another potential criticism is that, in allowing consideration of so many features, action systems are more complex than some other approaches. Rigidly fixing such aspects as the system interface from the very top level of specification might be too constraining in some circumstances.

Action systems are similar to a number of other notations combining state description and actions on state, for example TLA [6] and Unity [3]. However, these notations and the state-based approach to action systems [1] allow communication between components based on shared state. Our event-based view models communication by synchronisation of commonly-labelled actions. Parallel components can be refined independently, unlike the state-based approach where constraints are placed on the environment. Unlike the state-based approach, the failures of a system may be observed and internal (nondeterministic) and external choice are distinguished. The event-based view associates action systems with CSP [5], and the two notations are thus very similar in many respects. However, action systems give equal consideration to both state and events, with both being treated uniformly in refinement [9,2,8]. Using action systems can also improve clarity of specification since, unlike CSP, the inputs or outputs connected with a single channel are gathered in one action. This makes them easily identifiable, a feature which is particularly useful for parallel composition.

Action systems also have a clear link with purely state-based description techniques such as Z, but go further in stating explicitly when events are enabled. This is different from the Z notion of precondition which may be weakened through refinement. Action systems provide additional structure to state-based approaches, admitting the definition of traces, failures and divergence. Issues of concurrency and distributed implementation can be addressed.

References

1. Back R.J.R., Kurki-Suonio R. (1983) Decentralisation of process nets with centralised control. In *2nd ACM SIGACT-SIGOPS Symposium on Principles of Distributed Computing*, pp 131–142
2. Butler M.J. (1992) *A CSP Approach to Action Systems.* PhD thesis, Oxford University, UK
3. Chandy K.M., Misra J. (1988) *Parallel Program Design.* Addison-Wesley
4. Dijkstra E.W. (1976) *A Discipline of Programming.* Prentice Hall, Englewood Cliffs, NJ
5. Hoare C.A.R. (1985) *Communicating Sequential Processes.* Prentice Hall, Englewood Cliffs, NJ
6. Lamport L. (1994) The temporal logic of actions. *ACM Transactions on Programming Languages and Systems*, 16:872–923
7. Morgan C.C. (1990) Of wp and CSP. In D. Gries et al. editors, *Beauty is our business: a birthday salute to Edsger W. Dijkstra.* Springer-Verlag, pp 319–326
8. Sinclair J., Woodcock J. (1995) Event refinement in state-based concurrent systems. *Formal Aspects of Computing*, 7:266–288
9. Woodcock J.C.P., Morgan C.C. (1990) Refinement of State-based Concurrent Systems. *Proceedings of the VDM Symposium.* Springer-Verlag, LNCS 42
10. Spivey J.M. (1992) *The Z Notation: A Reference Manual*, 2nd edn. Prentice Hall, Englewood Cliffs, NJ

6 Using UML with a Behaviour-Driven Method

Sophie Dupuy, Agnès Front-Conte, and Christophe Saint-Marcel

6.1 Overview of the UML Notation and of the CSO Method

UML (Unified Modelling Language [1]) is a standard notation for object-oriented modelling. UML is composed of nine diagram types which support the modelling of a problem from requirement analysis to implementation. In this work, we only use the following UML diagrams:

- use case diagrams which are used to capture requirements;
- sequence diagrams illustrating use cases or describing them in a temporal view of objects interactions;
- collaboration diagrams which show in a spatial view how objects collaborate to perform use cases;
- class diagrams representing the system structure;
- state diagrams which describe the local behaviour of classes.

To use UML, many methods have been proposed. We have chosen a behaviour-driven approach inspired by the Objectory method [2]. This method named CSO (Conception des Systèmes à Objets) is taught at the Grenoble institute of technology (France). Its modelling process is simplified to take into account only the first two process components of Objectory.

It starts by defining use cases and scenarios introduced by Ivar Jacobson in the OOSE method [3]. These diagrams help to define the system limits by specifying the functionalities requested from the system. For each use case, one or more scenarios are described. A scenario presents the typical interactions between the actors and the system to give an idea of the system behaviour. The goal of this first step, called requirements capture, is to describe what the system should do.

The analysis and design steps determine how use cases are realised in terms of collaborating objects. In this work, we will use collaboration diagrams which introduce a spatial view of collaborations between objects. These diagrams are also the basis for the generation of Partial Class Diagrams (PCD). A PCD is the minimal structure which satisfies a collaboration. Each collaboration diagram is mapped into a PCD according to some basic rules which have been defined in the CSO method. The PCDs are merged to produce a global class diagram.

Object-oriented concepts like polymorphism can be used to improve the final class diagram. Finally, describing the local behaviour of some classes using state diagrams may complete the modelling work.

6.2 Case 1

6.2.1 Requirements Capture

The CSO method starts requirements capture by defining use cases. The use case diagram expresses the functional requirements of the system and aims to define the limits of the system.

Defining Use Case Diagrams. A use case expresses who the users are and what their needs are. It has to be simple in order to be easily understood by users. So a use case diagram has only two concepts: use cases which represent needs and actors which symbolise everything interacting with the system. Specifying use case diagrams determines the system functionalities and the actors which activate these functionalities. The specifier must then ask the user to make precise the system functionalities and their actors.

Question 1: Does the system deal with order management in general (invoicing an order becomes in this case a subproblem of this management) or does it only deal with invoicing?

Answer: As the user requirements provide no answer, we assume that in Case 1 the system is an order invoicing system.

Question 2: Who uses the system?

Answer: No information is given about the system entries and outputs in the user requirements. As we do not know who or what triggers the invoicing functionality, we consider invoicing like an internal process, so no actor is needed. No assumption is made about the choice of the order to invoice. We consider that we have some order to invoice and we only manage its invoicing.

On the basis of these answers, the use case diagram shown in Figure 6.1 can be produced.

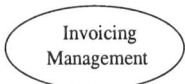

Fig. 6.1. Use case diagram - Case 1

Defining Scenarios. Now the CSO method leads us to identify scenarios describing more precisely the "Invoicing Management" use case. A scenario can be seen as a sequence of operations which represents the system behaviour. So in order to identify scenarios for the "Invoicing Management" use case, the process of order invoicing must first be understood. The user must make some choices about the invoicing process.

Question 3: What activities are undertaken for invoicing?

Answer: The user requirements specify that "the state of an order will be changed into "invoiced" if the ordered quantity is either less than or equal to the quantity which is in stock according to the reference of the ordered product". So invoicing an order consists of checking if the order can be satisfied, i.e. if the ordered quantity of products is less than or equal to the quantity in stock. If so, the stock is updated and the order is invoiced ("it changes from state "pending" to "invoiced"").

Question 4: What about an order which cannot be satisfied?

Answer: The user requirements specify that to invoice is to change the state of an order from the state "pending" to "invoiced". So if the order cannot be satisfied, it is left pending.

The answers to these questions determine the scenario of order invoicing. A scenario is composed of a textual and a graphical part. The textual part is given by the answers to the two previous questions and a sequence diagram (Figure 6.2) formalises the graphical part of the scenario. It is composed of objects and their interactions. As invoicing is considered as an internal process, the sequence diagram has only a "System" object which communicates with itself.

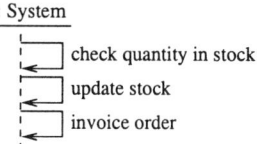

Fig. 6.2. "Order Invoicing" sequence diagram for "Invoicing Management" - Case 1

This first step permits us to identify the invoicing system needs and its limits. The next section presents how this requirement analysis can be satisfied in terms of objects.

6.2.2 Analysis and Design

The analysis and design phase starts by studying how use cases can be realised in terms of interactions between objects. Objects are concrete manifestations of abstractions. Objects which share the same attributes, operations, relationships and semantics are grouped into a class. Interactions between objects define the system behaviour and thus show how use cases can be realised. These interactions are described by collaboration diagrams which show objects communicating by message passing. Potentially, the main concepts of the user requirements (invoice, order, reference, product, stock) can be represented by objects. But according to the CSO method, we consider only objects required to realise use cases. So we have to identify the objects mandatory to realise an order invoicing. This is done by studying how the objects collaborate to invoice an order. So the user must specify how he wants the system to invoice an order. In particular, he must determine if the system has to manage invoicing.

Question 5: To invoice an order, does the system have to manage invoices?

Answer: Two solutions can be envisaged to invoice an order:

- if the system has to send invoices, invoice is considered as an object which has particular attributes like its price. So invoicing an order consists of creating a new object "invoice" whose customer should be known;
- otherwise, invoicing is only considered as an action on the order state. So there is no "Invoice" class and the "Customer" class is not mandatory to realise invoicing. This seems to be the minimal specification for order invoicing.

We think that the invoice should be a domain object but in the user requirements, nothing about an invoice is specified. In particular, there is no specific information like price, customer etc. So we choose the second solution which better corresponds to the user requirements.

Then in our solution, the order has to manage the invoicing attempt (Figure 6.3): it asks the product if the quantity in stock is sufficient to satisfy the order; if so the order can be invoiced and the quantity in stock is updated. We choose to have a "Product" object which is a model of the managed products: invoicing an order only manages the product category and not its physical instances.

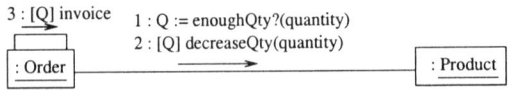

Fig. 6.3. Collaboration diagram for "Invoicing Management" - Case 1

In object-oriented formalisms, each object has a unique object identity which enables to identify it implicitly. Nevertheless identifiers can be added when they are required to design a coherent collaboration. In the CSO method, they are introduced to create the connection between concrete domain objects and computer objects and they are generally introduced as association qualifiers that identify objects in comparison with their associated objects. In our model (Figure 6.3), we guess that the link between an order and a product has been made without making assumptions about who has made it or how it has been made. So as the system knows the order and the product to invoice, the collaborations between "Order" and "Product" do not need to specify them. Orders and products do not need to be explicitly identified by references.

At this level of abstraction we do not arbitrarily define identifier formats. These will be constructed for instance with object attributes and might be discussed with users themselves.

Collaboration diagrams are the basis of a PCD which describes the system static structure in terms of classes and relationships between these classes. Classes, attributes and operations of the PCD are obtained following these rules:

- A domain class is created for all semantically identical objects used in collaboration diagrams (here we obtain the "Order" and "Product" classes).
- An operation in a class corresponds to a message sent to an object of this class in a collaboration diagram. For instance, the "enoughQty?" operation of "Product" is triggered by the "enoughQty?" message sent to a product.
- Attributes and associations are deduced from message parameters.
- Association direction in a class diagram corresponds to message direction. The navigability of the association between the "Order" and "Product" classes is deduced from the message direction between these classes.
- Class identifiers are deduced from message parameters. A class is specified with an identifier when an object of this class receives a message with an identifier value as a parameter and then accesses the identified object. For instance, the customer identifier sent to the "OrderManagement" class in Figure 6.10 implies that a qualifier exists in the PCD for the association between the "OrderManagement" and "Customer" classes.

As there is only one PCD for the invoicing functionality, it is the global class diagram (Figure 6.4). Its structure needs to be completed by defining the cardinalities of the association between the "Order" and the "Product" classes. So this brings the questions:

Question 6: Can an order address several products?

Answer: The user requirements specify that: "on an order, we have one and one only reference to an ordered product of a certain quantity". This sentence is ambiguous. It can be interpreted as: an order may reference several products, but each product is referenced only once per order; or an order may reference only one product. We choose the second interpretation.

According to this answer, the cardinality of the role from "Order" to "Product" is "1".

Question 7: Can a product be referenced in several orders?

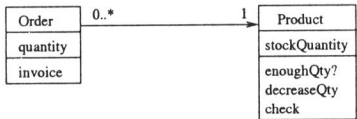

Fig. 6.4. Class diagram - Case 1

Answer: According to user requirements ("The same reference can be ordered on several different orders.") a product can be referenced by several orders. Then the cardinality of the role from "Product" to "Order" is "0..*".

By this point, the global system has been studied: its static structure with the class diagram (Figure 6.4) and its global behaviour with the collaboration diagram (Figure 6.3). Now the local behaviour of some classes can be examined. To describe it, UML provides state diagrams that are based on the Statecharts formalism [4]. As the user requirements give elements of behaviour only for ordering ("To invoice is to change the state of an order"), the order state diagram can be detailed.

A state diagram is composed of states and transitions between these states. The state of an object is an abstraction of the value of this object at a particular time. A transition represents the change from one state to another. It can be associated with an event that triggers it, with a condition and with actions to execute. So the method raises questions about the states in which an order may be.

Question 8: In what states may an order be?

Answer: According to the user requirements ("to invoice is to change the state of an order (to change it from state "pending" to "invoiced")"), two states are identified: "Pending" and "Invoiced". Initially, an order is "Pending" and it becomes "Invoiced" if the "Invoice" operation is called and if the product has enough quantity so if the condition (quantity in stock>=ordered quantity expressed by "enoughQty?= true") holds.

Question 9: Does the system store an invoiced order?

Answer: After being invoiced, an order can be deleted or kept in a database. We choose to keep it so as to be able to use it for statistics or other treatments. So "Invoiced" is not a final state for an order.

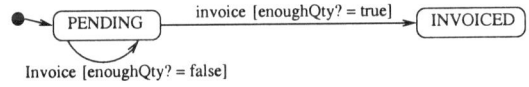

Fig. 6.5. State diagram of the "Order" class - Case 1

6.3 Case 2

6.3.1 Requirements Capture

Whereas the first case reduces the problem to an internal process, Case 2 can be considered as a global architecture of a system based on the invoicing functionality. This solution is presented as an extension of the invoicing use case defined in Case 1.

Defining Use Case Diagrams. In Case 2, the new entries of the system induce new functionalities, i.e. new use cases. So new questions must be asked of the user.

Question 10: What are the new functionalities of the system?

Answer: The user requirements do not give any explicit answer, but specify three external entries: Order Entry, Order Cancellation and Product Entry. Each of them triggers a new functionality.

A new architecture suited to these entries has to be defined. So we define a global use case named "Order Management" which uses "Invoicing Management" (Figure 6.6). The *uses* relationship implies that the behaviour defined in a use case is used in another one [1]. Moreover, "Product Entry" induces a "Stock Management" use case.

The user must then help to identify the actors and must answer the following question:

Question 11: Who interacts with the system to manage an order, to invoice an order or to manage the stock?

Answer: We guess that an order is made by a customer, that an order is invoiced by the system itself if it can be satisfied and that a new person called "Supplier" interacts with the stock management.

We can then easily identify two actors called "Customer" and "Supplier". "Customer" and "Supplier" interact respectively with "Order Management" use case and "Stock Management" use case.

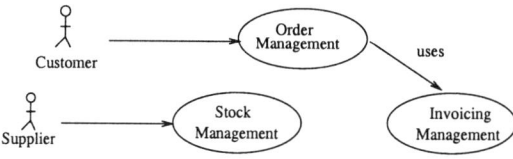

Fig. 6.6. Use case diagram - Case 2

Defining Scenarios. Three external entries must be taken into account. Each of them triggers a functionality represented by, at least, a scenario in the CSO approach. So three scenarios are introduced: "Order entry", "Order cancellation" and "Product entry". Each scenario must be associated with one of the use cases defined above. The Table 6.1 represents the use cases, their associated scenarios and the actors.

Table 6.1. Scenarios and actors associated to use cases

Use Case	Scenario	Actor
Order Management	Order entry	Customer
Order Management	Order cancellation	Customer
Invoicing Management	Order invoicing	
Stock Management	Product entry	Supplier

The three scenarios introduced in this part specify the external view of the system. They complete the first "Invoicing Management" use case introduced in Part 2. The following sections describe the scenarios presented in the Table 6.1. As in Case 1, questions on a scenario deal firstly with the activities made during this scenario.

Scenario 1: Order Entry.

Question 12: How does the system react to an order entry?

Answer: When an order entry is received, an internal order is created and saved.

Question 13: Which information must a customer give when sending an order?

Answer: According to the user requirements ("on an order, we have one and only one reference to an order product of a certain quantity"), the reference and the quantity of the product should be known.

So a "sendOrder" event (Figure 6.7) should have as parameters a reference and a quantity that defines the ordered quantity of the referenced product.

Question 14: Must the system check that a product reference is valid?

Answer: We consider that the system must check if a product reference is valid in order to reject an order and inform the customer if needed.

Question 15: When must the system check that the product reference is valid?

Answer: We choose to check the reference validity before creating an order.

Question 16: What happens when the product reference is not valid?

Answer: We choose to reject an order if the product reference is not valid.

So if the reference is valid, the order is ready for further treatment like invoicing. The sequence diagram below (Figure 6.7) describes the system activities required for order creation.

6 Using UML with a Behaviour-Driven Method   105

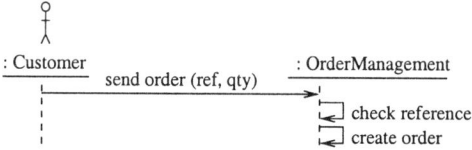

Fig. 6.7. Sequence diagram for "Order entry" - Case 2

Scenario 2: Order Cancellation.

Question 17: How does the system react to an order cancellation?

Answer: As no answer is given in the user requirements, we assume that when a customer wants to cancel an order, the system checks that the customer can cancel the order and if it is the case, cancels the order (Figure 6.8).

Question 18: Which orders can a customer cancel?

Answer: As no answer is given in the user requirements, we guess that a customer can cancel only one of his orders, not the order of another customer.

Question 19: Which information must a customer give to cancel an order?

Answer: As no answer is given in the user requirements, we guess that a customer must identify the order he wants to cancel.

So a "cancelOrder" event has as parameter the identifier of the order to cancel (Figure 6.8).

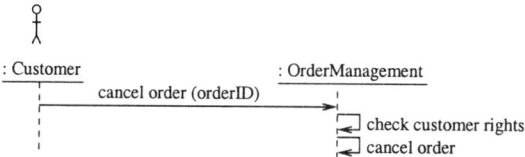

Fig. 6.8. Sequence diagram for "Order cancellation" - Case 2

Scenario 3: Product Entry. This scenario introduces a new actor, namely supplier. Its interaction with the system is basic since the supplier only adds quantities of products.

Question 20: How does the system react to a product entry?

Answer: When a supplier sends a new quantity of product to the system ("productEntry" event), the product quantity is updated (Figure 6.9).

Question 21: What information must a supplier give when he supplies a product?

Answer: As the user requirements give no answer to this question, we assume that there is only one product delivered at each time and that a supplier gives the reference of the product he supplies.

According to this answer, the "productEntry" event has as parameters a product identifier and its quantity (Figure 6.9).

Question 22: Can the system accept a unknown product?

Answer: No answer to this question being given in the user requirements, we assume that all products are already referenced in the system. Introducing a new product is the subject of another use case that is not studied here.

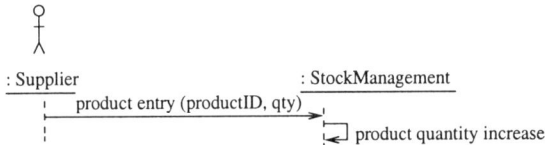

Fig. 6.9. Sequence diagram for "Product entry" - Case 2

6.3.2 Analysis and Design Phase

Collaboration 1: Order Entry. The user requirements specify that an order is made by sending a reference and a quantity to the system. So the method leads us to define a behavioural [1] class namely "OrderManagement", which takes into account this entry and acts like an interface for the " Order Management" use case. Here, an "OrderManagement" object is in charge of saving internal orders. We have to identify the exchanges between "OrderManagement" and the other classes to enter an order. In particular, comes the question about creating identifiers for customers in comparison with "OrderManagement": the "OrderManagement" class finds the identified customer with a "getCustomer" message sent to its customer collection. So we choose to send an order with a customer identifier as parameter (Figure 6.10).

Figure 6.11 represents a PCD generated from the collaboration diagram in Figure 6.10 according to the rules introduced in Section 6.2.2.

Collaboration 2: Order Cancellation. The specifier must wonder how the system will manage an order cancellation. Two answers can be given here. In the first answer, the cancellation is viewed as a response to the appropriate customer. A second solution is to manage cancellation at the "OrderManagement" level. The solution we choose here is the first one because it improves the cancellation process when a customer wants to cancel orders. Moreover, this solution seems to be more realistic and adapted to the management of cancellation privileges.

6 Using UML with a Behaviour-Driven Method   107

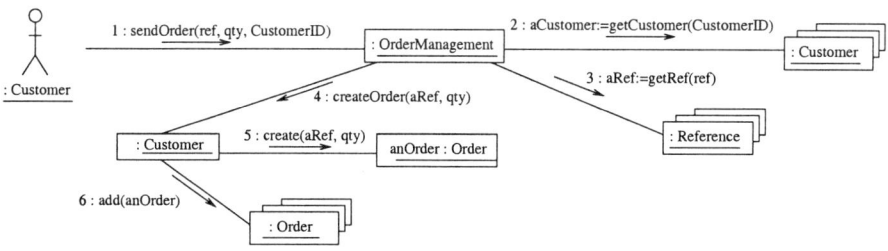

Fig. 6.10. Collaboration diagram for "Order entry" - Case 2

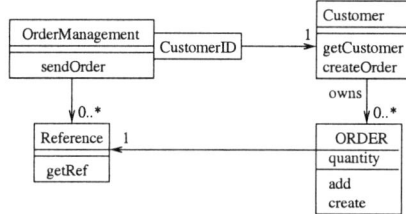

Fig. 6.11. Partial class diagram for "Order entry" - Case 2

This solution is relevant for the cancellation of one order, but the user may want the system to cancel several orders at once.

Question 23: May a cancellation address several orders?

Answer: As no answer is given in the user requirements, we assume for simplicity, that a cancellation addresses a unique order.

Then, the solution proposed to cancel one order is illustrated in Figures 6.12 and 6.13.

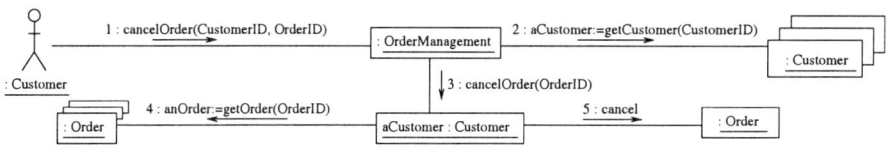

Fig. 6.12. Collaboration diagram for "Order cancellation" - Case 2

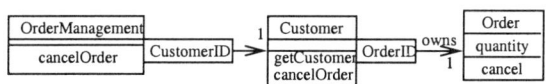

Fig. 6.13. Partial class diagram for "Order cancellation" - Case 2

Collaboration 3: Product Entry. An entry for a product can be created by a message from a supplier which provides a quantity of a given product. So the system must find which product is referenced. For this goal, we introduce arbitrary identifiers that associate one stock and one productID to a unique product. Moreover the system could be simplified if the customers and the suppliers have the same product identifier because the system would only have to manage one identifier for each product. But this is a management choice which must be made by the users.

Question 24: Are the product identifiers shared by customers and suppliers?

Answer: As no information is given in the user requirements, we guess that the product identifiers are different for customers and suppliers.

Question 25: Does the system manage information about suppliers?

Answer: It may be interesting to store information about suppliers in the system. A supplier would be associated with products to know where the products come from. We can imagine that an entry in stock is always associated with an identified supplier. But no choice of supplier data management is made here, and the collaboration represents the minimal information required to fulfil the user requirements.

A second behavioural class namely "StockManagement" is introduced (Figures 6.14 and 6.15). This design typically results from analysis choices where order and stock management are distinguished. Actually managing orders and products are very different. Both can be realised in different places, so they are not bound to share references. With this approach, it appears that we do not manipulate the same entities in those collaborations. So the derived class diagram is independent from the previous ones (Figures 6.11 and 6.13).

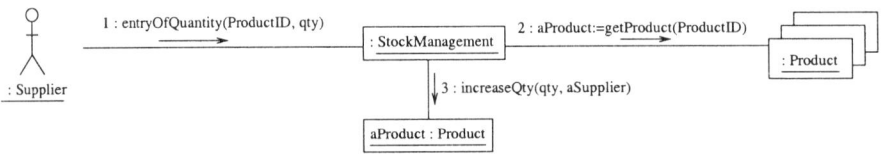

Fig. 6.14. Collaboration diagram for "Product entry" - Case 2

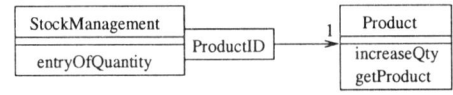

Fig. 6.15. Partial class diagram for "Product entry" - Case 2

6 Using UML with a Behaviour-Driven Method 109

Global Class Diagram: Order Invoicing. We have obtained the PCDs associated with the four distinct scenarios. The final step of design consists of merging them in a complete class diagram (Figure 6.16). First, we must identify classes that share the same semantics and then we have to merge their attributes, methods and associations in a coherent way. For the invoicing problem, we should know if there is a semantic equivalence between references and product identifiers.

Question 26: Can the references (Figures 6.11 and 6.13) and the product identifiers (Figure 6.15) be merged in a unique attribute of a product?

Answer: Yes, if the references are shared by suppliers and customers. We assumed previously that it was not the case here.

The deduced class diagram does not take advantage of object mechanisms. So, the second step that is not described here is to improve the global class diagram by introducing new abstract classes and using design patterns.

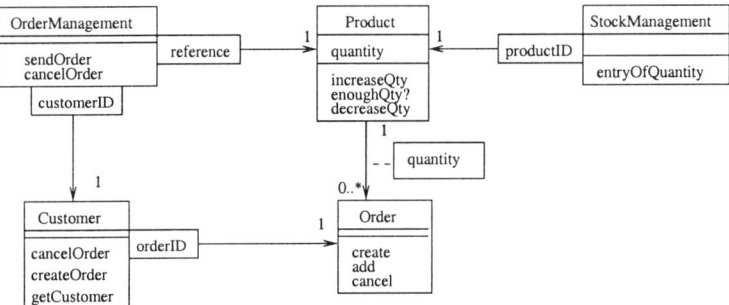

Fig. 6.16. Class diagram - Case 2

Global Behaviour. "Invoicing Management" introduced in Case 1 is a single collaboration, which needs entities handled in the order management and in the "StockManagement" use case. The other scenarios described in this part are independent. They are the basis for more complex scenarios which lead to questions on scenario synchronisation:

Question 27: When is an order invoiced?

Answer: A product entry may trigger the study of the pending orders. But interactions between the scenarios induce many management rules. So we choose to not study them.

Question 28: What happens when a customer wants to cancel an order that is already invoiced?

Answer: As no answer is given in the user requirements, in order to be more realistic we choose to let a customer cancel an order even if the order is already invoiced. But we do not say how this situation is resolved because this is an important problem which can be solved only by the user.

Even if the method does not allow the description of the interaction between scenarios, the behaviour of the system can be defined by describing state diagrams. Nevertheless, we cannot check that the behaviour of the state diagrams is consistent with the collaboration diagrams. As for Case 1, the behaviour of the "Order" class can be further studied.

Question 29: What actions can be carried out on an order?

Answer: According to the user requirements, two entries of the system can influence an order: invoicing and cancellation.

So an "Order" object can receive two kinds of messages: "invoice" and "cancel". From the answers to these questions, the "Order" state diagram (Figure 6.17) can be defined. As in Case 1, this diagram shows a unique transition between the "Pending" and "Invoiced" states which represents the invoicing of an order. But this diagram also considers the functionality to cancel an order: the "Invoiced" state of case 1 is specialised here into two states, "Invoiced" and "Conflict". A cancelled order which has not yet been invoiced becomes "Aborted". Moreover, the "Conflict" state represents the problematic case of a cancelled invoiced order. If the conflict can be resolved, the order becomes "Aborted"; the case when the conflict is unresolved must still be treated by the user.

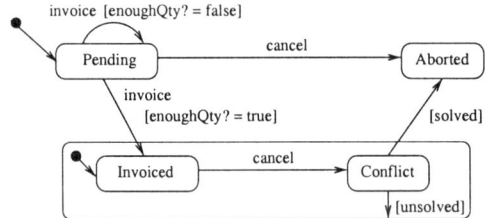

Fig. 6.17. State diagram of the class "Order" - Case 2

6.4 Natural Language Description of the UML Specifications

6.4.1 Case 1

In Case 1, invoicing is an internal functionality that concerns only one order at once. To invoice a set of orders, this functionality must be invoked once for each order. Invoicing requires to check if the order can be satisfied, i.e. if the ordered quantity of products is less than or equal to the quantity in stock. If so, the stock is updated and the order state changes from the state pending to the state invoiced. If the order cannot be satisfied, it is left pending. This case is a subproblem of the order invoicing itself. So definitions of orders and products that need to be deduced from the invoicing functionality are minimal.

6.4.2 Case 2

Case 2 needs a global architecture centred on the invoicing functionality described in Case 1. New functionalities are provided to take into account the system entries. There is no concurrency in the system: it is assumed that the functionalities are invoked in sequence.

The first functionality consists of considering a new order. To realise this functionality, the customer must send the reference and the quantity of the product ordered.

The second functionality is to cancel an order. A customer can only cancel his personal orders. The order is cancelled if it is still pending. When the order is already invoiced, the conflict must be resolved manually by the user.

The third functionality deals with adding a quantity of product in the stock. In our solution, the product must be already registered in the system because the system does not consider entries of unreferenced products. So for each product entry, the supplier must specify the product provided and its quantity.

The system class definitions are adapted from Case 1 to take into account these new functionalities. No information is held about suppliers, whereas the system manages customers and their orders. The system manages distinct product references for the customers and the suppliers.

6.5 Conclusion

Our approach has the advantage of being based upon a dialogue between users and specifiers of the system. As a matter of fact, user requirements relating to invoicing raised 29 questions. Moreover, our method is based upon an incremental process where each phase is clearly specified. So it provides a progressive way of analysing the user requirements: the questions range from user needs to technical questions.

The great majority of questions (17) took place during the requirements capture phase. This permitted us to determine the user needs early in the system definition, avoiding the design of an inadequate system. In the invoicing requirements, the method led to a quick definition of what invoicing is. In the user requirements, its definition was abstracted and given in terms of states and transitions whereas our method is first interested in the concrete world around the invoicing problem. That is why the first questions raised are all about precisely defining what exactly the system is and what its limits are. So many questions concern the functional decomposition: how to choose good use cases for the invoicing problem, what are their interactions with the environment and how do they work? Moreover our work highlights new functionalities not defined in the informal statement of the user requirements to take into account new products, new customers, new suppliers, etc.

In the analysis and design phase, the problems we encountered are more technical so that there are only a few questions. Typical technical problems concern the relevance of creating objects like invoice, supplier, customer. The management of identifiers is also an issue. The reason is again that the user requirements only describe the invoicing process and do not consider problems of order management itself.

Another interest of our approach is to generate class diagrams which exactly specify problems arising from the requirement analysis. The whole class diagram is justified by the realisation of use cases and not simply given from scratch. Both seamlessness of the modelling process and specification reuse are increased when using this method. Indeed, each functionality formalised with interaction and class diagrams is a solution to one problem elicited in the user requirements.

Nevertheless, in the CSO method, an effort must be made to associate use cases and to be sure that the result is globally coherent. The simplicity of the use case formalism which is a strength in the requirements capture phase seems to be a weakness in the other phases as it lacks in formality and expressiveness. A lot of recent research deals with this problem and aims to formalise use cases [5]. The same remark is valid for all UML diagrams. The lack of precise semantics does not enable system checks as formal methods do. Moreover, even if our approach tends to produce mutually consistent diagrams by following rules, it does not make explicit links between the local and global behaviours of the system.

References

1. Jacobson I., Booch G. and Rumbaugh J. (1998) Unified Modelling Language - User Guide. Addison-Wesley
2. Rational Software Corporation (1997) Rational Objectory Process 4.1. Technical report http://www.rational.com
3. Jacobson I., Christerson M., and Overgaard G. (1992) Object-Oriented Software Engineering - A Use Case Driven Approach. Addison-Wesley
4. Harel D. (1987) Statecharts: A visual formalism for complex systems. Science of Computer Programming 8(3):231–274.
5. Wills A. C. and D'Souza D. F. (1998) Objects, components, and frameworks with UML - the CATALYSIS approach. Addison-Wesley

7 VHDL: A Hardware Description Language and its Simulation Semantics

Laurence Pierre

7.1 Overview of VHDL

VHDL [8,2] is not a formal language like many of the formalisms considered in this book; it is a Hardware Description Language i.e., a language devoted to the description of hardware components at various levels of abstraction. This language has been standardised by the IEEE under the names *VHDL'87* and *VHDL'93* [5,6]; the VHDL'87 version is considered here. VHDL and another standardised language Verilog [7,9] are used widely by the community of hardware designers. A variety of commercial CAD tools support these languages, providing complete design environments with capabilities for schematic capture, simulation , gate-level or high-level synthesis. VHDL is often used in three different styles of description: the "behavioural" style (clocked or asynchronous concurrent "processes" execute algorithmic specifications and communicate through common "signals"), the "dataflow" style (the architecture of the device is described by means of a set of equations, this style roughly corresponds to the "Register Transfer" level of abstraction), and the "structural" style (the device is described as a set of interconnected components). In this chapter, we consider only the behavioural style.

VHDL has a "simulation semantics" i.e., a semantics based on an event-driven simulation engine. Since the publication of the first official VHDL Language Reference Manual, many efforts have been made to define the language formally (see for instance [3,1]). The semantics of the VHDL constructs introduced hereafter give their meaning in terms of the successive simulation cycles; a physical time and a logical time are attached to each simulation cycle.

A VHDL description is composed of an "entity" and one or several "architectures". The *entity* is a black box that only specifies the interface of the device (i.e., the input/output ports also called primary inputs and outputs). It can have "generic" parameters that parameterise a description; for instance the size of some structures (vectors, arrays) can be specified using generic parameters. Usually, the *specification* of such a description (the behaviour intended by the designer) is an *observable behaviour* which expresses a relationship between the primary inputs and outputs (the values that the primary outputs must take given input stimuli). Each *architecture* gives a particular view of the structure or behaviour of the system, depending on its style of description. An *architecture* contains a set of concurrent statements. The only concurrent statement that we use in the rest of this chapter is the "process" . A *process* includes a set of sequential statements that are executed at each simulation cycle in which the *process* is *active*. There are two ways of specifying when a *process* should be active: the keyword "process" is followed by a *sensitivity list*, or the *process* includes at least one "wait" statement. Only the construct of *sensitivity list* will be used below.

Prior to explaining the role of a *sensitivity list*, we have to define what a "signal" is. Signals are used to model hardware communication channels (wires, buses) or storage elements (latches, flipflops); they allow for the communication between the *processes*. Usual algorithmic "variables" can also be used, but have to be local to the *processes*. When a *variable* is modified (assignment operator :=), its new value is immediately available in the current simulation cycle. Conversely, the value assigned to a *signal* (assignment operator <=) during a simulation cycle is only available in a future cycle. More precisely, if the assignment statement includes no "after" clause to specify an explicit delay then the signal value is available in the next simulation cycle, otherwise it is available in the simulation cycle which corresponds to the physical time computed by adding the delay of the *after* clause to the current simulation time. A *sensitivity list* is a list of *signals*, the *process* sensitive to these *signals* resumes each time there has been an *event* on at least one of these *signals* (the value of the *signal* has changed). Upon resumption, it executes its sequential statements and then it suspends its execution until the next reactivation event. This is the usual way *processes* asynchronously communicate in VHDL: each time a *process* updates a *signal*, the *processes* that are sensitive to that *signal* resume (in the future) because of that event, and take into account this new value. They do not have to synchronize with sending/receiving actions. The *sensitivity list* can include primary inputs, hence external events can also be taken into account.

While *variables* are declared locally to *processes*, *signals* are shared by *processes*. Their values can be read by every *process* but only one of them is allowed to modify the value of a *signal*, unless a *resolution function* is defined, to manage conflicts in case of *multi-source signals*. A *resolution function* is a user-defined function that is used by the simulator to determine unambiguously the value to be assigned to the *signal* (for instance, in circuit descriptions, resolution functions often represent wired ORs or ANDs).

VHDL is a strongly typed language with some predefined data types (Boolean, natural,...). By default, the initial value of an object is the "lowest" value of range for its type. The user can define other types and sub-types, in particular enumerated types, records and arrays. Array types can be unconstrained (i.e. their size is not fixed), but instances of these types must be constrained. The user can also define functions/procedures. Type definitions and function/procedure signatures are given in a "package", function/procedure definitions are given in the corresponding "package body".

7.2 Analysis and Specification of Case 1

The goal of the invoicing system is to consider a stock of products and a set of orders, and to invoice orders when it is possible (i.e., if the ordered quantity is less or equal to the quantity in stock). In Case 1, we simply have to consider that the stock and the set of orders are given in a up-to-date state.

7.2.1 Identifying Data Structures

VHDL is a strongly typed language. Thus, the first questions we ask are related to the data types.

Question 1: Which data type can be used to represent the orders?

Answer: An order is characterized by a number, the reference of the ordered product, and the quantity ordered. These elements can be the fields of a record type Orders; these fields are represented by natural numbers. When an order is invoiced, its state has to be changed from "pending" to "invoiced". Thus, we have another field stat whose value is either pending or invoiced. We define an enumerated type State_of_order for these values.

```
type State_of_order is (pending, invoiced);
type Orders is record      -- record type for the orders
    number, ref, quant : natural;
    stat : State_of_order;
end record;
```

Question 2: Which data type can be used to represent the products?

Answer: Products can also be modelled as records. The type St_states has two fields that represent the reference of the product and the quantity in stock.

```
type St_states is record   -- record type for the products
    s_ref, s_quant : natural;
end record;
```

Question 3: Which data types can be used to represent the set of orders and the set of products?

Answer: They can be modelled using one-dimensional arrays. The types List_of_orders and State_of_stock are unconstrained (i.e. their size is not specified) one-dimensional arrays of Orders and St_states respectively.

```
type List_of_orders is array(natural range <>) of Orders;
type State_of_stock is array(natural range <>) of St_states;
    -- "natural range <>" means that
    -- the arrays are unconstrained
```

All these types, together with the associated functions, are declared in a package called Invoice. The function definitions will be given in the corresponding package body we show in the next section.

7.2.2 Identifying Operations

As explained in the introductory section, the VHDL description of a component starts with the definition of its *entity* (external view) which is associated with the notion of its observable behaviour.

Question 4: What should the external view of the invoicing system be?

Answer: The user should be able to observe on the **output** of the system a response (which orders have been invoiced) to the up-to-date state of stock and of orders. The system should also give information about the modifications it has made to the stock and to the orders. Therefore, we decide that the system **inputs** the up-to-date state, and **outputs** every order that can be invoiced, as well as the modified state. This corresponds to the external view depicted on Figure 7.1. The device has two inputs, the current state

Fig. 7.1. External view of Case 1

of orders (port ord of the VHDL description), and the current state of the stock (port st of the VHDL description). It outputs the invoiced orders (port outord of the description), and updates the state of orders and the state of stock (the ports ord and st are consequently declared as inout ports in the VHDL description). This corresponds to the following entity invoicing1 which has two generic parameters nbord and nbst that parameterise the description on the number of orders and on the number of products that can be considered:

```
entity invoicing1 is
      generic (nbord,nbst:positive);
      port (ord: inout List_of_orders(0 to nbord);
            st: inout State_of_stock(0 to nbst);
            outord: out Orders);
end invoicing1;
```

Question 5: How are the orders processed?

Answer: The orders contained in the list ord are iteratively scanned (using a for..loop VHDL statement) in order to try to invoice the pending orders. For each order, if the quantity ordered is less or equal to the quantity that is in stock for the ordered product, then the order is output on the port outord, its state (field stat) becomes invoiced, and the corresponding quantity is removed from the stock st.

7 VHDL: An HDL and its Simulation Semantics 117

Question 6: Which operators/functions are needed?

Answer: The first two actions, i.e. the order is output on the port outord and its state becomes invoiced, only require the use of the assignment statement. For the last action, i.e. the corresponding quantity is removed from the stock, we define a simple function called s_update1.

```
function s_update1(s:State_of_stock; r,q:natural)
return State_of_stock is
   -- returns the stock s where the quantity
   -- q of the product r has been removed
variable sres:State_of_stock(s'range);
begin
   for i in 0 to s_actualsize(s) loop
      sres(i).s_ref:=s(i).s_ref;
      if s(i).s_ref=r then
        sres(i).s_quant:=s(i).s_quant-q;
      else
        sres(i).s_quant:=s(i).s_quant;
      end if;
   end loop;
   return sres;
end s_update1;
```

Other functions are needed, **actualsize** computes the actual size of a vector of orders (used in the for..loop which scans the orders), **s_actualsize** computes the actual size of a vector of products (used in s_update1), and **s_extract_quant** returns the available quantity of a product, given its reference. Thus, here is the complete definition of the package Invoice and of its package body:

```
package Invoice is
  type State_of_order is (pending, invoiced);
  type Orders is record      -- record type for the orders
     number, ref, quant : natural;
     stat : State_of_order;
  end record;
  type St_states is record   -- record type for the products
     s_ref, s_quant : natural;
  end record;
  type List_of_orders is array(natural range <>) of Orders;
  type State_of_stock is array(natural range <>) of St_states;
  function actualsize(o:List_of_orders) return integer;
  function s_actualsize(s:State_of_stock) return integer;
  function s_extract_quant(s:State_of_stock; r:natural)
      return natural;
  function s_update1(s:State_of_stock; r,q:natural)
```

```
      return State_of_stock;
  end Invoice;

  package body Invoice is
    function actualsize (o: List_of_orders) return integer is
        -- computes the actual size of the vector of orders o
      variable i:natural;
    begin
      i:=0;
      while (i<=o'right) and (o(i).ref/=0)
        loop
          i:=i+1;
        end loop;
      return i-1;
    end actualsize;

    function s_actualsize (s: State_of_stock) return integer is
        -- computes the actual size of the vector of products
      variable i:natural;
    begin
      i:=0;
      while (i<=s'right) and (s(i).s_ref/=0)
        loop
          i:=i+1;
        end loop;
      return i-1;
    end s_actualsize;

    function s_extract_quant(s:State_of_stock; r:natural)
        return natural is
        -- returns the available quantity of
        -- the product r in the stock s
    begin
      for i in s_actualsize(s) loop
        if s(i).s_ref=r then
          return s(i).s_quant;
        end if;
      end loop;
      return 0;
    end s_extract_quant;

    function s_update1(s:State_of_stock; r,q:natural)
    return State_of_stock is
    variable sres:State_of_stock(s'range);
    begin
```

```
      for i in 0 to s_actualsize(s) loop
         sres(i).s_ref:=s(i).s_ref;
         if s(i).s_ref=r then
            sres(i).s_quant:=s(i).s_quant-q;
         else
            sres(i).s_quant:=s(i).s_quant;
         end if;
      end loop;
      return sres;
   end s_update1;
end Invoice;
```

Question 7: How many VHDL processes are required?

Answer: Our specification corresponds to the behaviour of a single process, called operative_part, which is sensitive to the signals ord and st. It resumes each time an event occurs on one of these signals. This process is the body of the architecture behavioural of the entity invoicing1:

```
architecture behavioural of invoicing1 is
begin
   operative_part:process(ord,st)   -- sensitive to ord and st
   variable s:State_of_stock(st'range);
   begin
      s:=st;
      -- tries to invoice every pending order
      -- in the set of orders:
      for i in 0 to actualsize(ord) loop
        -- for every pending order
        if (ord(i).stat=pending) then
           -- if the available quantity of product
           -- is sufficient
           if (ord(i).quant <= s_extract_quant(s,ord(i).ref))
             then
               -- the invoiced order is output,
               outord <= ord(i);
               -- its state changes,
               ord(i).stat <= invoiced;
               -- ord(i).quant articles are removed
               -- from the stock:
               s:=s_update1(s,ord(i).ref,ord(i).quant);
           end if;
        end if;
      end loop;
      st <= s;
   end process;
end behavioural;
```

Remark: Our aim is to emphasize the *dynamic* aspects of VHDL (behaviours, communications). It could have been possible to consider the fact that the same reference can be requested on several different orders, but we have not explicitly taken this into account, as it is simply related to *static* aspects (data). By default, our implementation arbitrarily selects the *oldest* order, since our type List_of_orders behaves as a FIFO.

7.3 Analysis and Specification of Case 2

Now we have to take into account the entries of new orders/cancellations of orders and the entries of quantities in the stock.

Question 8: What should the external view of the system be?

Answer: Now, we should observe on the output outord a response to these entries: new orders (port neword), order cancellations (port cancel), and new quantities in the stock (port newst). This corresponds to the entity invoicing given; the sizes of the vector of orders and of the vector of products are generic parameters. The port cancel receives the numbers of the orders to be cancelled.

```
entity invoicing is
      generic (nbord,nbst:positive);
      port (neword: in Orders; newst: in St_states;
            cancel: in natural; outord: out Orders);
end invoicing;
```

Question 9: How are the new entries processed?

Answer: With our encoding of the specification, we can identify three cases:

- if a new order is received, then it must be added to the current set of orders;
- if an existing order is cancelled, then we simply change its state from pending to invoiced;
- if a new quantity of a given product is to be added to the stock, then the state of the stock is updated accordingly.

Question 10: Do we need additional operators/functions?

Answer: For the first two cases of the answer to Question 9, only the use of the assignment statement is required. For the third case, we define an ad hoc function called s_update2.

```
function s_update2(s:State_of_stock; r,q:natural)
return State_of_stock is   -- returns s with the additional
                           -- quantity q of the product r
variable sres:State_of_stock(s'range);
```

```
variable found:boolean:=false;
variable k:integer;
  begin
    k:=-1;
    for i in 0 to s_actualsize(s) loop
       sres(i).s_ref:=s(i).s_ref;
       if s(i).s_ref=r then
          sres(i).s_quant:=s(i).s_quant+q;
          found:=true;
       else
          sres(i).s_quant:=s(i).s_quant;
       end if;
       k:=i;
    end loop;
    if (not found) then
       sres(k+1):=St_states'(r,q);
    end if;
    return sres;
  end s_update2;
```

Question 11: How many VHDL processes will be involved?

Answer: The behaviour of the whole system can be decomposed as illustrated by Figure 7.2:

- a process, referred to as the "operative part", takes into account the stock and the set of orders, and is in charge of invoicing the orders if possible (this corresponds to the process described in Section 2);
- another process, subsequently referred to as the "control part", receives the entries of new orders or cancellations of orders, and the entries of quantities in the stock, and its role consists in updating the set of orders or the state of stock as specified in the answer to Question 9.

The concurrent composition of these two processes fulfils the requirements of Case 2. Note that each process must keep the other one informed about the modifications it has made to the state of orders ord and to the state of the stock st; this bi-directional communication is shown as double arrows in the figure.

Question 12: How do the processes access to the common data ord and st?

Answer: VHDL requires great care with multi-source signals. For the state of stock st we leave complete control to the control part, and for the list of orders ord we will use a resolution function .

The internal signal ord will be a resolved signal, associated with the resolution function ord_resolv. The name of the resolution function will simply

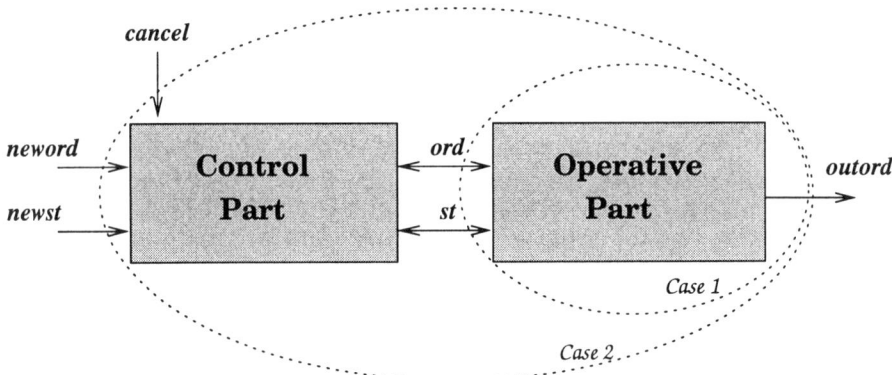

Fig. 7.2. Representation of Case 2

be written in the declaration of the signal, before the identifier of its type and the simulator will automatically use it when necessary. The number of possible sources for the same signal is never fixed (it depends, at each simulation cycle, on the number of processes that try to modify the signal), but a VHDL function cannot be declared with a variable number of formal parameters. Hence the parameter of a resolution function is an unconstrained one-dimensional array of elements of the type of the resolved signal. (type LO_res here, see its definition in the package Invoice below). The function must be written in such a way that it guarantees that its result is unchanged whatever the order of the sources is when the function is called. In case of conflict between several records, the following rules are used in the definition of the function ord_resolv:

- the state is invoiced if the state of at least one source is invoiced,
- the number and the reference are identical and unmodified by the processes of the description, thus any value can be used as the source,
- and the quantity is computed as the maximum of the quantities of the sources.

```
function ord_resolv(sources:LO_res) return List_of_orders is
variable res:List_of_orders(sources(0)'range);
variable maxq:natural;
begin
    for i in sources(0)'range loop
      res(i).stat:=pending; maxq:=0;
      for j in sources'range loop
        if sources(j)(i).stat=invoiced then
          res(i).stat:=invoiced;
        end if;
        if sources(j)(i).quant>maxq then
          maxq:=sources(j)(i).quant;
        end if;
```

```
      if sources(j)(i).number/=0 then
        res(i).number:=sources(j)(i).number;
      end if;
      if sources(j)(i).ref/=0 then
        res(i).ref:=sources(j)(i).ref;
      end if;
    end loop;
    res(i).quant:=maxq;
  end loop;
  return res;
end ord_resolv;
```

Now we can give the updated definition of the package Invoice and of its package body:

```
package Invoice is
  type State_of_order is (pending, invoiced);
  type Orders is record       -- record type for the orders
     number, ref, quant : natural;
     stat : State_of_order;
  end record;
  type St_states is record    -- record type for the products
     s_ref, s_quant : natural;
  end record;
  type List_of_orders is array(natural range <>) of Orders;
  type State_of_stock is array(natural range <>) of St_states;
  constant n:natural:=100;
  type LO_res is array(natural range <>) of
    List_of_orders(0 to n);
    -- used by the resolution function
  function actualsize(o:List_of_orders) return integer;
  function s_actualsize(s:State_of_stock) return integer;
  function s_extract_quant(s:State_of_stock; r:natural)
    return natural;
  function s_update1(s:State_of_stock; r,q:natural)
    return State_of_stock;
  function s_update2(s:State_of_stock; r,q:natural)
    return State_of_stock;
  function ord_resolv(sources:LO_res)
    return List_of_orders;
end Invoice;

package body Invoice is
  function actualsize (o: List_of_orders) return integer is
  variable i:natural;
```

```
begin
  i:=0;
  while (i<=o'right) and (o(i).ref/=0)
    loop
      i:=i+1;
    end loop;
  return i-1;
end actualsize;

function s_actualsize (s: State_of_stock) return integer is
variable i:natural;
begin
  i:=0;
  while (i<=s'right) and (s(i).s_ref/=0)
    loop
      i:=i+1;
    end loop;
  return i-1;
end s_actualsize;

function s_extract_quant(s:State_of_stock; r:natural)
return natural is
begin
  for i in s_actualsize(s) loop
    if s(i).s_ref=r then
      return s(i).s_quant;
    end if;
  end loop;
  return 0;
end s_extract_quant;

function s_update1(s:State_of_stock; r,q:natural)
return State_of_stock is
variable sres:State_of_stock(s'range);
begin
  for i in 0 to s_actualsize(s) loop
    sres(i).s_ref:=s(i).s_ref;
    if s(i).s_ref=r then
      sres(i).s_quant:=s(i).s_quant-q;
    else
      sres(i).s_quant:=s(i).s_quant;
    end if;
  end loop;
  return sres;
```

```
end s_update1;

function s_update2(s:State_of_stock; r,q:natural)
return State_of_stock is
variable sres:State_of_stock(s'range);
variable found:boolean:=false;   variable k:integer;
begin
  k:=-1;
  for i in 0 to s_actualsize(s) loop
     sres(i).s_ref:=s(i).s_ref;
     if s(i).s_ref=r then
       sres(i).s_quant:=s(i).s_quant+q;
       found:=true;
     else
       sres(i).s_quant:=s(i).s_quant;
     end if;
     k:=i;
  end loop;
  if (not found) then
    sres(k+1):=St_states'(r,q);
  end if;
  return sres;
end s_update2;

function ord_resolv(sources:LO_res) return List_of_orders is
                                  -- resolution function
variable res:List_of_orders(sources(0)'range);
variable maxq:natural;
begin
 for i in sources(0)'range loop
   res(i).stat:=pending; maxq:=0;
   for j in sources'range loop
     if sources(j)(i).stat=invoiced then
       res(i).stat:=invoiced;
     end if;
     if sources(j)(i).quant>maxq then
       maxq:=sources(j)(i).quant;
     end if;
     if sources(j)(i).number/=0 then
       res(i).number:=sources(j)(i).number;
     end if;
     if sources(j)(i).ref/=0 then
       res(i).ref:=sources(j)(i).ref;
     end if;
```

```
        end loop;
        res(i).quant:=maxq;
      end loop;
      return res;
    end ord_resolv;
  end Invoice;
```

As expressed by the answers to the previous questions, the architecture behavioural of the entity invoicing should include two processes, one for the operative part (called operative_part below) and one for the control part. For the sake of clarity, we divided the control part into two processes, that play distinct roles: control_part_ord manages new orders/cancellations, and control_part_st manages new items into the stock. Each process is only sensitive to its relevant input signals.

```
  architecture behavioural of invoicing is
  signal ord: ord_resolv List_of_orders(0 to nbord);
                                          -- resolved signal
  signal st,st2: State_of_stock(0 to nbst);
  begin
```

The process operative_part is only sensitive to the two internal signals ord and st. Each time an event occurs on one of these signals, the process resumes and behaves as the process operative_part of the description of Section 2. However, in order to let the process control_part_st have the entire responsibility of managing the stock, the process operative_part only updates an auxiliary signal st2 (with the function s_update1), so the process control_part_st can make the necessary modification in the actual stock.

```
    operative_part:process(ord,st)   -- sensitive to ord and st
    variable s:State_of_stock(st'range);
    begin
      s:=st;
      -- tries to invoice every pending order
      -- in the set of orders
      for i in 0 to actualsize(ord) loop
        if (ord(i).stat=pending) then
          if (ord(i).quant <= s_extract_quant(s,ord(i).ref))
            then
              -- the invoiced order is output
              outord <= ord(i);
              -- its state changes
              ord(i).stat <= invoiced;
              -- ord(i).quant articles are removed
              -- from the stock:
              s:=s_update1(s,ord(i).ref,ord(i).quant);
```

```
            st2 <= s;
        end if;
      end if;
    end loop;
end process;
```

The process control_part_st is sensitive to the port newst and to the local signal st2 (an event on st2 indicates that modifications in the stock are requested by the operative part). The modifications (if any) induced by the operative part are taken into account in a local variable s. Then, if there has been an event on the port newst, a new stock is computed with the corresponding modification (function s_update2).

```
--sensitive to newst and st2
control_part_st:process(newst, st2)
variable s:State_of_stock(st'range);
begin
  if (st2'event) then
    -- modifications induced by the operative part
    s:=st2;
  else
    s:=st;
  end if;
  if (newst'event) then
    -- a new quantity in stock is entered
    -- a new stock is computed,
    -- with the additional quantity
    s:=s_update2(s,newst.s_ref,newst.s_quant);
  end if;
  st <= s;  -- the actual stock is updated
end process;
```

Finally, the process control_part_ord is sensitive to the input ports neword and cancel. If a new order is input on neword then it is added at the end of the vector ord, and if an order is cancelled then its state becomes invoiced (but this order is not output on outord).

```
control_part_ord:process(neword, cancel)
begin
  if (neword'event) then
    -- a new order is received
    ord(actualsize(ord)+1) <= neword;
  end if;
  if (cancel'event) then
    -- an order cancellation is received
    for i in 0 to actualsize(ord) loop
```

```
          if (ord(i).number=cancel) then
            -- instead of removing the
            -- order, we give it the status "invoiced"
            ord(i).stat <= invoiced;
          end if;
        end loop;
      end if;
    end process;
  end behavioural;
```

Remark: the process operative_part iterates on the whole set of pending orders and this iteration is atomic from the point of view of the simulation engine. Inside a process, the statements are sequentially executed within the same simulation cycle (the simulation time is unchanged). Thus, the operative part examines the complete set of orders every time the process resumes.

7.4 The Natural Language Description of the Specification

7.4.1 Case 1

An order is characterized by a number, the reference of the ordered product, and the ordered quantity. All of these data are natural numbers. When an order is invoiced, its state changes from pending to invoiced. A product is represented by its reference and its quantity in stock. The set of orders and the stock (set of products) are encoded by one-dimensional arrays.

The system has two inputs, the current state of orders (port ord), and the current state of the stock (port st). It outputs the invoiced orders (port outord), and updates the state of orders and the state of stock. Each time there has been an external event (the state of orders or the state of stock has changed), the orders are iteratively scanned to invoice the pending ones: for each order, if the quantity ordered is less or equal to the quantity that is in stock for the ordered product, then the order is output by the device, its state becomes invoiced, and the corresponding quantity is removed from the stock.

7.4.2 Case 2

The behaviour described for Case 1 becomes the behaviour of the *operative part* of the system. Modifications to the state of orders or stock no longer correspond to external events but to events from the *control part*.

This *control part* reacts to external events (new orders, cancellations, or new products are input on the ports neword, cancel or newst) and to the events from the *operative part* (orders have changed from pending to invoiced, or quantities have been removed from the stock). Each time there is a new order, it is added to the set of orders (i.e. is put into the corresponding vector). When an order is cancelled, its state is changed to `invoiced`. When a new product or a new quantity is entered, the stock is modified accordingly.

7.5 Conclusion

VHDL provides direct mechanisms to partition and specify this example problem. This example involves elaborated types and their operators, communication between the system and its environment, and communication between sub-systems. VHDL can deal with all these aspects. The fact that VHDL is a strongly-typed language with user definable data types was valuable. The required data were concisely encoded using records and arrays, and it was easy to write elementary access and modification functions. Another interesting aspect of VHDL, highlighted by this case study, is that it allows modelling of asynchronously communicating processes, and it helps identify the problems that arise when several processes want to modify common data. To resolve the issue of different commands for specific orders, we have used a simple resolution function. For the management of the stock, we have adopted a description style that gives complete control to the control part.

Using the behavioural style of VHDL, one can develop abstract specifications and these specifications can be debugged by simulation . This is a significant advantage of using a Hardware Description Language and an associated CAD environment, whereas most formal languages or calculi are not supported by execution/simulation tools. A high-level synthesis tool can also be used to synthesize a VHDL specification into a more concrete realisation, provided that a *synthesisable subset* of VHDL is used. The high-level description proposed here is not restricted to this VHDL subset. It could be transformed into a *synthesisable* description by application of specific guidelines, among them the presence of a master clock and the use of constant bounds for the "for" loops. This simply reflects the fact that reasonable design rules have to be respected in a high-level specification for a realistic implementation.

The main disadvantage of VHDL is certainly its lack of formal semantics. The meaning of VHDL descriptions can be understood in terms of the event-driven simulator, but VHDL has not officially been given a formal semantics (though significant results have been proposed in that direction [3,1]).

In addition to debugging by simulation, one may want to use the VHDL specification to *formally prove* properties such as "if there is enough quantity in stock (and if this condition remains true) then a pending order will eventually be invoiced", or "if there is not enough quantity in stock then the product will not be removed from the stock until a sufficient quantity becomes available". Assuming a discrete time scale, such properties can be formalized using a temporal logic and can be verified by *model checking* techniques. Various public domain tools can be of valuable help, provided that we restrict the sets of data to *finite* sets.

Some of them include a Hardware Description Language front-end, for instance VIS [4] that supports a synthesisable subset of Verilog.

References

1. Kluwer Academic Publishers (1995) *Formal Methods in System Design.* 7(1/2)
2. Bergé J.M., Fonkoua A., Maginot S., Rouillard J. (1993) *VHDL'92 : The New Features of the VHDL Hardware Description Language.* Kluwer Academic Publishers
3. Delgado Kloos C., Breuer P. (Eds.) (1995) *Formal Semantics for VHDL.* Kluwer Academic Publishers
4. The VIS Group (1996) VIS: A system for verification and synthesis. In Alur R., Henzinger T. (Eds.) *8th International Conference on Computer Aided Verification.* LNCS 1102, Springer-Verlag
5. IEEE (1988) *Standard VHDL Language Reference Manual.* IEEE
6. ANSI/IEEE (1993) *Standard VHDL Language Reference Manual, IEEE Standard 1076-1993.* IEEE Computer Society
7. IEEE (1995) *1364-1995 IEEE Standard Description Language Based on the Verilog(TM) Hardware Description Language.* IEEE
8. Mazor S., Langstraat P. (1995) *A Guide to VHDL.* Kluwer Academic Publishers
9. Thomas D.E., Moorby P.R. (1998) *The Verilog Hardware Description Language (Fourth Edition).* Kluwer Academic Publishers

8 Estelle: A Formal Description Technique

Eric Lallet and Jean-Luc Raffy

8.1 Overview of the FDT Estelle

Estelle is a Formal Description Technique standardised by ISO[3,6,2]. Its main application field is the formal specification of distributed systems such as communication protocols[1]. Estelle permits a clear split between the definition of the global architecture of the system and the internal behaviour of its components.

An Estelle specification describes a collection of hierarchical communicating components that can be nested in a parent/child relationship. A component is an instance of a generic module definition composed of a single header definition and one or more associated body definitions. These instances may be statically or dynamically created by means of a header/body pair.

The header definition describes the external communication part of the module and specifies a synchronous parallel or a non-deterministic serial execution. The communication interface of a module is defined by ports called interaction points (IPs). Each IP refers to a channel which defines two sets of interactions (messages sent and received). Nested modules can also communicate by sharing exported variables. The attribute declared in the header part may be either **systemprocess** (or process) and it leads to a synchronous parallel execution or **systemactivity** (or activity) and it leads to a non-deterministic serial execution.

The body definition describes the behaviour of the component. It uses the extended finite state machine (EFSM) paradigm. It is composed of three parts : a declaration part, an initialisation part and a transition part where the EFSM is described. Within the EFSM, each transition part is made of two different parts, a clause group and a transition block. The clauses within a clause group define the transition firing conditions where the transition block defines the action part of the transition.

8.2 Analysis and Specification of Case 1

As stated above, we have to specify the architecture and then describe the behaviour of the different components.

We must first, clarify some points because of the incompleteness of the user requirements.

Question 1: Could an order contain several products?

Answer: We assume that, as it is only stated that "on an order, we have one and only one reference to an ordered product", an order could contain several products.

Moreover, as the user requirements states that a same reference can be ordered on several different orders and that an order will be changed to "invoiced" if the ordered quantity is either less than or equal to the quantity which is in stock, two more remarks arise.

- Firstly, the orders have to be invoiced one by one.
- Secondly, as no specific sequence among the orders is given, we must use a non-deterministic structure.

8.2.1 Defining the Architecture of the Specification

Identifying the Independent Systems. The first question one should ask is:

Question 2: How many independent systems must be specified?

Answer: The only system required is **invoiceCase1**. This system will contain sub-systems called modules.

Identifying the Global Behaviour and the Sub-Systems. As stated above, we will use a non-deterministic behaviour. In Estelle, it is expressed by the attribute "systemactivity".

Question 3: What are the sub-systems within the system?

Answer: As, in the first case study, the stock and the set of orders are given in a up-to-date state, we can use a static structure. Different choices could be made. In order to show some features of Estelle, we chose to have as many Order modules as actual orders. As in Estelle, we only declare generic modules, we need only one Order module. Thus, the sub-systems are the Stock module and the Order module. All the orders will be instances of the generic Order module.

Identifying the Information Sent and the Communication Links. Estelle permits some decisions to be left to the implementation phase. As we do not know how many orders are given, or how many products (and in which quantity) are in stock, we will use the keyword **any** to state that it may be any value taken in a range of values.

> **TYPE**
> *(we declare a new type with a range of values).*
> Max = 0..100000;

Comments can be added in Estelle code under 2 forms:

{this is a comment}
(*this is a comment, as well*)

CONST
  { *All the constants may take one of the values in range of Max.* }
  MaxOrder = any Max;
  MaxRef = any Max;
  MaxInList = any Max;
  MaxInStock = any Max;
  MaxOrdered = any Max;

TYPE
  { *We do not know at the specification phase, either the actual number of orders or the number of products referenced* }
  NbOrder = 0..MaxOrder;
  Reference = 1..MaxRef;
  { *We assume that a product is known by its reference number and its quantity* }
  Product = **RECORD**
      ref : Reference;
      nb : 1.. MaxOrdered
  END;
  { *We assume that an order is made of an array of Product* }
  ProductList = **ARRAY** [0..MaxInList] **OF** Product;

We have now to decide which messages are exchanged by the modules.

Question 4: What kind of information does an order send to the stock?

Answer: Let assume that the Order module sends only the list of products (with their quantities).

Question 5: What is the answer of the stock?

Answer: We assume that the Stock module answers a Boolean to indicate if the order can be executed (thus invoiced) or not.

A channel of communication is first declared with 2 opposite roles. Second, the messages to be sent are given for each role.

  CHANNEL OrderStockChan (order,stock);
      { *Parameters can be sent within messages* }
      BY order: destock (list:ProductList);
      BY stock: result (ack:boolean);

We can now declare the headers of the modules. They represent the external interface of the modules. We specify the interactions points (IPs) and the role they have, related to the channel declaration.

The Stock module has an array of IPs because of the number of orders it has to deal with. As the dimension of the array is not known, it is set to NbOrder. The parameter *stockList* is initialised with the initial stock. An exported variable, **Done**, is provided to communicate with the specification level. When all the orders have been taken into account the variable **Done** will be set to true. It will stop the execution.

> **MODULE** Stock **ACTIVITY** (stockList:ProductList);
> **IP**
>   ToOrder:**ARRAY**[NbOrder] **OF** OrderStockChan (stock);
> **EXPORT**
>   Done: **BOOLEAN**;
> **END**; { *MODULE HEADER Stock* }

As said previously, we have to declare only one Order module. It has a single interaction point because it exchanges messages only with the Stock module. It uses an exported variable to indicate if the order is invoiced or not. The parameter *order* is initialised with the list of product to be ordered.

> **MODULE** Order **ACTIVITY** (order:ProductList);
> **IP**
>   ToStock: OrderStockChan (order);
> **EXPORT**
>   Invoiced: **BOOLEAN**;
> **END**; { *MODULE HEADER Order* }

8.2.2 Defining the Behaviour

Defining the Initialisation of the Architecture. We first, have to declare the module variables with the keyword **modvar**. The initialisation part is a normal transition beginning by the keyword **initialize**. It is the first transition to be fired. In this transition, we have to initialise the modules, i.e. associate a body to the module variable (which has a type "module header"). Then connections have to be made. Recall that in Estelle, dynamic creation and deletion of modules is permitted. We will see the use of this feature in the second case.

> **MODVAR**
>   { *We declare the module variables before instantiation* }
>   ProductsInStock : Stock;
>   OrderForm: **ARRAY** [NbOrder] **OF** Order;
> **VAR**
>   itemsList : ProductList;
>
> **STATE**
>   wait, stop; {*The EFSM is composed of 2 states*}

INITIALIZE TO wait
NAME initPart:
BEGIN   {*Initialisation of a Stock module*}
    itemsList := fillStock;
    INIT ProductsInStock **WITH** StockBody(itemsList);
    { *StockBody is the part of the specification where the behaviour of the module Stock is specified* }
    ProductInStock.Done := **FALSE**;
    ALL nbOfOrderForms : NbOrder **DO**
        {*Initialisation of Order modules* }
        BEGIN
        itemsList := fillOrder(nbOfOrderForms);
        INIT OrderForm[nbOfOrderForms]
            WITH OrderBody (itemsList);
        OrderForm[nbOfOrderForms].Invoiced := FALSE;
        { *We create the links between Order modules and the Stock module* }
        CONNECT OrderForm[nbOfOrderForms].ToStock
        TO ProductsInStock.ToOrdel[nbOfOrderFormS];
        END;
END;

We use a function *fillOrder()* to fill in the order form. As nothing is said about it, we leave it for the implementation. In Estelle, such function is declared as follows.

FUNCTION fillOrder(nbOrd: NbOrder):ProductList; **PRIMITIVE**;

We use the same for the function *fillStock()*.

FUNCTION fillStock:ProductList;   **PRIMITIVE**;

When all the orders are taken into account, the result of the invoicing operation will be printed out.

TRANS
    FROM wait
    TO stop
    PROVIDED ProductsInStock.Done
    BEGIN
    END;

    FROM stop
    TO stop
    BEGIN
        ALL oo:NbOrder **DO**
            printResults (oo, OrderForm [oo].Invoiced);
    END;

Defining the Behaviour of the Modules. The Stock module receives a message from an order module with a list of products as parameter. It answers a Boolean depending of the state of the stock.

As stated above, no ordering is given to the orders. Thus we use a non-deterministic feature of Estelle given by the keyword **any**.

Question 6: What to do if an order can only be partly served?

Answer: As no information is given in the informal specification to explain what to do, we will use a function removeFromStock() whose description is postponed to the implementation.

The Stock module must take into account all the orders and then tell the specification module that it has ended. The behaviour can be described by means of an EFSM with 2 states, exec and close. The transition part is made of 2 transitions. The first one allows to take all the orders into account, the second one permits to tell the specification module that the job is done. As these 2 transitions start from the same state, *exec*, we have to specify which one will be first fired. In Estelle, we will use the clause **Priority**; that clause is used with a positive integer. The smaller the integer, the higher the priority.

BODY StockBody **FOR** Stock;
{behaviour of the Stock Module }
STATE
  exec, close; *{ The EFSM is composed of 2 states}*

TRANS
 FROM exec
 TO exec
 PRIORITY 0 *{ The highest priority}*
 { The any clause permits to specify a non-deterministic behaviour}
 ANY oo:NbOrder DO
 WHEN ToOrder[oo].destock(list)
 VAR
  ack:**BOOLEAN**;
 NAME checkAndUpdate:

 BEGIN
  { *removeFromStock() description is postponed to the implementation* }
  ack := removeFromStock(list,stockList);
  OUTPUT ToOrder[oo].result(ack)
 END;

 FROM exec
 TO close
 NAME closing;

8 Estelle: A Formal Description Technique   137

```
        BEGIN
            Done := TRUE;
        END;
END;{ MODULE BODY StockBody }
```

Each Order sends a message to the Stock module to destock. Then depending on the answer given by the Stock module, the order will be set to invoiced or not by means of the exported variable **Invoiced**.

BODY OrderBody **FOR** Order;
STATE pendingState, invoicedState; {*The EFSM is composed of 2 states*}
{*The Order module asks the Stock module if it can provide the required products*}
INITIALIZE TO pendingState
    NAME destock:
    BEGIN
        OUTPUT ToStock.destock(order);
    END;

TRANS

    FROM pendingState
    TO invoicedState
    WHEN ToStock.result(ack)
    NAME ackInvoice:
    BEGIN
        IF ack **THEN**
            Invoiced := **TRUE**;
    END;

END; { *MODULE BODY OrderBody*}

8.3 Analysis and Specification of Case 2

Question 7: What are the new required operations?

Answer: In Case 2, Orders can be added or deleted and products can be added to the Stock.

Thus, we have to add some new functions and procedures. As nothing is said about how and when all these operations could occur, we leave the description of these functions and procedures to the implementation.

FUNCTION initial_nb_of_order: NbOrder; **PRIMITIVE**;
{*permits to begin the job with a set of orders*}

FUNCTION NewItemsForStock: **BOOLEAN**; **PRIMITIVE**;

FUNCTION NewItemList: ProductList ; **PRIMITIVE**;
PROCEDURE AddToStock(list:Productlist,**VAR** stock:ProductList);
   PRIMITIVE;
{permit the addition of products to the stock}

FUNCTION OrderToDelete: **BOOLEAN**; **PRIMITIVE**;
FUNCTION OrderToDeleteId:NbOrder; **PRIMITIVE**;
FUNCTION NewOrderId:NbOrder; **PRIMITIVE**;
FUNCTION NewOrderToCreate: **BOOLEAN**; **PRIMITIVE**;
{permit to add or delete orders}

8.3.1 Defining the New Architecture

As we don't know how many orders would be added or cancelled, we will have to use a dynamic architecture. It means that order modules will be connected one after the other to the Stock module.

Question 8: What happens to the order module which cannot be invoiced?

Answer: We assume that the order could be presented later because of the possible refilling of the stock by the system.

Question 9: How many times could it be presented?

Answer: We assume that the process could last a certain period of time. The exact amount of time is left to the implementation. Thus, the exported variable *Done*, declared in the header of the Stock module (in the first case) becomes useless.

We use a clause called **DELAY** in a transition of the system. That clause postpones the firing of the transition until the delay given by a positive integer. This integer represents a number of time units defined by the **TIMESCALE** statement.

   TIMESCALE Second;

   TRANS
      TO stop
      DELAY (MaxTimeToFinish)
      PRIORITY 0
      NAME stop_with_some_orders_not_invoiced:
      BEGIN
      END;

Identifying the Information Sent and the Communication Links. The Stock module has to deal with the system to update its stock. Thus we have to add another interaction point to the Stock module and an internal interaction point to the system. We have to declare a channel of communication between the System and the Stock modules. We assume that the Stock module accepts any refilling of its stock. Thus, a single message has to be declared.

CHANNEL SystemStockChan (system,stock);
    BY system:
        addstock (list:ProductList);

MODULE Stock **ACTIVITY** (stockList:ProductList);
    IP
        ToOrder : OrderStockChan (stock);
        ToSystem: SystemStockChan (stock);
END; { *MODULE HEADER Stock* }

IP {*Internal interaction point of the system* }
    ToStock: SystemStockChan(system)

8.3.2 Defining the Behaviour

Defining the Initialisation of the Architecture. We assume that the process begins with some orders. First, we initialise the Stock module and connect it to the System module. Then we initialise the order modules. The System automaton is composed of 3 states, no_order_connected, stop and one_order_connected.

    INITIALIZE TO no_order_connected
    VAR
        OrderId: NbOrder;
        itemsList: ProductList;

    NAME initPart:
    BEGIN
        itemsList := fillStock;
        INIT ProductsInStock **WITH** StockBody(itemsList);
        CONNECT ProductsInStock.ToSystem **TO** ToStock;
        FOR OrderId := 1 **TO** initial_nb_of_order **DO**
            BEGIN
            itemsList := fillOrder(OrderId);
            INIT OrderForm **WITH** OrderBody (itemsList);
            OrderForm.OrderId := OrderId;
            END;
    END;

The system must connect one Order module to the Stock module. It has to look for Order modules whose exported variable to_do is set to to_wait. It is done in Estelle by the statement **Exist .. Suchthat**. If at least one such an Order module exists, the system has to select one and only one to connect it to the Stock module. It is done in Estelle by the statement **Forone .. Suchthat**.

TRANS

FROM no_order_connected
TO one_order_connected
PROVIDED EXIST oo: Order **SUCHTHAT** (oo.to_do = do_wait)
PRIORITY 1
NAME system_connects_order:
BEGIN
    FORONE oo: Order **SUCHTHAT**
        (oo.to_do = do_wait)
    DO
        BEGIN
        CONNECT oo.ToStock **TO** ProductsInStock.ToOrder;
        oo.to_do := do_order;
        OrderConnected := oo.OrderId;
        END;
END;

As soon as the Order module has got its answer, the system disconnects it.

FROM one_order_connected
TO no_order_connected
PROVIDED EXIST oo: Order **SUCHTHAT**
((oo.OrderId = OrderConnected) **AND** (oo.to_do <> do_order))
NAME system_deconnects_order:
BEGIN
    DISCONNECT ProductsInStock.ToOrder;
END;

The system stops either when all the orders are invoiced or when the timeout is expired.

As the following transition has no Priority clause, it will be fired only if the transition with the priority set to 1 is not fireable.

FROM no_order_connected
TO   stop
NAME all_orders_are_Invoiced:
BEGIN
END;

TRANS
TO stop
DELAY (MaxTimeToFinish)
PRIORITY 0

NAME stop_whith_some_order_not_invoiced:
BEGIN
END;

In Estelle, dynamic creation and deletion of modules are permitted. The deletion is done by the statement **Terminate**. The creation is done exactly as in the static case.

TRANS
FROM no_order_connected
TO no_order_connected
PROVIDED OrderToDelete
PRIORITY 0
VAR
    OrderId: NbOrder;
NAME System_deletes_order:

BEGIN
    OrderId := OrderToDeleteId;
    FORONE oo: Order **SUCHTHAT**
        ((oo.OrderId = OrderId) **AND** (oo.to_do = do_wait))
    DO
        TERMINATE oo;
END;

The two following transitions have neither **from** clause nor **to** clause. The meaning of this structure is that these transitions may be fired from any state to the same one.

TRANS
PROVIDED NewOrderToCreate
VAR
    OrderId: NbOrder;
    itemsList : ProductList;
NAME System_Creates_new_order:
BEGIN
    OrderId := NewOrderId;
    ItemsList := fillOrder(OrderId);
    INIT OrderForm **WITH** OrderBody (itemsList);
    OrderForm.OrderId := OrderId;
END;

The following transition permits the addition of some products to the stock.

    PROVIDED NewItemsForStock
    VAR

        itemsList : ProductList;
NAME System_adds_items_to_stock:
BEGIN
        itemsList := NewItemList;
        OUTPUT ToStock.AddStock(itemsList,stockList);
END;

Defining the Behaviour of the Stock Module.

Question 10: What new operation must be done by the Stock module?

Answer: The only new operation is the update of the stock done by the system. Thus we have to add a new transition.

WHEN ToSystem.addstock(list)
NAME add_to_stock:
BEGIN
        AddToStock(list,stockList);
END;

Defining the Behaviour of the Order Module. Order modules can have different status:

- waiting for connection;
- waiting for the answer from the stock module after being connected;
- waiting for the end of the transaction.

We use an exported variable, **to_do**, to state the status. To describe the behaviour we need 3 states:

- **initState**, when the module is not connected and not invoiced;
- **pendingState**, when the module is connected and waiting for the answer from the stock;
- **invoicedState**, when the order is invoiced.

        {*Body of Module Order*}
        BODY OrderBody **FOR** Order;
        STATE InitState, PendingState, InvoicedState;
        INITIALIZE TO InitState
        NAME init_of_order:
        BEGIN
                to_do := do_wait;
        END;

        TRANS

        FROM InitState

TO PendingState
PROVIDED (to_do = do_order)
NAME send_order:
BEGIN
 OUTPUT ToStock.destock(order_list);
END;

FROM PendingState
TO InitState
WHEN ToStock.result(ack)
PROVIDED NOT ack
NAME order_fail:
BEGIN
 to_do := do_wait;
END;

FROM PendingState
TO InvoicedState
WHEN ToStock.result(ack)
PROVIDED ack
NAME order_success:
BEGIN
 to_do := do_end;
END;
END; { *MODULE BODY OrderBody* }

8.4 Validating the Specification

Once the decisions left to the implementation are made, a simulation can be performed to validate the specification. Some tools, such as EDT (Estelle Development Toolset) [4], permit a random and/or a user-driven simulation. Moreover, with EDT what you simulate is what you implement; it is not necessary to rewrite the validated specification. It means that it is the same code you use to test and to implement the specification. It is also possible to implement your specification as a distributed system with no change [5]. Unfortunately you cannot use formal proof tools or model checking for validation (see drawbacks below).

8.5 The Natural Language Description of the Specifications

8.5.1 Case 1

The system is composed of two modules. An Order module which is instantiated as many times as the number of orders to serve and a Stock module which has only one instance. A product list is given to each Order module instance as a parameter. An initial stock is given to the Stock module. Each Order module sends its order list to the Stock module. Depending of the state of the stock, the Stock module sends back an acknowledgement. When an order is invoiced its variable called *invoiced* is set to true. The system stops when the Stock module has sent all the acknowledgements.

8.5.2 Case 2

As new orders as well as refilling of stock can happen during execution, the specification level has to control it. Thus its behaviour changes. One and only one Order module is now connected at a time to the Stock module. Either it can be invoiced or not. If not it could be reconnected later. The number of successive connections is not set. The system stops when a timer is out. At any time the system can add some products to the stock.

The behaviour of the Stock module remains the same except the adding of new products. An intermediate state has been added to the behaviour of order modules. It permits to come back to the initial state in case of non invoicing.

8.6 Conclusion

Although the fact that the use of a formal description technique such as Estelle is not usual for this kind of specification, it does work. But as said in the introduction, Estelle is more appropriate to formally specify communicating distributed systems. Nevertheless, we have shown some interesting features of Estelle:

- the possibility to postpone some decisions to the implementation which permits to test several different scenarios without changing the core of the specification;
- the possibility to express the non-determinism;
- the possibility to implement the specification as a distributed system[5].

We must point out some drawbacks:

- the use of Estelle does not prevent incorrect descriptions of the user requirements, even if it permits to clarify some points;
- it does not provide any formal method to validate operations on data.

Finally, we think that it could be worthwhile to combine formal methods, such as the B method, and Estelle, to be able to cover all the aspects of the formal specification problem.

References

1. Bredereke J. (1997) Communication Systems Design with Estelle. Thesis D 386, Kaiserslautern University, Shaker Verlag, Aachen

2. Budkowski S. (1985) Generation of a global system description from the description of cooperating subsystems. In: Yemini Y., Strom R., Yemini S. (Eds.) IFIP WG 6.1 Fourth International Workshop on Protocol Specification, Testing, and Verification, June 11-14, 1984, North-Holland
3. Budkowski S., Dembinski P. (1987) An Introduction to Estelle: A Specification Language for Distributed Systems. Computer Networks and ISDN Systems 14:3–23
4. Budkowski S. (1992) Estelle Development Toolset. Computer Networks and ISDN Systems 25:63-82
5. Catrina O., Lallet E., Budkowski S. (1997) Automatic implementation using Estelle Development Toolset (EDT). In: research report, Institut National des Télécomunications, RR 97 10 01 October 1997
6. ISO/IEC (1997) Information technology – Open Systems Interconnection – Estelle: A formal description technique based on an extended state transition model. ISO/IEC 9074:1997, International Organization for Standardisation, Geneva, Switzerland

9 SDL: A Language Based on Extended Finite State Machines with Abstract Data Types

P. Poizat

9.1 Overview of SDL

SDL (Specification and Description Language) is a specification language with a formal semantics that has been developed and standardised [2] by ITU-T[1]. It is based on an extended finite state machine (EFSM) model for the description of system behaviour together with abstract data types (ADT) features. Recent developments such as non-determinism and object-oriented features have led to the definition of SDL-92 [3]. SDL comes with two equivalent notations, GR (Graphical Representation) and PR (Phrase Representation). Here we use the GR representation since it is more readily understood. Please refer to SDL related literature [2,3] for GR and PR equivalence.

SDL is mainly used for the specification of telecommunication protocols and services but may be used more widely on any reactive system. SDL is supported by several tools, like Verilog ObjectGEODE and Telelogic Tau.

General Semantic Aspects. SDL is a "mixed specification language" in the sense that it has both a dynamic part – for communication aspects – and a static part – coping with data types.

An SDL specification describes a *system* as several communicating extended finite state machines. These machines exchange messages called *signals* that may carry typed data values (and hence provide a simple way for data exchange between them). The machines support the *process* concept. A process is a common description of the behaviour that is shared by its *instances*. Each process instance has a single different process identifier (PId). These PIds are particularly useful for addressing messages between processes instances. The processes own data values (hence the term "extended" for the machines). Exchange of data between processes is possible by way of signals or variable sharing.

The system may also communicate with the external environment which is assumed to behave like any SDL process instance (for example, it is assumed to own a PId different from all the system components PIds).

SDL offers basic types (types are called *sorts* in SDL) for use in process behaviours. These include the usual ones like integers or Booleans but also time

---

[1] International Telecommunication Union, has replaced in 1993 the former International Telephone and Telegraph Consultative Committee (CCITT).

(to model timers), duration and PId (to work on process instances). User-defined sorts can be defined by means of *abstract data types*: constants (called *literals*), typed signatures for the operations (called *operators*) available on the sort and equations (called *properties*) for their semantics. SDL-92 defines object-oriented concepts. We will not present them here since we do not use them.

9.2 Analysis and Specification of Case 1

There are various ways to make a specification from scratch (informal requirements) in SDL as in other formal description techniques that have both a dynamic and a static (data type) part [7,8]. Following the usual approach, we will first work on the system structure, then we will make the process graphs and finally define the sorts used in the previous steps.

9.2.1 System Structure

The first task is to find out all the system functionalities (signals triggered by the system environment). The system is about invoicing orders and the unique available functionality is `invoice`. A user (in the environment) is assumed to send the corresponding signal to the system.

This operation raises several questions. We will give them together with the solution we adopted.

Question 1: What are the `invoice` operation parameters? Does the user just ask the system to invoice all the orders it can or does the user ask the system to invoice a particular order?

Answer: (1) The user asks to invoice a particular order. The `invoice` signal carries some information on the order that is to be invoiced (its identifier to stay at an abstract level). (2) The user asks to invoice all invoiceable orders (but in which order?). (3) The system runs independently to invoice one (or several orders); in this case, the `invoice` operation is not triggered by the environment. We choose the first solution.

We then have to give the `invoice` operation dynamic semantics in more detail.

Question 2: What shall the system do if the order does not exist?
Answer: Return a specific signal (named `error`) to the user.

Question 3: What shall the system do if the order cannot be invoiced?
Answer: Return an error signal. Another solution would have been to save the `invoice` signal for later use.

Question 4: May the user ask to invoice the same order several times?

Answer: Surely not. This should output the `error` signal.

We also have to give more details on the operation conditions.

Question 5: Under which conditions is invoicing an order possible?

Answer: At this (abstract) level, we assume an `invoiceable` Boolean operation in some SDL sort to check if an order may be invoiced. Questions on this operation's semantics will be deferred to the work on sorts in Section 9.2.3.

Question 6: Do there exist wrong orders (i.e. orders with products not referenced in stock)?

Answer: This could have been the case, and an error message could have been sent, somewhere! Since we do not have an operation to create orders in this case, this would make no sense. This question and related ones will be delayed to Case 2.

Now that we have the system functionalities, we split the system into subparts to have a good architecture to work on. This split may be done several times until we have a good level of detail with sequential processes running in parallel.

SDL offers the means to structure a specification. The system is made up of several connected *blocks*. There are *block substructures* and *block diagrams*. They differ only in the fact that block diagrams are at the end of the decomposition process. Whereas block substructures may contain other block substructures or block diagrams, a block diagram may only contain processes.

The connections are modelled by *channels*. Channels may not connect more than two blocks. They may carry the signals defined in their *signal list*. Channels are uni- or bi-directional. A signal list is associated to each direction. Channels between processes are called *signal routes*.

Connection points link block channels with their enclosing superstructure. Like the blocks, the channels may be decomposed into subcomponents (blocks and channels). This may be used for example when modelling unreliable media.

As with processes, blocks (including the system) and channels give a common definition shared by their instances. SDL has a simple name scope rule: any definition is available in the current and sub-blocks. Note that in blocks one may use definitions or references to remote specifications. References are useful as placeholders. They also provide a more readable structuring of systems and blocks by separating abstraction levels.

We model the case study with two subcomponents: a process that manages the stock and a process that manages the set of orders. We will have a single block for the system. This block will contain references to a STOCK process and a SET_ORDERS process. Note that this is a matter of choice. We might also have used a single component.

In order to model the other types (orders and products), we have to make a choice between active (process) and passive (sort) objects. We here make the choice to use passive objects. Orders could have been modelled using active objects with different PIds as identifiers.

This decomposition leads us to ask questions about the subcomponent signal exchanges (between each other and the environment):

- What are the channels and signal routes between the system and the environment?
  The invoice signal comes from the external environment (user) and is received by the SET_ORDERS process. If the order is not correct, an error signal is sent back.
- What are the channels and signal routes between inner blocks?
  The SET_ORDERS process when receiving a correct invoice signal asks the STOCK using an ask signal if the order may be invoiced. The STOCK may then reply using either an ok or a not_ok signal.
- What are the new signal parameters?
  The whole order information is to be used by the STOCK. Full orders will then be used as parameters for the ask signal. ok and not_ok (return signals) have no parameters.

All these questions and the corresponding answers lead to the system architecture given in Figures 9.1 and 9.2. SDL notations are given in Figure 9.2.

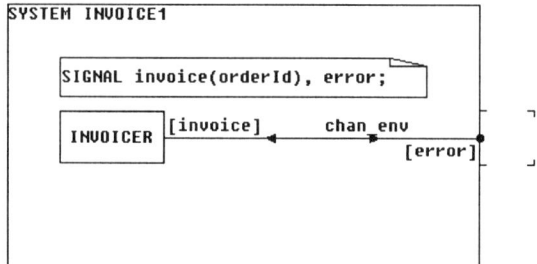

Fig. 9.1. The system architecture for Case 1

SDL allows one to give an initial and a maximum number of instances in process references. In the case study, there is a unique STOCK instance and a unique SET_ORDERS instance.

9.2.2 Process Graphs

In this part, we specify the behaviour of the processes.

Process behaviours are given by means of process graphs. A process instance may be in several *states* where it may receive or send different sets of signals. Process instances are created (at system initialisation or dynamically by another process instance in the same block) in a special state called the *initial state* (the states without names on the process graphs). The semantics for the behaviour of the system is given in terms of its instance process behaviours.

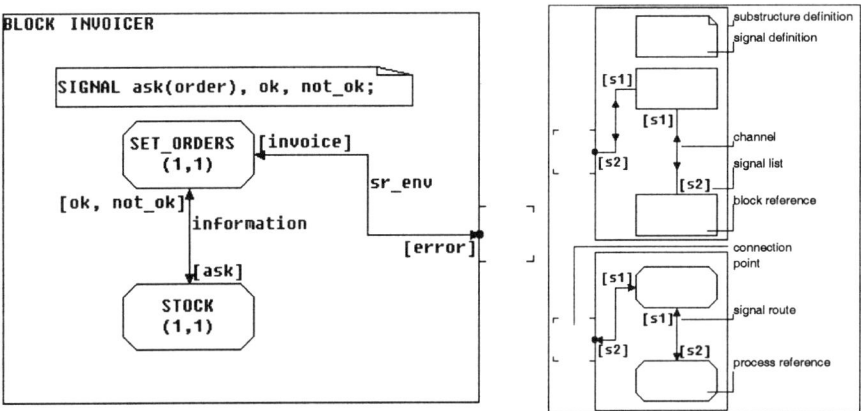

Fig. 9.2. The INVOICER block for Case 1/system structuring notation

Process instance communication is *asynchronous*. Senders do not block on signal sending. Receivers own an (unlimited) buffer where valid signals (i.e. signals the process may treat in some state) are held until consumption or discard. If a message may be treated in the current state, the process instance initiates a *transition*, consumes the signal, does some optional *activity* and goes into the target state. If the message cannot be treated in the current state, the instance discards it (there is also a way to save the message for later). The buffers, also called *input ports*, behave in a first-in/first-out way (except for saved signals).

Signals are a way to exchange values. A process instance p may send signals (i) implicitly to the unique process instance connected to it via the system structure, (ii) to all processes instances linked to a certain signal route (via signal routes and channels), or (iii) to a specific process instance using process identifiers (remember there is a unique identifier for each process). Destination keywords include: *self* (the process instance itself), *sender* (the process instance that sent the last message), *offspring* (the last process instance created by p) or *parent* (the process instance that created p).

STOCK. The STOCK process receives requests from the SET_ORDERS process to ask if some order is invoiceable. As we have already said, we assume that the sort associated with the stock has an operation to reply to this question.

Question 7: What happens when an order may be invoiced?

Answer: We assume there is an invoice operation defined on sort orderStock for this. This keeps abstraction at this level and delays the real answer to this question to the work on the sorts.

The STOCK process behaviour is then very simple. It receives requests via the ask signal and answers them. SDL, being asynchronous, does not force the STOCK process to reply when the ask signal is received. There may be already some other signal in its buffer. So the question arises: to which process instance does STOCK reply? Using the to sender keywords of SDL, the STOCK, when treating a given ask signal, is able to reply to the exact sender of the signal.

The behaviour of the STOCK process is given in Figure 9.3.

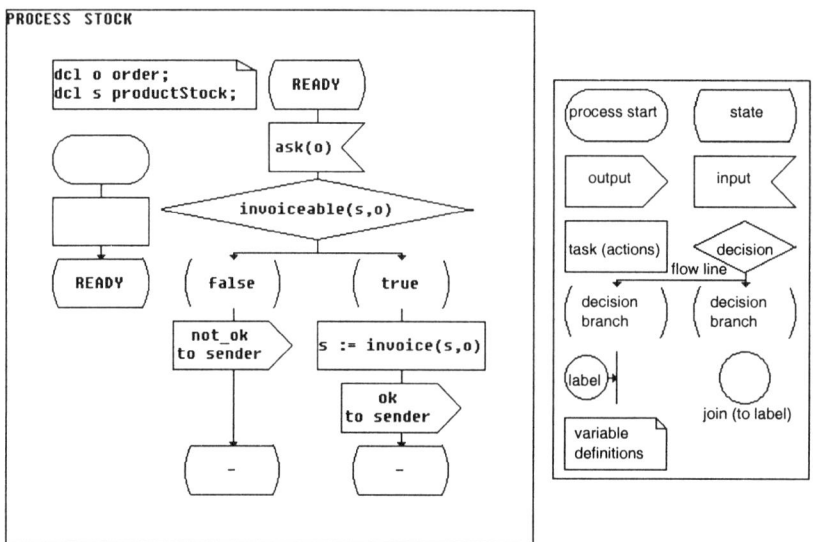

Fig. 9.3. The STOCK process behaviour for Case 1 / process notation

SET_ORDERS. The SET_ORDERS process receives invoice requests from the environment. If the order does not exist or has already been invoiced, an error signal is output. Otherwise, the STOCK is asked for the order invoiceability. If the order is not invoiceable an error signal is output, otherwise the order is invoiced. Errors are returned (as signals) to the sender of the invoice signal. The PId of this sender has to be kept in a variable (lastsender).

Question 8: Apart from passing the order from state pending to invoiced, what becomes of the order?

Answer: (1) The order may be suppressed or (2) it may be kept in the set of orders. We chose the second solution.

We saw that the SET_ORDERS process sends ask signals to the STOCK in order to check the invoiceability of orders. Thereafter, the SET_ORDERS process may either work on other invoicing requests after sending this signal or wait until reception of an ok or not_ok signal. Since the first approach could lead to orders affecting the stock several times before being invoiced, we will choose the first one.

The behaviour of SET_ORDERS is given in Figure 9.4.

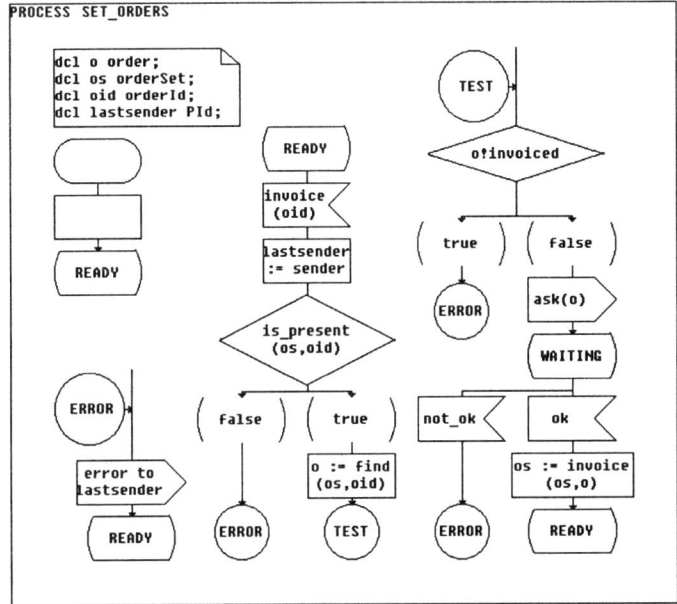

Fig. 9.4. The SET_ORDERS process behaviour for Case 1

9.2.3 Sort Definitions

In earlier phases we focused on system decomposition or signal exchange conditions. Here we give the corresponding operator properties. For each sort we use a constructive approach. Basic operators are defined and then semantics for all other operators used in process graphs are given in terms of these basic operators.

The sorts used in earlier phases (process graphs) are: orderId, order, orderSet, and productStock. Other sorts are SDL predefined sorts (PId). Each non-SDL predefined sort has to be defined.

Sorts orderId (and productId[2]). These two sorts are used as identifiers. This may be achieved using the Natural sort. We use the SDL *syntype* concept that enables one to define (rename) a sort with a restricted (or here equal) set of values with respect to the type it is based on.

```
syntype orderId = Natural        syntype productId = Natural
endsyntype;                      endsyntype;
```

Sort order. Orders have an identifier. We assume identifiers are unique. Orders also contain references to certain quantities of products. Orders may be

---
[2] The productId sort will be used later on.

invoiced or (alternatively) pending. Therefore, we will use a *structure* type (close to records in programming languages) for orders. Elements in a structure may be accessed using a "!" notation (e.g. o!id yields the identifier of the order o).

Question 9: How many references are there to an order?

Answer: (1) Only one reference or (2) a set of references (with the constraint that the products in these references are all different). Both solutions cope with the informal specification stating that "on an order we have one and only one reference to an ordered product of a certain quantity". For simplicity, we choose to model orders with only one reference to a given product. Solution number two would have led us to take into account complex things such as "partially invoiceable" orders.

Sort productRef. This sort models product references.

Question 10: What is a productRef?

Answer: A productRef is made up of a product identifier and a quantity.

Question 11: What is a quantity? May it be negative?

Answer: A quantity may not be negative.

In SDL, we may model such numbers using naturals.

```
newtype order struct
    id orderId;
    ref productRef;
    invoiced Boolean;
endnewtype;
```

```
newtype productRef struct
    id productId;
    qty Natural;
endnewtype;
```

Sorts orderSet and productStock. These two sorts are sets. SDL enables one to define sets by means of the *powerset* generator. The usual operations on sets (incl to add an element, del to remove an element, in to test if an element is in a set, and empty for the empty set) are available (amongst others).

```
newtype basicOrderSet
    powerset(order)
endnewtype;
```

```
newtype basicProductStock
    powerset(productRef)
endnewtype;
```

These basic sorts must be extended to define operators used in the process graphs that are not defined in basic sets. This can be done using the SDL *inheritance* concept. All that is defined in the parent sort is inherited, and more can be defined using the adding keyword. Partial inheritance (or renaming) can be specified on literals and/or operators.

The operators needed for sort orderSet are the following. An operator invoice: orderSet, order → orderSet (it takes an orderSet, an order, and it returns an orderSet) marks the order in the order set as invoiced. An operator is_present: orderSet, orderId → Boolean will be used to check if an order of a certain orderId is in the set. An operator find: orderSet, orderId → order is also needed to find the order corresponding to a certain identifier.

```
newtype orderSet
inherits basicOrderSet
   literals all;
   operators all;
adding
   operators
      invoice : orderSet, order -> orderSet;
      find : orderSet, orderId -> order;
      is_present : orderSet, orderId -> Boolean;
axioms
 for all os in orderSet (
 for all o1,o2 in order (
 for all oid in orderId (
  invoice(empty, o2) == empty;
  (o1!id = o2!id)==> invoice(incl(o1,os),o2) == incl(invoice(o1),os);
  (o1!id /= o2!id)==> invoice(incl(o1,os),o2) ==
      incl(o1,invoice(os,o2));

  is_present(empty, oid) == false;
  (o1!id = oid)==> is_present(incl(o1,os),oid) == true;
  (o1!id /= oid)==> is_present(incl(o1,os),oid) ==
      is_present(os,oid);

  (o1!id = oid)==> find(incl(o1,os),oid) == o1;
  (o1!id /= oid)==> find(incl(o1,os),oid) == find(os,oid);
 );););
endnewtype;
```

The operators needed for sort productStock are the following. Operators invoice: productStock, order → productStock and invoiceable: productStock, order → Boolean are needed.

Question 12: When is an order invoiceable?

Answer: When the product it references is present in the stock and in a sufficient quantity.

Question 13: What is the effect of invoicing an order on the stock?

Answer: There are several solutions: (1) no effect, (2) the stock may be reduced by a corresponding amount, or (3) the corresponding amount of the required product may be marked as being reserved (for example until some customer pays for it). We choose the second solution

```
newtype productStock
inherits basicProductStock
```

```
       literals all;
       operators all;
    adding
       operators
          invoice : productStock, order -> productStock;
          invoiceable : productStock, order -> Boolean;
    axioms
     for all s in productStock (
     for all o in order (
     for all p in productRef (
       invoice(empty,o) == empty;
       (o!ref!id = p!id)==> invoice(incl(p,s),o) ==
          incl(subtractQty(p,o!ref!qty),s);
       (o!ref!id /= p!id)==> invoice(incl(p,s),o) ==
          incl(p,invoice(s,o));

       invoiceable(empty,o) == false;
       (o!ref!id = p!id)==> invoiceable(incl(p,s),o) ==
          (o!ref!qty <= p!qty);
       (o!ref!id /= p!id)==> invoiceable(incl(p,s),o) ==
          invoiceable(s,o);
    );););
    endnewtype;
```

Modifications in productRef. An operator subtractQty: productRef, Natural → productRef is needed due to prior sort definitions. Its definition makes use of *! operators. These operators are to be used in structure type definitions. The operator *Make!(...)* builds a structure from its fields, an operator like *IDExtract!(record)* is used to extract the value of some field *ID* in the record, and an operator like *IDModify!(record,value)* is used to replace the value of some field *ID* in the record.

```
    newtype productRef struct
       ...
    adding
    operators
       subtractQty : productRef, Natural -> productRef
    axioms
     for all pr in productRef (
     for all qtySub in Natural (
       (qtyExtract!(pr) >= qtySub)==> subtractQty(pr,qtySub) ==
          qtyModify!(pr,qtyExtract!(pr) - qtySub);
    ););
    endnewtype;
```

Modifications in order. An operator invoice: order → order is needed due to prior sort definitions.

```
newtype order struct
  ...
adding
operators
   invoice : order -> order
axioms
 for all o in order (
  invoice(o) == invoicedModify!(o,true);
 );
endnewtype;
```

9.2.4 Comments on the First Case Study

The first case-study specifies that the stock and set of orders are always up to date. On the other hand, it is said that no other operation than invoicing should be defined. This causes a problem since SDL is dynamic and does not specify static properties (invariants) of the system. In order to have a fully working system, we should have modelled operations for initialisation and adding of orders/products in stock.

9.3 Analysis and Specification of Case 2

Case 2 is an extension of Case 1. This is reflected in the SDL specification.

9.3.1 System Structure

There is still the `invoice` functionality. New ones are `addProduct` to add a certain quantity of a given product in stock, `createOrder` to create new orders and `cancelOrder` to cancel an order.

Question 14: What are their parameters?

Answer: `addProduct` takes a product identifier and a certain quantity as parameter. This pair is of sort productRef as seen earlier. `createOrder` takes an order as parameter. `cancelOrder` takes an order identifier (of sort orderId) as parameter.

Question 15: Are there any conditions on `addProduct`?

Answer: We choose to impose non-negative quantities. Another choice would have been to treat negative quantities and to either return an error when there is not a sufficient product quantity in stock, or to keep the request for later (saving the signal).

Question 16: What shall be done when `addProduct` is used to add a quantity of a product that does not exist in stock (yet)?

Answer: The product is created in stock with an initial amount equal to the quantity given in `addProduct`.

Question 17: Are there any conditions on `createOrder`?

Answer: This is not said in the informal specification. We assume the product reference should exist in stock, and if this is not the case return an error. Another choice would have been to save the `createOrder` signal.

Question 18: What shall be done if the order identifier already exists?

Answer: Return an error signal.

Question 19: What is/should be the initial status of orders?

Answer: Orders may be created in (1) any status or (2) in a pending state. We choose the second solution. If the order given as parameter for `createOrder` is invoiced, return an error signal.

Question 20: Are there any conditions on `cancelOrder`?

Answer: The order with the given identifier has to exist. If this is not the case, an error signal is returned.

Question 21: Can invoiced orders be cancelled?

Answer: No. Return an error signal if a `cancelOrder` is received for an invoiced order.

As far as the system structure is concerned, the architecture of Case 1 is still relevant for Case 2. Again (see Case 1) the structuring leads us to reply to the questions:

- What are the channel and signal routes?
  The channel and signal routes for Case 1 are kept. New signals corresponding to the new operations are added where needed. A new channel and a new signal route are created between the environment and the STOCK concerning the `addProduct` operation. A new signal is created for SET_ORDERS to ask the STOCK if the product referenced in a newly created order is valid or not. This signal will be called `askValid`. The STOCK will use `valid` and `not_valid` signals to answer.
- What are the new signal parameters?
  Information needed for testing the validity of a product consists of a product identifier. Return signals have no parameters.

The architecture of Case 2 is given in Figures 9.5 and 9.6.

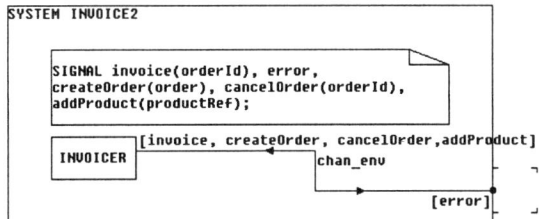

Fig. 9.5. The system architecture for Case 2

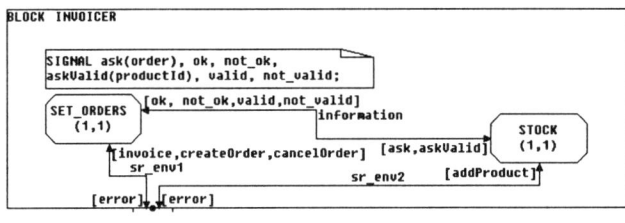

Fig. 9.6. The INVOICER block for Case 2

9.3.2 Process Graphs

STOCK. We have to take into account the new communication scheme corresponding to the SET_ORDERS process asking the STOCK process if a given product identifier is valid or not. This will be modelled using a transition, a decision to test the validity, and corresponding output signals. As far as the addProduct signal is concerned, we just call an addProduct operation that has to be defined on the sort productRefStock: as usual, the exact semantics of operations are to be defined latter, in the sorts part of the specification, the dynamic conditions being in the process graph.

Figure 9.7 gives only what should be added to the definition given in Figure 9.3.

SET_ORDERS.

Question 22: What happens when cancelling an order?

Answer: There are two solutions: (1) mark it as being cancelled, or (2) remove it from the set of orders. The first solution would require modifications to the existing process graph (when invoicing, we should verify that the order is not cancelled). So we choose the second solution.

As with STOCK, Figure 9.8 gives only what should be added to the definition given in Figure 9.4.

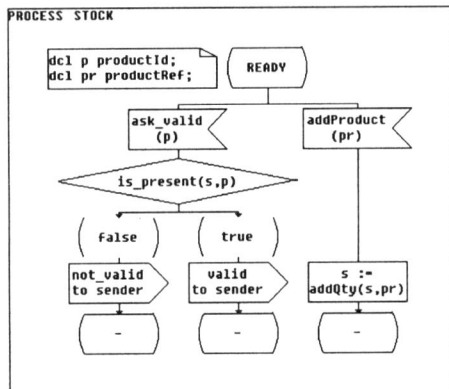

Fig. 9.7. The STOCK process (added) behaviour for Case 2

9.3.3 Sort Definitions

The new process graphs introduce new operators. We herein give the parts that are to be added to the sorts defined in Section 9.2.3. Another solution would have been to use the SDL inheritance concept to define the new sorts, and to modify the process graphs to take this into account.

Sorts orderSet and productStock. As far as sort productStock is concerned, new operators is_present : productStock, productId → Boolean and addQty : productStock, productRef → productStock are needed. Operator is_present is like the operator with the same name defined in orderSet (we may have defined a new set type constructor by specializing Powerset).

```
newtype productStock
inherits basicProductStock
   literals all;
   operators all;
adding
   operators
       ...
       is_present : productStock, productId -> Boolean;
       addQty : productStock, productRef -> productStock;
axioms
 for all s in productStock (
 for all p1,p2 in productRef (
 for all id in productId (
   ...
   is_present(empty, id) == false;
   (p1!id = id)==> is_present(incl(p1,s),id) == true;
   (p1!id /= id)==> is_present(incl(p1,s),id) == is_present(s,id);
```

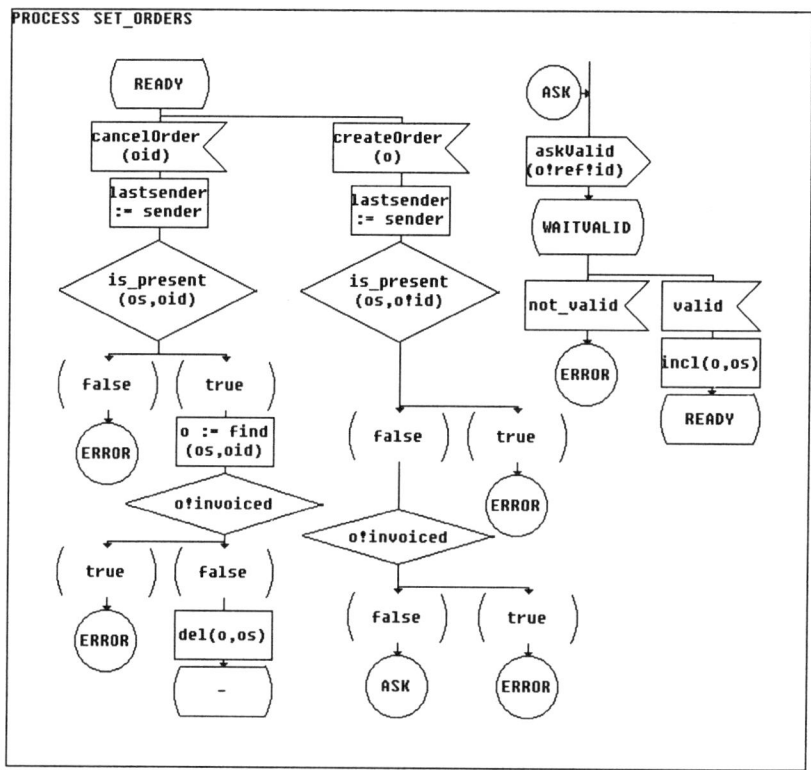

Fig. 9.8. The SET_ORDERS process (added) behaviour for Case 2

```
    addQty(empty,p2)  == incl(p2,empty);
    (p!id = p2!id)==> addQty(incl(p,s),p2) == incl(addQty(p,p2!qty),s);
    (p!id /= p2!id)==> addQty(incl(p,s),p2) == incl(p,addQty(s,p2));
    ...
);););
endnewtype;
```

Sort productRef. Due to prior sort definitions, an operator addQty: productRef, Nat → productRef is needed.

```
newtype productRef
operators
    ...
    addQty : productRef, Natural -> productRef;
axioms
    for all pr in productRef (
      for all qtyAdd in Natural (
        addQty(pr,qtyAdd) == qtyModify!(pr,qtyExtract!(pr) + qtyAdd);
    );078);
```

```
endnewtype;
```

9.4 The Natural Language Description of the Specifications

9.4.1 Case 1

In Case 1, the only functionality is `invoice`.

Orders are made up of an order identifier, a status ("pending" or "invoiced") and a unique product reference. A *product reference* is made up of a product identifier and a non-negative quantity. A *stock* is a set of product references. The orders are in a *set of orders*.

To invoice means: change the status of the order from "pending" to "invoiced" and reduce the quantity of product in stock by an amount corresponding to the amount in the product reference of the order being invoiced. Invoiced orders are kept in the set of orders.

An order is said to be *invoiceable* if it is in "pending" status and if the product it references exists (in a quantity superior or equal to the one in the order) in stock.

The `invoice` functionality takes a unique order identifier as parameter. Its effect is to invoice the order if it is invoiceable. If it is not, a specific signal (`error`) is returned. Orders are invoiced in sequence.

9.4.2 Case 2

Case 2 is an extension of Case 1. New functionalities are `addProduct`, `createOrder` and `cancelOrder`.

`addProduct` takes a product identifier and a certain non-negative quantity as parameters. If the product does not exist in stock, it is created (with the given quantity as initial amount), elsewhere, the quantity of the product in stock is increased by the given quantity.

`createOrder` takes an order as parameter. The product in the order must exist in stock or a specific signal (`error`) is returned. This signal is also returned if the order identifier exists in the set of orders or if the order is created in invoiced status.

`cancelOrder` takes an order identifier as parameter. If the order does not exist in the set of orders or if it has already been invoiced then a specific signal (`error`) is returned, elsewhere the order is removed from the set of orders.

9.5 Conclusion

As shown by the invoicing system, informal specifications, even of small case studies, are inherently incomplete and not precise. Being formal, SDL enables us to express the system requirements in a more precise way (raising questions) and to validate the specification using a wide range of tools (theorem provers for the data part, simulation, model-checking).

Like other "mixed" formal specification languages or methods [4,5], SDL enables one to describe both the dynamic and the static parts of systems. This is really a great advantage as the semantics of operations and the order and conditions under which they may be applied are equally important. Clearly separating the specification into structuring, process graphs and data types makes mixed specification easy.

SDL comes with both a textual and a graphical representation. This provides the specifier with a wider specification toolbox. The SDL graphical concepts are intuitive. They enable the specifier to work at different abstraction levels using the structuring mechanisms. They also make the extension of existing specifications easier (see the passage from Case 1 to Case 2 for example). The system structuring may be extended adding blocks and channels. The process graphs may be extended adding new transitions. Finally, data types may be extended using the SDL inheritance concept.

SDL asynchronous buffered communication semantics are closer to real-world communication mechanisms - closer to an implementation in terms of (asynchronously) communicating objects - than some other specification languages such as LOTOS. Moreover, requirements involving time may be expressed in SDL using timers.

If these SDL strengths were used in Case 2, Case 1 showed its main weakness. Unlike model-based specification methods such as Z [6] or B [1], SDL is inherently dynamic and requirements like "the set of orders and the stock are always given in an up-to-date state" (a state invariant) cannot be expressed.

Acknowledgements

I would like to thank Prof. K. J. Turner for his careful reading and comments about an earlier version of this chapter.

References

1. J.-R. Abrial. (1996) *The B Book - Assigning Programs to Meanings.* Cambridge University Press
2. CCITT. (1992) *Recommendation Z.100: Specification and Description Language SDL,* blue book, volume x.1 edition
3. J. Ellsberger, D. Hogrefe, and A. Sarma. (1997) *SDL : Formal Object-oriented Language for Communicating Systems.* Prentice-Hall
4. ISO/IEC. (1989) ESTELLE: A Formal Description Technique based on an Extended State Transition Model. ISO/IEC 9074, International Organization for Standardization
5. ISO/IEC. (1989) LOTOS: A Formal Description Technique based on the Temporal Ordering of Observational Behaviour. ISO/IEC 8807, International Organization for Standardization

6. D. Lightfoot. (1991) *Formal Specification using Z*. Macmillan
7. P. Poizat, C. Choppy, and J.-C. Royer. (1999) Concurrency and Data Types: A Specification Method. An Example with LOTOS. In J. Fiadeiro, editor, *Recent Trends in Algebraic Development Techniques, Selected Papers of the 13th International Workshop on Algebraic Development Techniques WADT'98*, volume 1589 of *Lecture Notes in Computer Science*, pages 276–291, Lisbon, Portugal. Springer-Verlag
8. K. J. Turner, editor. (1993) *Using Formal Description Techniques, An introduction to Estelle, Lotos and SDL*. Wiley

10 (E)-LOTOS: (Enhanced) Language of Temporal Ordering Specification

Kenneth J. Turner and Mihaela Sighireanu

10.1 Overview of the LOTOS Notation and Method

This section introduces the LOTOS and E-LOTOS languages, and how they may be used in requirements capture.

10.1.1 The LOTOS and E-LOTOS Languages

LOTOS (Language of Temporal Ordering Specification [7]) is a standardised FDT (Formal Description Technique) originally intended for the specification of communications and distributed systems. Several tutorials for LOTOS are available [1,16]. The design of LOTOS was motivated by the need for a language with a high abstraction level and a strong mathematical basis, suitable for the specification and analysis of complex systems. LOTOS consists of two integrated sub-languages for specifying data types (ADTs –Abstract Data Types) and behaviour (process algebra). LOTOS has been used to specify and analyse a variety of systems. Many of these have been communications standards, but LOTOS has been successfully used in a number of other fields. LOTOS is supported by tools for specification, simulation, compilation, test generation and formal verification. LOTOS toolsets include CADP (CÆSAR/ALDÉBARAN Development Package [4]), LITE (LOTOS Integrated Tool Environment) and LOLA (LOTOS Laboratory). More information about LOTOS, tools, applications and publications can be found online [19].

Although LOTOS has proved to be widely applicable, ISO has been developing a revised version called E-LOTOS (Enhancements to LOTOS [8]). New language features of particular relevance to the invoicing case study include modularity, functional (constructive) data types, classical programming constructs, a controlled imperative style and strongly typed gates. Since E-LOTOS standardisation was not quite complete at the time of writing, the authors have used a snapshot of the language.

In LOTOS and E-LOTOS, a system (the entity being specified) is modelled as one or more processes that communicate with each other and with their environment (whatever is outside a process, e.g. its user). The communication ports of a process are called (event) gates. LOTOS processes are parameterised by their gates and the values they maintain. Inputs and outputs correspond to LOTOS events, i.e. interactions at a gate between two processes such as the system and its environment. It will be seen later that the inputs of Figure 10.1

correspond to event offers made in the specifications. In LOTOS, an event occurs when two parties synchronise on matching event offers. An event offer indicates a willingness to communicate at a gate. Since several events may be offered, a choice may have to be made of which event offers are synchronised and therefore which event actually occurs. This choice may affect the future behaviour of the system.

10.1.2 Requirements Capture in LOTOS

LOTOS is often used to specify a system as a black box, and therefore to concentrate on its boundary, inputs and outputs. A LOTOS specifier will try to write a high-level specification of requirements, avoiding implementation-oriented concerns. The emphasis will be on specifying the partial ordering of (observable) events. Other factors that influence the approach include the balance chosen between processes and data in the specification, and the choice of specification style (if one is explicitly adopted). Various methods have been investigated for LOTOS, e.g. [2,15], but because the case study was so small, the authors followed only general LOTOS principles:

- delimit the boundary of the system to be specified;
- define the interfaces of the system (inputs, outputs, parameters);
- define the functionality of the system (the relationship among inputs and outputs);
- for incomplete requirements, choose an abstract or simple interpretation that will give some freedom later for adopting a more specific interpretation.

LOTOS is a constructive specification language: any specification will exhibit some structure (usually hierarchic, though a monolithic style is also possible). The subject of specification style has been investigated in considerable depth for LOTOS. Indeed it might be fairly said that LOTOS specifiers are pre-occupied with specification style! The choice of style for specifying requirements has a big impact on how the specification is structured. Another way of putting this is to say that LOTOS specifiers care about the high-level architecture of a system. (In the sense of [17], the architecture of a specification means its structure and style.) Several LOTOS workers have considered general 'quality' principles for specification architecture [12,17].

Because LOTOS combines a data type language with a process algebra, the specifier must choose an appropriate balance when using these two aspects of the language [9]. This partly depends on the preferred specification style, partly on the intended use of the specification (e.g. for analysis or refinement), and partly on the application. Some applications focus on the representation and manipulation of data (e.g. a database), and so are more naturally specified using the data part of LOTOS. Other applications focus on dynamic (reactive) behaviour, and so are more naturally specified using the process algebra part of LOTOS.

The case study treated in this book is data-oriented in nature since it effectively describes a database. For this reason, its LOTOS specification makes significant use of data types. However, there is a modelling choice to be made of whether to represent stocks and orders as processes or as data values. For this reason, *two* specification approaches were used by the authors. These give some idea of the range of styles open to the LOTOS specifier.

A LOTOS-based approach to requirement capture raises the following kinds of questions:

Environment: Who are the users of the system? What is the context of the system? What is the boundary of the system? What functions can the system rely on in the environment?

Interfaces: What are the interfaces to the environment? What are the data flows into and out of the system? What is the structure and content of these data flows?

Functionality: What functions must the system perform? What is the relationship among inputs and outputs?

Limitations: What limits apply to system inputs, outputs and functions?

Non-functional aspects: What timing and performance aspects must be specified? What other organisational issues should be considered?

Methodology: How should the formal model be developed? Which specification style is appropriate? How should the specification be validated (by testing and/or verification)?

The case study deals with requirements capture, analysis, specification and verification of the invoicing system. Of necessity this chapter presents only an overview of the specifications and their verification. Full details can be found in [14]. The act of formalisation typically raises many questions that would normally be discussed with the client. In a realistic situation, the systems analyst would raise such questions with the client. This would allow ambiguities, errors and omissions in the requirements to be resolved. As in this case study, it is sometimes not possible to approach a client with questions. For example, it may be necessary to carry out a *post hoc* formalisation of something that already exists (e.g. a legacy system or an international standard).

It was necessary for the authors to raise questions about the invoicing requirements and to provide answers in a sensible fashion. Analysis was performed according to the method outlined above. Some answers (**Answer** in the following) came from a common-sense reading of the requirements. Others (**Answer+**) required interpretation or extension of the requirements. As will be seen, the volume of questions is much greater than the informal problem statement! Of course, this demonstrates the value of a formal method.

Each portion of a formal specification is preceded by an informal explanation. In the specifications that follow, the authors have used their own convention for the case of identifiers (keywords in bold, variables in lower case, other identifiers with an initial capital).

10.2 Analysis and Specification of Case 1

The first case is discussed in this section though, as will be seen, it is treated as a simple abstraction of the second case.

10.2.1 Analysis

Methodology

Question 1: Is Case 1 a simplification/abstraction of Case 2? Is Case 2 an extension/refinement of Case 1?

Answer+: It is not clear what the relationship between the cases is meant to be. In the authors' opinion, Case 1 does not make sense in isolation from Case 2. Note that this is a methodological issue, not a LOTOS issue. From the LOTOS point of view, Case 1 could have been specified without reference to Case 2. Orders cannot realistically be satisfied from stock under all circumstances, even if the informal problem statement permits this assumption. Sometimes it is better if the analyst does not literally accept everything the client says! The system could be placed in an impossible situation if the assumption were violated. The informal description of Case 1 also supposes some unidentified agency that maintains orders and stocks. For both these reasons, the authors do not regard Case 1 as meaningful in its own right – only as a simplification of Case 2. It was therefore decided to treat Case 2 as primary, with Case 1 being an abstraction of this. The analysis in this section is therefore confined to those questions that arise from Case 1 alone.

Interfaces

Question 2: What does being 'given stock and the set of orders' imply?

Answer: This means that the first case study deals with a closed system that does not directly accept stock or order changes. It also means that the system has direct access to the current stock and orders. It follows that these must be maintained by some other sub-system.

Functionality

Question 3: Why is it said that all ordered references are in stock?

Answer+: This is presumably a hint that stock levels should not be checked before an order is invoiced. However it is not a realistic assumption. It is therefore prudent to check stock levels in this case, even if the check proves to be redundant.

10 (E)-LOTOS: (Enhanced) Language of Temporal Ordering Specification   169

Question 4: It is said that there will be no entry flows to the system, yet the system is 'given stock and orders in an up-to-date state'. Being 'given' such information is equivalent to an entry flow. How should such apparently contradictory requirements be resolved?

Answer+: The only interpretation that begins to make sense is that the information is somehow separate from the invoicing function and is updated by some other agency. The system can then consult this information at any time. Presumably the information is up-to-date only in respect of current stocks and order requests. That is, the order status is presumably not up-to-date or the system would be pointless! This interpretation does not directly affect the specification, but is a necessary stage in understanding the requirements.

10.2.2 Specification

Case 1 is viewed as an abstraction of Case 2. There is therefore no externally observable behaviour since the system is closed. For Case 2, the process-oriented style introduces some internal structure to the specification. The structure of the specifications to be presented is pictured in Figure 10.1. The outer ovals in this figure represent the boundaries of alternative models. These correspond to the specifications for Case 1, Case 2 in data-oriented form, and Case 2 in process-oriented form. In each specification, the inner details are hidden from external view. There are thus three alternative levels of abstraction. Case 1 has no inputs, and thus has no externally observable behaviour. The inputs in Case 2 are *Request* (place an order), *Cancel* (remove an order) and *Deposit* (supply new stock). The process-oriented version of Case 2 introduces an internal communication *Withdraw* (satisfy an order from stock).

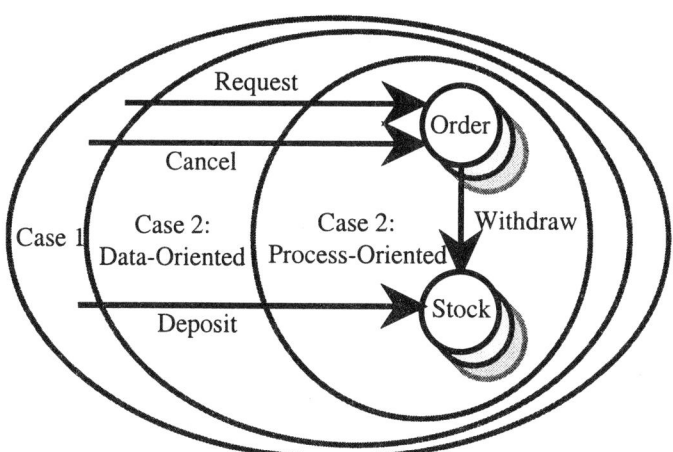

Fig. 10.1. Structure of the alternative models/specifications

Since Case 1 is treated as a simple modification of Case 2, the primary specifications are given in Section 10.3. Note that this was a modelling choice and is not intrinsic to how LOTOS might have been used. In fact the modifications for Case 1 are trivial, requiring only the internal communication channels to be hidden. For example, the process-oriented E-LOTOS specification has the following added:

hide Request:(Reference, Product, Amount)   (* hide internal gates *)
  Cancel:Reference, Deposit:(Product, Amount),
  Withdraw:(Product, Amount) **in** ...   (* in remainder of specification*)

10.3 Analysis and Specification of Case 2

The meat of this chapter lies in analysing and specifying the second case. Four specifications will be presented, using E-LOTOS and LOTOS in process-oriented and data-oriented styles.

10.3.1 Analysis

Environment

Question 5: Is it necessary to know how many users there are?

Answer: This is not stated in the informal requirements. If there were only one user it would not be necessary to identify orders (assuming that they were processed in sequence). If there were several users and it were necessary to issue invoices (or other messages to users), it would be necessary to identify users or orders. Invoices and the like would then have to carry an identification. Since the informal requirements do not ask the system to do anything (e.g. produce an invoice or deliver a product), this question is purely for understanding the requirements. It does not affect the LOTOS specifications directly.

Interfaces

Question 6: At what point is the status of an order updated? If the status is updated when the stock or set of orders changes, how does the system know that there has been a change? If the status is updated following a periodic check, how frequently should the system check?

Answer+: Updating on change of stocks or orders is a simpler interpretation and is therefore preferred. It follows that the system must be told of new stocks or orders. This information thus becomes input to the system. The system must update the stock and orders, which by implication are stored within the system since no outputs are mentioned. The system to be specified is thus an embedded sub-system of some larger system.

Question 7: Are new stocks or orders notified individually or in batches to the system?

Answer+: For simplicity it is assumed that inputs occur individually.

Question 8: How is invoicing triggered, how is the information obtained, and how is the decision made to update orders?

Answer+: Since the requirements imply that some internal agency manages the stocks and orders, it is presumed that this agency supplies information to the system as required and triggers an update.

Question 9: How is it possible to identify an order to be cancelled?

Answer+: The only sensible solution is if an order carries a reference that can subsequently be quoted in a cancellation. Other information such as the original product code or requested quantity would be redundant on cancellation and so is omitted.

Question 10: Who, then, is responsible for creating an order reference?

Answer+: It could be supplied by the user or generated automatically by the system. In normal ordering practice the user generates the order number, so this might seem to be more natural. However it creates a new problem: how to handle a duplicate order number. Solving this would require mechanisms to force users to use unique numbers, or to reject a duplicate. In fact it is simpler to adopt a more abstract approach that simply requires unique numbers, whether generated by the user or the system (or both, in cooperation).

Functionality

Question 11: What is the meaning of being able to 'change the state of an order'?

Answer: It is presumed that the system merely inspects the state of current orders and adjusts their status according to the current stock.

Question 12: Should the system issue an invoice when 'changing the state of an order'?

Answer: Normally such a system would actually issue an invoice. However, there is no mention of this in the informal problem statement. The conclusion is that the system operates on a set of orders whose status is updated by the system. If an invoice had to be generated, there would be other questions about what it should contain: order reference, product code, quantity, price, etc. However these matters can be ignored in the case study.

Question 13: What is implied by the system changing the state of an order from 'pending' to 'invoiced'?

Answer+: It is not clear whether this means that orders should be explicitly associated with a status. Presumably so, though the status of an order might be implicit (e.g. if unfulfilled orders are held separately).

Question 14: It is said that several orders may cite the same product code. This seems an almost unnecessary remark, but it hints that several orders may be outstanding for the same product. In this case, how should stock be allocated to orders?

Answer+: The stock is limited by implication, so the choice of allocation strategy may lead to different results. For example the smallest – or the largest – outstanding order for a product might be satisfied first. In the interests of abstractness, it is presumed that orders are satisfied in some 'random' manner. Specifically, the allocation algorithm is not visible to or influenced by the system environment, i.e. it is non-deterministic.

Question 15: If an order can be fulfilled from stock, its state must be changed to 'invoiced'. What should happen if an order cannot be fulfilled because the stock is insufficient?

Answer+: In this situation the order might be ignored, it might be explicitly rejected, or it might be held until stock becomes available. The first possibility is rather unfriendly and is therefore not considered. As already concluded, the system produces no outputs so the second possibility is rejected. The third possibility is therefore adopted, and is more consistent with the informal requirements.

Question 16: What should be done if an order is held until stock becomes available?

Answer+: When the system is given new stock it must re-examine any unfulfilled orders to see if they can be satisfied. As discussed in Question 14, there is then an issue of how stock should be allocated. Again, a 'random' algorithm is assumed.

Question 17: What does cancelling an order mean?

Answer+: This suggests an explicit request rather than just omitting an order from the updated list. At what point can an order be cancelled: before it is received by the invoicing system, after reception but before invoicing, after invoicing but before delivery, after delivery? In a real system these questions would have to be answered concretely. However, as discussed above the purpose of the system seems to be just maintaining a set of current orders. Cancellation must therefore mean removing an order from the pending set. Cancelling a non-existent or invoiced order is assumed to be forbidden.

Question 18: Is any concurrent or distributed processing required?

Answer+: There is nothing explicit in the requirements, but some implicit possibilities exist. For example, the processing of stock and order updates might be handled concurrently. The invoicing system might also be subdivided into distributed components. Since these issues are open a decision should not be forced, though they may be permitted by the specification.

Limitations

Question 19: Is it required that an order carry a product code?

Answer: This is implicit.

Question 20: Is there any restriction on the product quantity carried by an order?

Answer+: Presumably the quantity must be a positive integer. Negative quantities might correspond to returned products. A zero-quantity order is conceivable, but does not seem very useful and should be forbidden. Fractional quantities might be meaningful for products that can be broken down into smaller units, but for simplicity this was not allowed. Similarly, stock deposits are assumed to be strictly positive integers.

Question 21: Are there any orders or stocks initially?

Answer+: This is not explicitly stated in the informal requirements. Conceivably there could be an initial setup of orders or stocks, but for simplicity it is presumed that these are empty at start-up.

Non-Functional Properties

Question 22: As would normally be expected, are there any non-functional requirements such as cost, delivery schedule, performance, reliability, integration and testing?

Answer: Performance specification and testing have been studied in LOTOS-based development. However, non-functional aspects can be ignored since the only requirements available are strictly functional.

Question 23: Must an uncancelled order be satisfied eventually?

Answer: It is assumed that the system behaves fairly, and does not indefinitely delay the processing of an order.

Question 24: Must the system be free from deadlocks?

Answer: This requirement is implicit, and leads to a formal property of the specification that should be checked.

Question 25: Must the system be free from livelocks (i.e. unbounded loops of internal actions)?

Answer: This requirement is implicit, and leads to a formal property of the specification that should be checked.

10.3.2 Specification

Since E-LOTOS is the future form of the language, the authors felt it would be interesting to show how its specification style differs from LOTOS. Both E-LOTOS and LOTOS specifications of the case study have therefore been prepared. Since the languages differ, each has been written in its native style; the specifications are not just syntactic translations of each other. There are thus eight specifications in total, corresponding to {Case 1, Case 2}×{process-oriented, data-oriented}×{E-LOTOS, LOTOS}. For space reasons, these have not been presented in full.

Process-Oriented Specifications.

Process-Oriented E-LOTOS Specification. Gates in E-LOTOS are typed, allowing static checks on the kinds of values that are communicated. E-LOTOS event offers such as *Request(!ref, ?prd, ?amt)* may be synchronised (matched) with others. A fixed value in an event offer is preceded by '!', whereas a value to be determined in an event offer is preceded by '?'. These notations are also used in pattern-matching of expressions. Although '!' and '?' in event offers can usually be interpreted as output and input respectively, there is technically no distinction between these in LOTOS. This is because '?' is just a shorthand way of offering all the values from a set (e.g. '?prd' means 'offer any product reference').

The process-oriented specification of the invoicing system might be regarded as object-based. Orders and stock items are individual objects that encapsulate an identity (order reference or product code), state (order or stock status) and services (request order, deposit stock, etc.). The identity of an order or stock item allows that object, out of the whole collection, to synchronise on the messages intended for it. The specification allows several pending orders to compete simultaneously for the same product (whose stock levels may not be sufficient to satisfy all the orders). Since these orders are handled concurrently, the sequence in which they are satisfied is non-deterministic.

The data types and processes are specified here in a separate module *Order-Stock* for convenience. As in normal software engineering practice, an E-LOTOS module is a re-usable and self-contained collection of definitions. Modules are maintained separately from the specification proper that describes the whole system.

For clarity, separate types are introduced for an order *Reference*, a *Product* code, and a product *Amount*. For simplicity, these types simply rename the natural number type (non-negative integers); library types like this can be used without explicit importing. If desired, structured types could be introduced for order references and product codes.

    module OrderStock **is**   (* order-stock definitions *)
       type Reference **renames** Nat **endtype**   (* order references *)
       type Product **renames** Nat **endtype**   (* product codes *)

type Amount **renames** Nat **endtype**   (* product amounts *)

The status of an order is defined using an enumerated type. Orders start out blank, i.e. their product and amount have not yet been defined. Such an order is said to have status *None*. The complete type for an order is given as a record containing product, amount and status fields.

type Status **is enum** None, Pending, Invoiced **endtype** (* order status *)
type Order **is**   (* order *)
  record Prod:Product, Amt:Amount, Stat:Status
endtype

A blank order is filled in when an *Order* object accepts an order *Request*. A pending order may accept a *Cancel* and be annulled. A pending order may also *Withdraw* from stock. A choice is made from these possibilities using the '[]' (choice) operator that offers alternative behaviours. One of these is selected by matching event offers with the environment of the *Order* object. Other common LOTOS operators include ':=' (for assignment) and ';' (for sequential behaviour).

An event offer may be qualified by a condition (written in brackets after the offer). For example, a new order is permitted only if the order is blank (status *None*) and the amount being ordered is positive (*amt > 0*); the order status then becomes *Pending*. Cancellation is allowed only if the order is pending, at which point the order ceases to exist (i.e. its status becomes *None*). A pending order may ask for withdrawal of stock. The stock object with the corresponding product will synchronise on this offer if there is sufficient stock. If the order cannot be currently satisfied, the withdrawal request remains open until sufficient stock exists. At this point the order becomes invoiced.

```
process Order [Request, Cancel, Withdraw]     (* order object gates, ... *)
  (ref:Reference, prd:Product, amt:Amount, sta:Status) is (* parameters *)
    loop                                       (* loop indefinitely *)
      Request(!ref, ?prd, ?amt)   (* new order if blank, amount positive *)
      [(sta == None) and (amt > 0)];
      ?sta := Pending                          (* set status pending *)
    []                                         (* or *)
      Cancel(!ref) [sta == Pending];           (* cancel order if pending *)
      ?sta := None                             (* set status not in use *)
    []                                         (* or *)
      Withdraw(!prd, !amt)     (* withdraw product for pending order *)
      [sta == Pending];
      ?sta := Invoiced                         (* set status invoiced *)
    endloop                                    (* end main loop *)
  endproc                                      (* end order object *)
```

A *Stock* object repeatedly accepts deposits from the environment and withdrawals from order objects. New stock (of positive amount) is added to the current stock-holding. Withdrawal is permitted if the requested amount can be taken from current stock.

```
process Stock [Deposit, Withdraw]            (* stock object gates, ... *)
  (prd:Product, amt:Amount) is                              (* parameters *)
  var newamt:Amount in                          (* variable declaration *)
    loop                                              (* loop indefinitely *)
      Deposit(!prd, ?newamt)         (* deposit stock if amount positive *)
      [newamt > 0];
      ?amt := amt + newamt                       (* increase stock amount *)
    []                                                               (* or *)
      Withdraw(!prd, ?newamt)  (* withdraw stock if sufficient amount *)
      [newamt <= amt];
      ?amt := amt − newamt                       (* decrease stock amount *)
    endloop                                            (* end main loop *)
  endvar                                       (* end variable declaration *)
endproc                                              (* end stock object *)
```

The module concludes by defining unbounded sets of processes for *Orders* and *Stocks*, each running independently in parallel (denoted '|||'). These are obtained by explicit recursion over the order reference and stock product code. An order is initialised with its reference and 'not in use' status. A stock item is initialised with its product code and a zero amount.

```
process Orders [Request, Cancel, Withdraw]         (* orders gates, ... *)
  (ref:Reference) is                                      (* parameter *)
    Order [Request, Cancel, Withdraw] (ref, 0, 0, None)   (* one order *)
  |||                                    (* independently in parallel with *)
    Orders [Request, Cancel, Withdraw] (ref + 1)       (* more orders *)
endproc                                                    (* end orders *)
process Stocks [Deposit, Withdraw]                   (* stocks gates, ... *)
  (prd:Product) is                                         (* parameter *)
    Stock [Deposit, Withdraw] (prd, 0)               (* one stock item *)
  |||                                    (* independently in parallel with *)
    Stocks [Deposit, Withdraw] (Succ(prd))         (* more stock items *)
endproc                                                    (* end stocks *)
endmod                                  (* end order-stock definitions *)
```

The overall specification imports the module for orders and stocks. The communication gates (all inputs in this case) are introduced, and the types of values they carry are specified.

```
specification Invoicing imports OrderStock is (* use order-stock module *)
  gates Request:(Reference, Product, Amount),  (* gates and their types *)
        Cancel:Reference, Deposit:(Product, Amount)
  behaviour                                      (* specification behaviour *)
```

Communication between orders and stocks is via an internal gate *Withdraw* (see Figure 10.1). The order and stock processes synchronise on withdrawal. An operator such as '|[*Withdraw*]|' names the gates on which parallel behaviours must synchronise. The first order reference and product code are given as 0.

10 (E)-LOTOS: (Enhanced) Language of Temporal Ordering Specification

As new orders and stocks arrive, the processes will update their state and will communicate to satisfy orders.

    hide Withdraw:(Product, Amount) **in**   (* hide withdrawal gate *)
      Orders [Request, Cancel, Withdraw] (0)   (* orders *)
      |[Withdraw]| (* synchronising on withdrawals with *)
      Stocks [Deposit, Withdraw] (0)   (* stocks *)
endspec   (* end specification *)

Process-Oriented LOTOS **Specification.** The equivalent process-oriented specification in LOTOS is similar, except that modules are not available. The specification is self-contained behaviour that continues indefinitely ('**noexit**').The natural number type is selected from the standard library. Since this type does not define subtraction, a definition of this is given (though not here, for brevity).

    specification Invoicing [Request, Cancel, Deposit] : **noexit**   (* gates *)
      library NaturalNumber **endlib**   (* use naturals in library *)

As for the E-LOTOS process-oriented specification, order references, product codes and product amounts are specified by renaming naturals. These types, along with the similar status type, are omitted here. The overall behaviour is also left out as it is similar to the E-LOTOS version. Except for syntactic differences, the *Order* and *Stock* objects are similar to their E-LOTOS counterparts. Loops must be achieved by explicit process recursion in LOTOS.

    process Order [Request, Cancel, Withdraw] (* order object gates, pars *)
      (ref:Reference, prd:Product, amt:Amount, sta:Status) : **noexit** :=
    [sta = None] →   (* status is blank order? *)
      Request !ref ?prd:Product   (* order request for positive amount *)
      ?amt:Amount [amt gt 0];
      Order [Request, Cancel, Withdraw]   (* set pending status *)
        (ref, prd, amt, Pending)
[]   (* or *)
    [sta = Pending] →   (* status is pending order? *)
    (
      Cancel !ref;   (* cancel order *)
      Order [Request, Cancel, Withdraw]   (* set blank status *)
        (ref, 0 **of** Product, 0 **of** Amount, None)
    []   (* or *)
      Withdraw !prd !amt;   (* withdraw stock *)
      Order [Request, Cancel, Withdraw]   (* set invoiced status *)
        (ref, prd, amt, Invoiced)
)
    endproc   (* end order object *)
    process Stock [Deposit, Withdraw]   (* stock object gates, ... *)
      (prd:Product, amt:Amount) : **noexit** :=   (* parameters *)
      Deposit !prd ?newamt:Amount   (* deposit if positive amount *)

```
            [newamt gt 0];
            Stock [Deposit, Withdraw]            (* repeat with increased stock *)
              (prd, amt + newamt)
        []                                                                   (* or *)
            Withdraw !prd ?newamt:Amount        (* withdrawal if sufficient amount *)
            [newamt le amt];
            Stock [Deposit, Withdraw]            (* repeat with decreased stock *)
              (prd, amt − newamt)
          endproc                                        (* end stock object *)
        endspec                                          (* end specification *)
```

Data-Oriented Specifications.

Data-Oriented E-LOTOS Specification. In this approach, orders and stocks are defined by data values rather than processes. Invoicing is then an operation on these values. The simple data types are not given here since they closely resemble the process-oriented E-LOTOS ones. A collection of orders is treated as an associative array indexed by order reference. A collection of stocks is similar, but the array is indexed by product code and the values are amounts. An array element is accessed by operation *Get* and stored by *Put*. Similar operations are used with record fields, e.g. *Get_Stat* and *Set_Stat* for the order status field.

Invoicing orders is performed by function *Invoice* that takes current orders and stocks. Each order is checked in a loop, from first reference number to last. The *Next* function finds the next array index since there may be gaps in order numbers. Orders are thus fulfilled in reference number sequence, whereas the process-oriented specifications deal with them non-deterministically. Non-determinism could have been achieved, but only by complicating the specification. The current reference is used to extract the product, amount and status of a record. The product code is used to extract the stock level. If the order is pending and there is sufficient stock, the order is marked as invoiced and the stock level is updated. After all orders have been processed, the function exits with the updated orders and stocks. If an order cannot be fulfilled, it may be satisfied later when invoicing is repeated on receipt of new stock.

```
        function Invoice(ords:Orders, stks:Stocks) :   (* invoicing parameters, ... *)
          (Orders, Stocks) is                                       (* results *)
          var ref:Reference, prd:Product, amt,         (* variable declarations *)
              stk:Amount, sta:Status in
            for (?ref := First(ords); ref <= Last(ords);    (* first to last order *)
                 ?ref := Next(ords, ref)) do
              (?prd, ?amt, ?sta) := Get(ords, ref);        (* get order details *)
              ?stk := Get(stks, prd);                   (* get stock for product *)
              if (sta == Pending) and                               (* pending ... *
                  (amt <= stk) then                                (* in stock? *)
                ?ords :=                                      (* set order invoiced *)
```

```
            Put(ords, ref, Set_Stat(Get(ords, ref), Invoiced));
        ?stks := Put(stks, prd, stk − amt)     (* decrease stock level *)
      endif                                     (* end pending order check *)
    endfor                                      (* end order loop *)
    (ords, stks)                                (* return resulting orders, stocks *)
  endvar                                        (* end variable declarations *)
  endfunc                                       (* end invoicing function *)
endmod                                          (* end order-stock definitions *)
```

The system specification is like that for the process-oriented E-LOTOS version except that local variables are introduced for orders, stocks, order reference and product code. Orders and stocks are initialised to be empty. The main behaviour repeatedly accepts order requests, order cancellations and stock deposits. The logic is as already seen, except that the existence of an order is checked against the *Orders* array. Each branch of the loop updates orders or stocks as appropriate. The *Invoice* function is then called to deal with pending orders and to alter stocks accordingly.

```
    loop                                        (* loop indefinitely *)
    (                                           (* choice of request, cancel, deposit *)
        Request(?ref, ?prd, ?amt)               (* new order, positive amount? *)
        [NotIn(ords, ref) and (amt > 0)];
        ?ords :=                                (* update orders with pending order *)
        Put(ords, ref, Order(prd, amt, Pending))
      []                                        (* or *)
        Cancel(?ref)                            (* cancel order if exists and pending *)
        [IsIn(ords, ref) andthen
         (Get_Stat(Get(ords, ref)) == Pending)];
        ?ords := Delete(ords, ref)              (* delete order *)
      []                                        (* or *)
        Deposit(?prd, ?amt) [amt > 0];          (* deposit positive amount *)
        ?stks := Put(stks, prd,                 (* update with extra/new amount *)
            if IsIn(stks, prd) then Get(stks, prd) + amt else amt endif)
    );                                          (* end choice *)
    (?ords, ?stks) := Invoice(ords,stks)        (* get new orders, stocks *)
    endloop                                     (* end main loop *)
  endvar                                        (* end variable declarations *)
endspec                                         (* end specification *)
```

Data-Oriented LOTOS Specification. This specification begins in much the same way as the process-oriented LOTOS version, except that Boolean equality for status values has to be defined. Boolean equality is defined for two status values so that compound Boolean expressions involving status can be written. Following normal LOTOS practice, equality is defined using an auxiliary function that maps values to the natural numbers. The reference, product, amount and status types are imported as components of an order. Stock is built from product and amount types. Since LOTOS does not have a record construct, *MkOrder* and *MkStock* operations are needed.

Orders and stocks might have been defined using the generic *Set* type in the library. However, orders and stocks have been specified from scratch since sets are not entirely appropriate. (Stocks of the same product need to be amalgamated, so stock is not strictly a set. Identical orders should be allowed, so a bag rather than a set is needed.) *NoOrders* is an empty collection of orders. An order may be added to or removed from this using the *AddOrder* and *RemOrder* operations. *StatOrder* is introduced to retrieve the status of an order in the collection. Each operation is defined by equations that show its evaluation for each pattern of parameters. In this case, the distinct forms of operation parameter to be considered are a collection with no orders and with at least one order. Conditional equations (*condition* ⇒ *equation*) apply only if the condition holds.

```
type Orders is Order, Status                       (* order list *)
   sorts Orders                                    (* name for order list *)
   opns                                            (* operations *)
      NoOrders : -> Orders                         (* empty list of orders *)
      AddOrder : Order, Orders -> Orders           (* add order to list *)
      RemOrder : Order, Orders -> Orders           (* remove order from list *)
      StatOrder : Reference, Orders -> Status      (* get status for reference *)
   eqns                                            (* equations *)
      forall ref1,ref2:Reference, prd1,prd2:Product,    (* global variables *)
         amt1,amt2:Amount, sta1,sta2:Status, ords:Orders
         ofsort Status                             (* operations yielding status *)
            StatOrder(ref1, NoOrders) = None;      (* no orders, no status *)
            ref1 eq ref2 =>                        (* order references match? *)
               StatOrder(ref1,                     (* get status *)
                  AddOrder(MkOrder(ref2, prd2, amt2, sta2), ords)) = sta2;
            ref1 ne ref2 =>                        (* order references differ? *)
               StatOrder(ref1,                     (* check other orders *)
                  AddOrder(MkOrder(ref2, prd2, amt2, sta2), ords)) =
                     StatOrder(ref1, ords);
         ofsort Orders                             (* operations yielding orders *)
            ref1 eq ref2 =>                        (* order references match? *)
               RemOrder(                           (* remove order from list *)
                  MkOrder(ref1, prd1, amt1, sta1),
                  AddOrder(MkOrder(ref2, prd2, amt2, sta2), ords)) = ords;
            ref1 ne ref2 =>                        (* order references differ? *)
               RemOrder(                           (* keep current order, check later ones *)
                  MkOrder(ref1, prd1, amt1, sta1),
                  AddOrder(MkOrder(ref2, prd2, amt2, sta2), ords)) =
                     AddOrder(MkOrder(ref2, prd2, amt2, sta2),
                        RemOrder(MkOrder(ref1, prd1, amt1, sta1), ords));
endtype                                            (* end order list *)
```

A stock collection is defined in a similar way. The operations particular to stocks are *InStock* (to check if a product is stocked) and *StockOf* (to check the stock level). As has just been seen, LOTOS data types are reasonably straightforward but lengthy. The *Stocks* type is therefore omitted here.

A LOTOS operation can return only one result, unless results are grouped in a composite type. Invoicing is therefore computed by two separate operations: *UpdateOrders* and *UpdateStocks*. In both cases, the collection of orders is processed one by one. As in the data-oriented E-LOTOS specification, this means that order fulfilment is deterministic, although not in the fixed order of reference numbers. If an order is pending and the stocks are sufficient for the requested amount, the order status is set to invoiced and the stock level is updated.

```
type Updates is Orders, Stocks            (* order-stock updates *)
  opns                                    (* operations *)
    UpdateOrders : Orders, Stocks -> Orders    (* update orders *)
    UpdateStocks : Orders, Stocks -> Stocks    (* update stocks *)
  eqns                                    (* equations *)
    forall ref:Reference, prd:Product, amt:Amount,  (* global variables *)
           sta:Status, ords:Orders, stks:Stocks
      ofsort Orders                       (* operations yielding orders *)
        UpdateOrders(NoOrders, stks) =         (* no orders, no update *)
          NoOrders;
        (sta eq Pending) and              (* pending order, sufficient stock? *)
        (StockOf(prd, stks) ge amt) =>
          UpdateOrders(          (* update orders by setting order invoiced *)
            AddOrder(MkOrder(ref, prd, amt, sta), ords), stks) =
              AddOrder(MkOrder(ref, prd, amt, Invoiced),
                UpdateOrders(ords, RemStock(MkStock(prd, amt), stks)));
        (sta eq Invoiced) or              (* invoiced or insufficient stock? *)
        (StockOf(prd, stks) lt amt) =>
          UpdateOrders(          (* update orders by leaving order alone *)
            AddOrder(MkOrder(ref, prd, amt, sta), ords), stks) =
              AddOrder(MkOrder(ref, prd, amt, sta),
                UpdateOrders(ords, stks));
      ofsort Stocks                       (* operations yielding stocks *)
        UpdateStocks(NoOrders, stks) =         (* no orders, no update *)
          stks;
        (sta eq Pending) and              (* pending order, sufficient stock? *)
        (StockOf(prd, stks) ge amt) =>
          UpdateStocks(          (* update stocks by decreasing stock *)
            AddOrder(MkOrder(ref, prd, amt, sta), ords), stks) =
              UpdateStocks(ords, RemStock(MkStock(prd, amt), stks));
        (sta eq Invoiced) or              (* invoiced or insufficient stock? *)
        (StockOf(prd, stks) lt amt) =>
          UpdateStocks(          (* update stocks by leaving stock alone *)
```

                    AddOrder(MkOrder(ref, prd, amt, sta), ords), stks) =
                    UpdateStocks(ords, stks);
endtype   (* end order-stock updates *)

The overall behaviour is similar to that for the E-LOTOS data-oriented specification, though the syntax is different. Explicit process recursion is used to express a loop. Each branch of the choice produces an updated pair of order-stock values. A recursive call to the *Invoice* process updates the orders and stocks following invoicing.

10.4 Validation and Verification of the LOTOS Specifications

The terms 'validation' and 'verification' are used with various meanings in the literature. The authors use these terms to mean testing and proof respectively. Since E-LOTOS had not quite reached its final form at time of writing, tools for the language were still under development. The E-LOTOS specifications should hence be regarded as preliminary, although they were statically checked using the TRAIAN compiler developed by INRIA Rhône-Alpes. However they are similar to the LOTOS specifications and have been independently reviewed, so there is a high degree of confidence in them. The following discussion therefore refers to automated analysis of only the LOTOS specifications.

10.4.1 Validation

The LOTOS specifications were initially validated using the LITE toolset in a form of white-box testing. The data type definitions were checked by evaluating operations on test values conforming to each distinct form of parameter. For example, *RemOrder* was checked with an empty list of orders (*NoOrders*) and a list containing at least one order (*RemOrder(SomeOrder, MoreOrders)*). The latter has two sub-cases: the order reference exists in the list of orders, and the order reference does not exist.

Behavioural aspects were checked using scenarios that exercised each significant case. For order requests the scenarios included duplicated references, zero amounts, products not currently in stock, amounts less than current stock, amounts exactly equal to current stock, and multiple orders for the same product. For order cancellations the scenarios dealt with non-existent references, pending and invoiced orders. For stock deposits the scenarios included new product codes, existing product codes, zero amounts, and stocks for pending orders. Validation was documented by executing the scenarios and recording the reactions of the specified system. Normally the client would be asked to confirm the completeness and correctness of testing, but that was not possible in this case study. Instead the authors reviewed the behaviour exhibited by the specifications. This uncovered some small specification errors, notably in the LOTOS data types (which are rather complex).

10.4.2 Verification

Model Generation. Validation cannot ensure the correctness of the specification. Neither is it possible to prove equivalence between various specifications. To achieve this requires formal verification, for which the authors used model-checking [3] and equivalence-checking [5]. These procedures are automated, but apply only to a system with a finite state space.

CADP (CÆSAR/ALDÉBARAN Development Package [20]) provides several tools for the design and verification of communications protocols and distributed systems. The CADP tools used in the case study will be mentioned only briefly. CÆSAR and CÆSAR.ADT are compilers that translate a LOTOS specification into a (possibly infinite) LTS (Labelled Transition System) that encodes all possible execution sequences. ALDÉBARAN is a verification tool for comparing or minimising LTSs with respect to various equivalence relations [10]. XTL (Executable Temporal Language) is a functional-like programming language for compact implementation of various temporal logics.

An LTS is formally defined as a quadruple $M = \langle Q, A, T, q_{init} \rangle$. Q is the set of states, A is the set of actions, and $T \subseteq Q \times A \times Q$ is the transition relation between the states. A transition $\langle q_1, a, q_2 \rangle \in T$ (also written $q_1 \xrightarrow{a} q_2$) means that it is possible to move from state q_1 to state q_2 by performing action a. State $q_{init} \in Q$ is the initial one. The translation of a LOTOS specification into an LTS respects the operational semantics of LOTOS. A state of an LTS represents a point in the behaviour of a specification, and each transition from a state is labelled with a possible action of the behaviour.

To compile data operations efficiently, CÆSAR.ADT needs to know which operations are the constructors (i.e. the primary operations that build values). Also, data type equations are considered as rewriting rules (that change the left-hand expression to the right-hand one), and equations between constructors are not allowed. For tool use, the data types are therefore annotated and some transformations are applied [6].

To ensure finiteness, the domains of various parameters were restricted for verification purposes. Specifically, an upper bound was set on the highest value for order references, product codes and order amounts (denoted *MaxRef*, *MaxProd*, and *MaxAmt*). An infinite number of parallel processes is implied by the specifications since the number of orders and stock items is unlimited. A specific number of process instances was used according to the upper bound chosen for the parameters. As a practical limitation, only certain combinations of parameter bounds were investigated: *MaxRef* values of 1 or 2, *MaxProd* values of 0 and 1, *MaxAmt* values of 1 and 2. In principle this generates 8 LTSs for each specification under consideration.

Verification requires knowledge of all the actions performed by the system. Specifications of Case 2 can be used directly. However, those for Case 1 cannot because visible actions are deliberately made internal. Models are therefore generated only for Case 2. Execution times in Tables 10.1 and 10.2 were obtained when using the CADP tools on a SUN computer (Ultra Sparc-1, 143 MHz processor, 256 MBytes memory).

Model generation for the process-oriented specification of Case 2 is summarised in Table 10.1. This is limited by state explosion. The three last rows of the table indicate the incomplete LTSs generated before memory is exhausted. The reason for the state explosion is the high degree of parallel interleaving in this specification. Note that the LTS size increases by one order of magnitude when *MaxRef* or *MaxAmt* is incremented. Moreover, it increases more sharply with *MaxAmt* than with *MaxRef*.

Table 10.1. Model generation for the process-oriented specification of Case 2

MaxProd	MaxRef	MaxAmt	States	Transitions	Time (mins.)
0	1	1	5,890	16,130	0.1
0	1	2	39,371	170,754	0.5
0	2	1	25,846	96,430	0.4
0	2	2	323,459	1,826,512	5.9
1	1	1	7,698,453	35,655,750	132.8
1	1	2	> 6,531,532	> 49,232,000	164.5
1	2	1	> 8,213,739	> 49,896,000	383.0
1	2	2	> 4,524,531	> 43,904,000	237.1

Model generation for the data-oriented specification of Case 2 is summarised in Table 10.2. The limit here is execution time not memory occupancy: the last row of the table stays within memory limits but takes an inordinate amount of time. The reason is that parallel interleaving in the process-oriented specification is replaced by data computations. The functions used by the data-oriented specification perform several traversals over the lists containing the orders and the stocks, and these are relatively complex structures. It is interesting to note that the LTS size increases by one order of magnitude when either *MaxRef* or *MaxAmt* is incremented. In the data-oriented case the model size increases more sharply with *MaxRef* than with *MaxAmt*.

Table 10.2. Model generation for the data-oriented specification of Case 2

MaxProd	MaxRef	MaxAmt	States	Transitions	Time (mins.)
0	1	1	14,975	20,195	0.5
0	1	2	88,023	165,792	4.0
0	2	1	82,403	117,386	5.6
0	2	2	848,067	1,603,478	165.3
1	1	1	> 5,236,886	> 9,761,401	31935.4

Verification using Model Checking. The generated LTSs are verified against formal properties stated in XTL. Since the informal requirements do not state formal properties, these have to be inferred. As the dynamic semantics of LOTOS is event-based, it is natural to express the properties as temporal logic formulae concerning actions. The XTL language supports data types for states, transitions and labels. It also supports functions for manipulating them.

The informal requirements were interpreted as described in Sections 10.2.1 and 10.3.1. The new requirements can be split into three (overlapping) classes: those that cannot be formalised, those are self-evidently reflected in the specifications, and those that lead to formal properties. The last class of requirements was formalised as safety or liveness properties. Safety properties state that something bad never happens, while liveness properties state that something good eventually happens.

For conciseness, only the first property below is presented in full detail. The text gives an informal statement, a more precise formulation (in italics), a formalisation in XTL, and an explanation of this. For the other properties, only the informal statement and the more precise formulation are given. The full formulation of these properties may be found in [14].

Property 1: A safety property is that the quantity carried by an order must be a positive integer. *All Requests have strictly positive amounts.*

  not exists L : **label in**
    L -> [Request _ _ ?amt : **integer where** amt $\leq$ 0]
  end_exists

The **exists** operator checks here for existence of a label in the LTS corresponding to a *Request* with an amount that is not positive. Of course, such a label should not exist. Formulae are written in brackets as above. XTL is able to access the parameters of an event; the '_' notation stands for any value of event parameter.

Property 2: A safety property is that an order reference must be unique. Duplicate references to an order (i.e. more than one *Request* with the same reference) are allowed only if the order has not been invoiced (i.e. a *Cancel* for the order reference has been accepted). *Between two subsequent Requests with the same reference ($0 \leq ref \leq MaxRef - 1$), a Cancel action with the same reference must occur.*

Property 3: A safety property is that only existing orders may be cancelled. *A Cancel action with some reference ($0 \leq ref \leq MaxRef - 1$) can appear only if there has been a Request with the same reference.*

Property 4: A liveness property is that an uncancelled order will eventually be invoiced. Note that this property makes a statement about the state variables of the specifications (i.e. the status of an order). Since the underlying model of LOTOS is an LTS, a state variable cannot be checked directly. Instead, only properties over transitions can be verified. It is therefore necessary to introduce an explicit *Invoice* event that notes when invoicing occurs. *After a Request with some reference ($0 \leq ref \leq MaxRef - 1$), if a Cancel with* *the same reference does not occur then eventually an Invoice action for the reference will occur.*

Property 5: System behaviour should always progress. *The system is free from deadlock.*

Property 6: System behaviour should not get stuck in an internal loop. The need for this property arises because of internal actions in the specifications. These are due to hiding gates (*Withdraw*) or indirectly due to the enabling operator ($\gg$). *The system does not livelock, i.e. there are no cycles of internal actions.*

The six properties were evaluated on the complete LTS models using the XTL model-checker. The models were first minimised using strong equivalence in order to reduce their size. In every case the properties were verified in less than one minute. Properties 1, 2, 3, 5 and 6 are true of all the models. With the introduction of an *Invoice* event to verify property 4, all the properties were shown to hold.

Verification using Bisimulation. As an alternative to model-checking, verification using bisimulation was also performed using ALDÉBARAN. The goal was to prove that the process-oriented and data-oriented LOTOS specifications of Case 2 are equivalent by checking their LTSs. ALDÉBARAN supports several notions of equivalence, ranging from strong bisimulation equivalence (each specification can mimic the other) to safety equivalence (neither specification violates safety properties of the other). The ALDÉBARAN tool was used to check all the possible forms of equivalence. Branching equivalence and observational equivalence cannot be checked since the specifications contain internal events.

It was found that the data-oriented specification is included in the process-oriented one, but not equivalent to it when using safety equivalence. This equivalence does not hold because the process-oriented specifications allow *Cancel* events after *Deposit* events if the order is not yet treated. In the data-oriented specification this cannot occur since the list of orders is immediately updated after each *Deposit* event.

This difference can be removed by not immediately updating the stocks and orders in the data-oriented specification. Instead, an internal event is required before updating can occur. This has the positive effect of making the data-oriented and process-oriented specifications safety equivalent. Unfortunately it also introduces livelock due to continual updating of stocks and orders. Although this violates Property 6, a more complex modification of the specification would avoid livelock.

10.5 Natural Language Description of the Specifications

The following summarises how the two cases have been interpreted in the (E-)LOTOS specifications.

10.5.1 Case 1

As discussed under Question 1, Case 1 is considered to be an abstraction of Case 2. Its specifications merely hide (make internal) the actions that *Request* orders, *Cancel* orders, and *Withdraw* products from stock. This applies equally to the LOTOS/E-LOTOS and process-oriented/data-oriented variants.

10.5.2 Case 2

The E-LOTOS variants have separate modules for handling orders and stocks. This cleanly separates the subsidiary operations from the main specification. Modules do not exist in LOTOS, so specifications have to be written in isolation. For E-LOTOS and LOTOS, basic types are defined for an order *Reference*, a *Product* code, a product *Amount*, and an order *Status*. These are used to define the main type for an *Order*

In the process-oriented E-LOTOS specification, *Order* and *Stock* items are represented as processes. A blank *Order* may be filled in by a *Request*. A pending *Order* may be annulled by a *Cancel* or it may *Withdraw* stock. A *Stock* item may accept the *Deposit* of new stock, or may allow an *Order* to *Withdraw* stock. Sets of *Orders* and *Stocks* synchronise on *Withdraw* actions that are hidden from external view. The process-oriented LOTOS specification is broadly similar to its E-LOTOS counterpart, except that the main loop must be specified using explicit process recursion.

In the data-oriented E-LOTOS specification, lists of *Orders* and *Stocks* are maintained as data values rather than as processes. An *Invoice* function is called to allocate pending orders to available stocks. The main behaviour simply loops, accepting *Request*, *Cancel* and *Deposit* actions. The data-oriented LOTOS specification is forced to use complex data types that achieve the effect of invoicing. Lists of *Orders* and *Stocks* are specified in data types with auxiliary operations on orders and stock items. The *Updates* type defines operations equivalent to the *Invoice* function. *UpdateOrders* yields the new order list following invoicing, while *UpdateStocks* does the same for the stock list.

10.6 Conclusion

This chapter has shown how E-LOTOS and LOTOS may be used for requirements analysis, formal specification, validation and verification. Through the procedure of formal specification and verification, 25 questions were raised about the informal requirements. This in itself is an indication of the value of applying a formal technique.

The LOTOS approach of black-box specification is useful in obtaining a high-level formalisation of a system. Although LOTOS shares its behavioural approach with other process algebras, LOTOS is relatively unusual in having an integration of behaviour with data specification. This is convenient for specification since different aspects of a problem can be treated as behaviour or data. The process-oriented and data-oriented specifications show that these aspects can be balanced according to the system being specified.

Of the four Case 2 descriptions, the authors are most satisfied with the E-LOTOS process-oriented specification. It is clear that E-LOTOS offers a much cleaner and more compact style of specification compared to current LOTOS. In particular modularity, typed gates, and functional data types are felt to be much preferable. The data types used in LOTOS have been rather disliked for the verbosity that is evident from the specifications of the case study. The LOTOS data type library is also somewhat distant from conventional programming practice. Some syntactic LOTOS data typing shorthands have been developed for these reasons [11].

The process-oriented and data-oriented specifications make an interesting comparison. In E-LOTOS there is little to choose between them regarding clarity or compactness. However in LOTOS, the data-oriented specification is tedious because of the verbose data part. In general, there are good reasons to prefer the process-oriented approach. It takes an object-based view, and is thus closer to conventional analysis. The approach also hints at possible concurrent or distributed implementation, and so allows a range of realisations.

Verification with CADP supports LOTOS with state-of-the-art techniques. As far as the authors know, CÆSAR and CÆSAR.ADT are the only model checkers that support dynamic data structures. It is useful to have the choice of verification through model-checking or equivalence-checking. Model-checking requires system properties to be explicitly formalised. It is not always obvious what these properties should be, nor whether 'enough' properties have been defined. Nonetheless, formulating system properties is a valuable exercise in its own right. For the case study, the properties highlighted some important issues that might otherwise have been overlooked.

The main difficulty with model checking is state-space explosion. This is, of course, not unique to LOTOS. To generate finite and tractable LTSs it is necessary to modify the original LOTOS specifications. Although these changes are relatively straightforward, they are nonetheless changes. The need to modify data types will disappear with E-LOTOS since this has constructive type definitions. However, it will continue to be necessary to limit the number of parallel processes considered during verification. Despite the restrictions imposed during verification, state-space explosion continued to be a problem. The source of this is the high degree of non-determinism in the process-oriented specifications and the complex data types in the data-oriented specifications. It is hoped that ongoing development of CADP will help to minimise state-space explosion by producing reduced LTSs.

Equivalence checking was relatively straightforward, although a minor change still had to be made in the specifications to prove equivalence. However this reflects the different ways that the process-oriented and data-oriented specifications were written. The need for a change was thus for modelling rather than theoretical reasons.

Acknowledgements

Thanks are due to the following for carefully reviewing the papers that formed the basis of this chapter: Hubert Garavel (INRIA Rhône-Alpes), Radu Mateescu (INRIA Rhône-Alpes) and Carron Shankland (University of Stirling). Mihaela Sighireanu was employed by INRIA Rhône-Alpes during most of the work reported here.

References

1. Bolognesi T., Brinksma E. (1988) Introduction to the ISO specification language LOTOS. Computer Networks and ISDN Systems 14(1):25–59
2. Bolognesi T., van de Lagemaat J., Vissers C. A., Eds. (1995) The LOTOSPHERE Project. Kluwer Academic Publishers, London, UK
3. Clarke E., Emerson E. A., Sistla A. P (1983) Automatic verification of finite-state concurrent systems using temporal logic. In: 10th Annual Symposium on Principles of Programming Languages
4. Fernández J.-C., Garavel H., Kerbrat A., Mateescu R., Mounier L., Sighireanu M. (1996) CADP (CÆSAR/ALDÉBARAN Development Package): A protocol validation and verification toolbox. In: Alur R., Henzinger T. A. (Eds.) 8th Conference on Computer-Aided Verification, Number 1102 in Lecture Notes in Computer Science. Springer-Verlag, Berlin, Germany, 437–440
5. Fernández J.-C., Mounier L. (1991) A tool set for deciding behavioral equivalences. In: CONCUR'91, Amsterdam, Netherlands
6. Garavel H. (1989) Compilation of LOTOS abstract data types. In: Vuong S. T. (Ed.) Formal Description Techniques II. North-Holland, Amsterdam, Netherlands
7. ISO/IEC (1989) Information Processing Systems – Open Systems Interconnection – LOTOS – A Formal Description Technique based on the Temporal Ordering of Observational Behaviour. ISO/IEC 8807, International Organization for Standardization, Geneva, Switzerland
8. ISO/IEC (2000) Information Processing Systems – Open Systems Interconnection – Enhancements to LOTOS – A Formal Description Technique based on the Temporal Ordering of Observational Behaviour. ISO/IEC 8807, International Organization for Standardization, Geneva, Switzerland
9. Leduc G. (1987) The intertwining of data types and processes in LOTOS. In: Rudin H., West C. H. (Eds.) Protocol Specification, Testing and Verification VII. North-Holland, Amsterdam, Netherlands, 123–136
10. Milner A. J. R. G. (1989) Communication and Concurrency. Addison-Wesley, Reading, Massachusetts, USA
11. Pecheur C. (1993) Vlib: Infinite virtual libraries for LOTOS. In: Danthine A. A. S., Leduc G., Wolper P. (Eds.) Protocol Specification, Testing and Verification XIII. North-Holland, Amsterdam, Netherlands, 29–44
12. Scollo G. (1993) On the Engineering of Logics. PhD Thesis, Department of Informatics, University of Twente, Enschede, Netherlands

13. Sighireanu M. (1998) Model-checking validation of the LOTOS descriptions of the invoicing case study. In: Allemand M., Attiogbé C., Habrias H. (Eds.) International Workshop on Comparing Systems Specification Techniques. University of Nantes, France, 99–114
14. Sighireanu M., Turner K. J. (1998) Requirement capture, formal description and verification of an invoicing system. Technical Report RR-3575, Institut National de Recherche en Informatique et Automatique, Le Chesnay, France
15. Turner K. J. (1990) A LOTOS-based development strategy. In: Vuong S. T. (Ed.) Formal Description Techniques II. North-Holland, Amsterdam, Netherlands, 157–174
16. Turner K. J., Ed. (1993) Using Formal Description Techniques — An Introduction to ESTELLE, LOTOS and SDL. John Wiley, New York, USA
17. Turner K. J. (1997) Specification architecture illustrated in a communications context. Computer Networks and ISDN Systems 29(4):397–411
18. Turner K. J. (1998) The invoicing case study in (E-)LOTOS. In: Allemand M., Attiogbé C., Habrias H. (Eds.) International Workshop on Comparing Systems Specification Techniques. University of Nantes, France, 83–98
19. Turner K. J. (2000) World-wide Environment for Learning LOTOS. http://www.cs.stir.ac.uk/well/
20. VASY (Validation des Systèmes) Team (1999) CADP (CÆSAR/ALDÉBARAN Development Package): A software engineering toolbox for protocols and distributed systems. http://www.inrialpes.fr/vasy/cadp/

11 Specifying a Cleanroom Black Box Using JSD

Marc Frappier and Richard St-Denis

11.1 Overview of the Method

The Cleanroom method [7,8] and the JSD (Jackson System Development) method [2,5] were proposed in the early eighties by Harlan Mills and Michael Jackson, respectively. Both methods cover all phases of the software development process. They propose, however, different notations and techniques for each phase. This chapter illustrates how these two methods can be combined at the specification phase for a more effective process.

The motivation behind Cleanroom is *defect prevention*. To achieve this, Mills proposed a structured process with precise notations at each phase. The first phase consists of two parallel activities: i) the functional specification of user requirements using the box structure notation and ii) the specification of system usage (also called *an operational profile*). The system then is decomposed into increments. The functional specification is refined for each increment until executable code is reached, again using the box structure notation. Statistical tests cases are concurrently developed for each increment. Statistical testing is conducted on each increment and a reliability measure is derived (MTTF – Mean Time to Failure).

Box structure notation has three levels. The *black box* is a function from sequences of inputs to outputs. It can be refined into a *state box*, which is a transition function from inputs and states to outputs and states. In turn, a state box is refined into a *clear box*, which is a state box defined using the fundamental constructs of structured programming (assignment, sequence, if-then-else, while-do) and other black boxes. Recursively, the newly introduced black boxes are refined until executable code is reached.

The JSD process is decomposed into the following phases: i) entity action; ii) entity structure; iii) initial model; iv) function; v) system timing; and vi) implementation. The first two steps, in which entities are identified and the valid sequences of actions for each entity are defined, are of interest for Cleanroom. Entities are specified using an *entity structure diagram*, which is essentially the abstract syntax tree of a regular expression.

In this chapter, an extension of JSD's entity structure diagram, constructed using process algebras like CSP [4], CCS [6], and LOTOS [1], is used to specify a Cleanroom black box. A complete description of the method can be found in [3].

11.2 Analysis and Specification of Case 1

Before solving the problem of Case 1, the method presented in this chapter should be related to the main characteristic of the problem. Essentially, this problem has been reduced to its bare essentials in the sense that the function Invoice_Order is described without any reference to a business domain. Case 1 is essentially a state-based description. It refers to the status of an order, which must be changed from *pending* to *invoiced*. Consequently, it would be better described by a state box in Cleanroom.

A state box is a function from $X \times Q$ to $Y \times Q$, where X, Y, Q denote the input set, output set, and set of states, respectively. It also includes an initial state $q \in Q$. Elements of X and Y are visible to the user (or the environment). Elements of Q are not visible to the user; they are internal. A black box abstracts from states by using the history of inputs to determine the output. It is a function from X^+, the set of input sequences, to Y.

In Case 1, the output depends on the *last* input only; a function form X to Y would therefore be sufficient. Nevertheless, for the sake of illustration, a solution is given in terms of a black box. The purpose is solely to give an idea of the following concepts: input and output spaces, entity type, input sequence, input-output trace, entity trace, constraint, and input-output behaviour. The description of the method is necessarily presented with many simplifications.

11.2.1 Declaration of Input-Output Space and Entity Types

The first two questions are closely related because responses to one can hold the answer to the other and vice versa. Indeed, a problem can be tackled by using different strategies: one in which emphasis is placed on entities, one in which emphasis is placed on operations, or one that is a mix of the two.

Question 1: What are the atomic operations (*transactions*, or *actions*) performed by the system?

Answer: The only atomic operation identified from Case 1 is Invoice_Order.

Question 2: What are the entities that perform this operation?

Answer: There are many entities that perform operation Invoice_Order, but they are of the same type: the entity type order.

The answers to the two previous questions establish the boundary of the software system. The next two questions concern the operation Invoice_Order.

Question 3: What are the input attributes of this operation?

Answer: The input attributes are "*order*" and "*stock*".

This answer leads to the following interpretation of operation Invoice_Order: invoice an *order* according to the quantity of the ordered products in *stock*.

Question 4: What are the output attributes of this operation?

Answer: The only output attribute is a confirmation message ("*msg*"). The reason behind this decision is essentially to introduce some aspects of the method to the reader earlier because the operation Invoice_Order is an update operation that normally has no output.

The questions below concern the type of input and output attributes. An attribute type is a set constructed using elementary sets and set operations. This allows the definition of sub-attributes.

Question 5: What is the type of the input attribute "*order*"?

Answer: The type of "*order*" is defined using the Cartesian product of three sets. The elements of the first set (denoted **ORDER**) are order identifiers. The elements of the second set (denoted **STOCK**) are total functions that associate a natural number (representing a quantity) with each product, that is, **STOCK** $\triangleq$ **PRODUCT** $\to$ **NAT**. A function that belongs to this set represents the ordered products (also called items) with their quantity. The last set is $\{Pending, Invoiced\}$, which denotes the current status of the order.

Question 6: What is the type of the input attribute "*stock*"?

Answer: The type of "*stock*" is **STOCK**, but a function that belongs to this set represents the quantity of each product in stock.

Question 7: What is the type of the output attribute "*msg*"?

Answer: The type of "*msg*" is $\{\text{"Order "}\} \cdot \textbf{ORDER} \cdot \{\text{" invoiced"}\}$, which represents the set of all strings obtained from the concatenation of a constant string, an order identifier, and a constant string.

All the previous answers lead to the following formal operation declaration.

$$X_1 : Y_1 \triangleq \langle \text{Invoice\_Order}, order : \langle order\_id : \textbf{ORDER}, items : \textbf{STOCK}, \\ status : \{Pending, Invoiced\}\rangle, \\ stock : \textbf{STOCK}\rangle : \\ \langle msg : \{\text{"Order "}\} \cdot \textbf{ORDER} \cdot \{\text{" invoiced"}\}\rangle$$

An operation declaration defines an input set and an output set. The set $X_1 \triangleq (\textbf{ORDER} \times \textbf{STOCK} \times \{Pending, Invoiced\}) \times \textbf{STOCK}$ is the input set of operation Invoice_Order and set $Y_1 \triangleq \{\text{"Order "}\} \cdot \textbf{ORDER} \cdot \{\text{" invoiced"}\}$ is its output set.

Generally, input space X (output space Y) is the union of all input (output) sets. In this simple case, the input space X (output space Y) and X_1 (Y_1) are interchangeable. Elements of input space X are concatenated to form system input sequences of the form (symbol "$\_$" denotes some value for an attribute)

$$\langle \text{Invoice\_Order}, \langle \_, \_, \_ \rangle, \_ \rangle \cdot \cdots \cdot \langle \text{Invoice\_Order}, \langle \_, \_, \_ \rangle, \_ \rangle$$

A program that implements a specification accepts each element of an input sequence s and delivers a response when the processing of an element has been completed. After processing the last input, the program delivers an output $y \in Y$. The pair $\langle s, y \rangle$ is an input-output trace.

The traces specific to each entity can be recognized from an input sequence. In this solution, each entity admits entity traces, which are one-element sequences necessarily of the form $\langle \mathsf{Invoice\_Order}, \langle oId, I, sts \rangle, S \rangle$. It means that an order can be invoiced only once.

11.2.2 Definition of Global Constraints

Question 8: What are the constraints on input sequences?

Answer: A valid input sequence is a sequence in which every invoice operation refers to an order that includes at least one ordered product. This means that there exists at least one product that belongs to **PRODUCT** such that its associated quantity is greater than zero. Moreover, the status of the order must be "Pending" and the ordered quantity of each product is either less than or equal to the quantity in stock.

These constraints are formally defined as follows.

$Check\_Order(s) \Leftrightarrow$
  $\forall oId, T, t, I, S :$
    $\mathsf{entity\_traces}(s, T) \wedge$
    $\mathsf{order}(t, oId, T) \wedge$
    $t = \langle \mathsf{Invoice\_Order}, \langle oId, I, sts \rangle, S \rangle$
    $\Rightarrow$
    $sts = Pending \wedge$
    $(\exists pId : pId \in \textbf{PRODUCT} : I(pId) > 0) \wedge$
    $(\forall pId : pId \in dom(I) : I(pId) \leq S(pId))$

Predicate $entity\_traces(s, T)$ holds if input sequence s is constructed from all the entity traces of T. In other words, it holds when T is the decomposition of s into entity traces. This makes it possible to extract entity traces that belong to s. In this solution, an element of T is a 3-tuple of the form

$\langle \mathsf{order}, \langle \mathsf{Invoice\_Order}, \langle oId, I, sts \rangle, S \rangle, oId \rangle$,

where $\langle \mathsf{Invoice\_Order}, \langle oId, I, sts \rangle, S \rangle$ is an entity trace specific to the entity of type order identified by the order identifier oId. Predicate $\mathsf{order}(t, oId, T)$ holds iff $\langle \mathsf{order}, t, oId \rangle \in T$.

Recall that the type of attribute *items* is a function from **PRODUCT** to **NAT**. Hence, expression $I(pId)$ denotes the ordered quantity of product pId in order oId. Function dom returns the domain of a function.

11.2.3 Specification of Input-Output Behaviour

Question 9: What is the relation between the input attributes and output attribute of the operation Invoice_Order?

Answer: The message "Order xxx invoiced" is displayed.

This is formally translated in the following input-output axiom.

$Check\_Order(s\vdash \langle\text{Invoice\_Order}, \langle oId, I, sts\rangle, S\rangle)$
$\Rightarrow$
$s\vdash \langle\text{Invoice\_Order}, \langle oId, I, sts\rangle, S\rangle \triangleleft R \triangleright \text{``}Order\text{ ''} \cdot oId \cdot \text{`` } invoiced\text{''}$

The expression $s\vdash \langle\text{Invoice\_Order}, \langle oId, I, sts\rangle, S\rangle$, which appears twice in this formula, represents an input sequence ending with an operation Invoice_Order. The variable oId denotes the order identifier, the variable I denotes the order's items, and the variable S denotes the quantity in stock of all products. An expression of the form $s \triangleleft R \triangleright o$ is a predicate stating that the tuple $\langle s, o \rangle$ is an element of the relation R.

A legitimate question that could be raised is "What is the output for an input sequence that does not satisfy the global constraints (denoted here by predicate $Check\_Order$)?". In this method, the convention is that some information message is issued to notify the user, but it is not mandatory to specify it at this point. A specific message can be defined later in the development process.

11.3 Analysis and Specification of Case 2

11.3.1 Declaration of Input-Output Space and Entity Types

Essentially, Case 2 raises the same questions as Case 1, but they are repeated for each entity, operation, and attribute. According to the text of Case 2, a new order is created from scratch and ordered products (items) are progressively added. Then, in addition to the operation Invoice_Order, two new atomic operations are introduced: Create_Order and Add_Item.

Question 10: Could the effect of the operations Invoice_Order, Create_Order, and Add_Item be cancelled by opposite actions?

Answer: This question cannot be completely answered from Case 2, but it is assumed that it is the case.

Therefore, the operations Cancel_Invoice, Delete_Order, and Remove_Item are also considered. All the previous operations are executed by entities of type order. Another entity type appears from Case 2, the type product.

Question 11: What are the operations performed by an entity of type product?

Answer: From the text of Case 2, different quantities of product can be added to or removed from the stock.

The identifiers Add_Stock and Remove_Stock denote these last two operations.

Question 12: What are the output attributes of these new operations?

Answer: The previous operations are update functions that normally deliver an invisible output (denoted by the symbol τ), since their only effect is to modify the internal system state, which is not visible to the user.

To display information about the system state, the user typically invokes inquiry functions, which do provide a visible output. Only one inquiry operation (List_Order_Status) is considered. It should be noted that this operation in not performed by any entity, since it concerns all the entities of type order. Inquiry operations that cannot be connected to specific entities are grouped together into a single entity of the type query.

The following definitions are obtained at the end of the requirements elicitation process and after a phase of formalisation. The set E denotes the set of entity types.

$E \triangleq \{\text{order}, \text{product}, \text{query}\}$

$X_1 : Y_1 \triangleq \langle \text{Add\_Stock}, \textit{product\_id} : \textbf{PRODUCT}, \textit{quantity} : \textbf{NAT} \rangle : \tau$

$X_2 : Y_2 \triangleq \langle \text{Remove\_Stock}, \textit{product\_id} : \textbf{PRODUCT}, \textit{quantity} : \textbf{NAT} \rangle : \tau$

$X_3 : Y_3 \triangleq \langle \text{Create\_Order}, \textit{order\_id} : \textbf{ORDER} \rangle : \tau$

$X_4 : Y_4 \triangleq \langle \text{Delete\_Order}, \textit{order\_id} : \textbf{ORDER} \rangle : \tau$

$X_5 : Y_5 \triangleq \langle \text{Add\_Item}, \textit{order\_id} : \textbf{ORDER}, \textit{product\_id} : \textbf{PRODUCT},$
$\quad \textit{quantity} : \textbf{NAT} - \{0\} \rangle : \tau$

$X_6 : Y_6 \triangleq \langle \text{Remove\_Item}, \textit{order\_id} : \textbf{ORDER},$
$\quad \textit{product\_id} : \textbf{PRODUCT} \rangle : \tau$

$X_7 : Y_7 \triangleq \langle \text{Invoice\_Order}, \textit{order\_id} : \textbf{ORDER} \rangle : \tau$

$X_8 : Y_8 \triangleq \langle \text{Cancel\_Invoice}, \textit{order\_id} : \textbf{ORDER} \rangle : \tau$

$X_9 : Y_9 \triangleq \langle \text{List\_Order\_Status} \rangle : (\textbf{ORDER} \times \{\textit{Pending}, \textit{Invoiced}\})^*$

Note that the signature of the operation Invoice_Order is not the same as in Case 1. It no longer includes the order status and stock. Input space X and output space Y of this list of atomic operations are simply the union of their input sets and output sets, respectively:

$$X \triangleq \bigcup_{i=1}^{9} X_i \text{ and } Y \triangleq \bigcup_{i=1}^{9} Y_i.$$

Given input space X and output space Y, the external behaviour of the order management system shall be given by a relation R, called a *trace-based specification*, which is a subset of $X^+ \times Y$, where X^+ denotes the set of non-empty input sequences built using elements of X. A *trace-based specification* defines how each input sequence is related to an output with the restriction that

Table 11.1. An input-output trace for the order management system

n°	Input Element	Output
1	$\langle \text{Add\_Stock}, p_1, 25 \rangle$	τ
2	$\langle \text{Create\_Order}, o_1 \rangle$	τ
3	$\langle \text{Add\_Item}, o_1, p_1, 3 \rangle$	τ
4	$\langle \text{Add\_Stock}, p_2, 50 \rangle$	τ
5	$\langle \text{Create\_Order}, o_2 \rangle$	τ
6	$\langle \text{Add\_Item}, o_2, p_1, 5 \rangle$	τ
7	$\langle \text{Add\_Item}, o_1, p_2, 1 \rangle$	τ
8	$\langle \text{List\_Order\_Status} \rangle$	$\langle o_1, Pending \rangle \cdot \langle o_2, Pending \rangle$
9	$\langle \text{Invoice\_Order}, o_2 \rangle$	τ
10	$\langle \text{List\_Order\_Status} \rangle$	$\langle o_1, Pending \rangle \cdot \langle o_2, Invoiced \rangle$

for every input-output trace $\langle s, y \rangle \in R$, $y \in Y_i$, if the last element of s belongs to X_i.

Consider Table 11.1. Assume that the system is just started and input n° 1 is submitted. The system processes the input and delivers output τ, which is not visible to the user. In the specification R of this system, the input-output trace corresponding to this behaviour is:

$\langle \text{Add\_Stock}, p_1, 25 \rangle \triangleleft R \triangleright \tau$.

When the second input is submitted, the system delivers τ again. The corresponding input-output trace of R is:

$\langle \text{Add\_Stock}, p_1, 25 \rangle \cdot \langle \text{Create\_Order}, o_1 \rangle \triangleleft R \triangleright \tau$.

When the first List_Order_Status input is submitted, the system delivers an output visible to the user:

$\langle \text{Add\_Stock}, p_1, 25 \rangle \cdot \langle \text{Create\_Order}, o_1 \rangle \cdot \langle \text{Add\_Item}, o_1, p_1, 3 \rangle \cdot$
$\langle \text{Add\_Stock}, p_2, 50 \rangle \cdot \langle \text{Create\_Order}, o_2 \rangle \cdot \langle \text{Add\_Item}, o_2, p_1, 5 \rangle \cdot$
$\langle \text{Add\_Item}, o_1, p_2, 1 \rangle \cdot \langle \text{List\_Order\_Status} \rangle$
$\triangleleft R \triangleright$
$\langle o_1, Pending \rangle \cdot \langle o_2, Pending \rangle$.

Finally, when the second List_Order_Status input is submitted, the system delivers $\langle o_1, Pending \rangle \langle o_2, Invoiced \rangle$. The corresponding input-output trace of R is:

$\langle \text{Add\_Stock}, p_1, 25 \rangle \cdot \langle \text{Create\_Order}, o_1 \rangle \cdot \langle \text{Add\_Item}, o_1, p_1, 3 \rangle \cdot$
$\langle \text{Add\_Stock}, p_2, 50 \rangle \cdot \langle \text{Create\_Order}, o_2 \rangle \cdot \langle \text{Add\_Item}, o_2, p_1, 5 \rangle \cdot$
$\langle \text{Add\_Item}, o_1, p_2, 1 \rangle \cdot \langle \text{List\_Order\_Status}, o_1 \rangle \cdot \langle \text{Invoice\_Order}, o_2 \rangle \cdot$
$\langle \text{List\_Order\_Status} \rangle \triangleleft R \triangleright \langle o_1, Pending \rangle \cdot \langle o_2, Invoiced \rangle$.

11.3.2 Description of Individual Behaviours of Entities

A set of *keys* must be identified for each entity type. As usual, a key uniquely identifies an entity.

Question 13: What are the sets of keys associated with entity types?

Answer: The sets of keys associated with the entity types order and product, denoted by K_{order} and $K_{product}$, are **ORDER** and **PRODUCT**, respectively.

The entity query does not have a "natural" key. Nevertheless, a key must be identified. By convention, the one-point set $\{1\}$ is used.

Question 14: What are the ordering constraints on the operations specific to each entity of type product?

Answer: The operations Add_Stock and Remove_Stock are processed in any order and as many times as necessary for any entity of type product.

This ordered constraint is formalized by a process expression over the alphabet X:

$$product(pId) \triangleq (\langle \text{Add\_Stock}, pId, \_\rangle \mid \langle \text{Remove\_Stock}, pId, \_\rangle)^*$$

Process expressions correspond, roughly speaking, to regular expressions extended with parallel composition and synchronization. They describe the behaviours of entities. The previous expression defines a set of entity traces containing zero or more occurrences (the Kleene star operation "*") of Add_Stock and Remove_Stock in any order (the choice operation " | "). A process expression may be graphically represented by a syntax tree, called a *structure diagram*. Figure 11.1 provides the structure diagram for the process expression $product(pId)$. Since some details are missing, one may examine the formal textual definition of the corresponding process expression to get precise information.

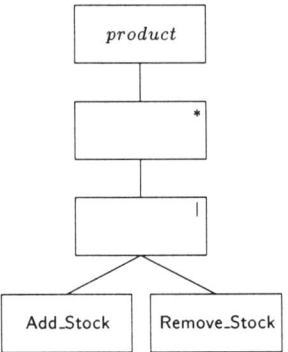

Fig. 11.1. The structure diagram for entities of type product

Question 15: What are the ordering constraints on the operations specific to each entity of type order?

Answer: There are four constraints that are formalized in a modular fashion. The behaviour of an order starts with the operation Create_Order and optionally ends with Delete_Order (first constraint). Items can be added and then optionally removed independently from each other. They evolve in parallel inside an order (second constraint). Items must, however, synchronize on invoicing operations (third constraint). This means that an item cannot be added or removed after the execution of the operation Invoice_Order, unless the operation Cancel_Invoice is eventually executed just after the operation Invoice_Order (fourth constraint).

The fourth constraint is formalized by the following process expression:

$$invoice(oId) \triangleq (\langle \text{Invoice\_Order}, oId \rangle \,.\, \langle \text{Cancel\_Invoice}, oId \rangle)^*$$

The concatenation operation (".") ensures that Cancel_Invoice is executed just after Invoice_Order. This process can be repeated any number of times (see operation "*" at the end of this expression).

The third constraint is formalized as follows:

$$item(oId, pId) \triangleq invoice(oId) \,.\, (\langle \text{Add\_Item}, oId, pId, \_\rangle \,.\, invoice(oId) \,.\, \langle \text{Remove\_Item}, oId, pId \rangle \,.\, invoice(oId))^*$$

The third and fourth constraints can be equivalently represented by a state transition diagram that shows how items evolve. This diagram is given in Figure 11.2. As usual, the initial state is identified by a wedge underneath it and final states are identified by a double circle.

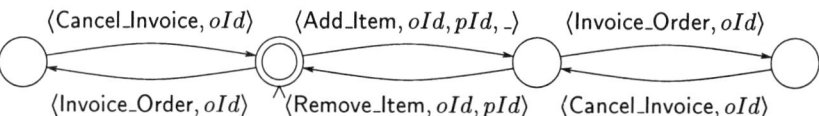

Fig. 11.2. The state transition diagram equivalent to the process expression $item(oId, pId)$

Finally, the following process expression takes into account the first and second constraints:

$$order(oId) \triangleq \langle \text{Create\_Order}, oId \rangle \,.\\ (\boxed{|[Inv\_Op]|}\; pId : \textbf{Product\_Id} : item(oId, pId)) \,.\\ \langle \text{Delete\_Order}, oId \rangle$$

Figure 11.3 provides the structure diagram for this process expression. For instance, an order's behaviour is structured as a concatenation. The first term is the operation Create_Order. The last term is the operation Delete_Order. Note that an order can be created only once. We assume that this is a business rule. The second term is more complex. It uses a *bounded quantification* that selects an

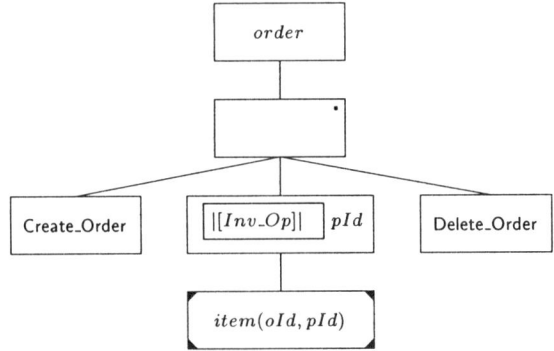

Fig. 11.3. The structure diagram for entities of type order

arbitrary finite set of ordered products and composes in parallel item processes, one for each product. Item processes must synchronize on operations given in the set Inv_Op, defined as {Invoice_Order, Cancel_Invoice}.

Question 16: What are the ordering constraints on the operations specific to the entity of type query?

Answer: Inputs that correspond to inquiry operations initiated by a user may be submitted at any time, since they typically do not have strong ordering constraints.

The corresponding process expression is generally the Kleene closure of a choice between inquiry operations:

$$query(1) \triangleq (\langle \text{List\_Order\_Status} \rangle)^*.$$

Entity traces are combined to form the set of well-formed input sequences. This set is automatically obtained from a process expression in conformity with the following semantics rules. All traces of entities of the same type are interleaved. It does not matter in which order entities of the same type evolve, because they are independent. The resulting traces for each entity type are then composed in parallel, but they are synchronized on common inputs. The parallel composition operation between entity types acts like a conjunction. As advocated in the JSD method, an input sequence must satisfy all the ordering constraints specified for each entity.

11.3.3 Definition of Global Constraints

Question 17: What are the global constraints on input sequences?

Answer: There are three constraints: i) to invoice an order, there must be at least one item with a strictly positive ordered quantity; ii) to invoice an order, there must be enough quantity in stock for each item; and iii) the quantity in stock must never be negative.

To formalize these three constraints, the predicates $entity\_traces(s, T)$ and $order(t, oId, T)$ are used again. They make it possible to extract entity traces from a well-formed input sequence. As an example, let s be the input sequence in Table 11.1. The predicate $entity\_traces(s, T)$ holds with:

$$T = \{\, \langle \text{product}, t_1, p_1 \rangle, \langle \text{product}, t_2, p_2 \rangle, \langle \text{order}, t_3, o_1 \rangle, \langle \text{order}, t_4, o_2 \rangle,$$
$$\langle \text{query}, t_5, 1 \rangle \,\},$$

where

$t_1 = \langle \text{Add\_Stock}, p_1, 25 \rangle,$
$t_2 = \langle \text{Add\_Stock}, p_2, 50 \rangle,$
$t_3 = \langle \text{Create\_Order}, o_1 \rangle \cdot \langle \text{Add\_Item}, o_1, p_1, 3 \rangle \cdot \langle \text{Add\_Item}, o_1, p_2, 1 \rangle,$
$t_4 = \langle \text{Create\_Order}, o_2 \rangle \cdot \langle \text{Add\_Item}, o_2, p_1, 5 \rangle \cdot \langle \text{Invoice\_Order}, o_2 \rangle,$
$t_5 = \langle \text{List\_Order\_Status} \rangle \cdot \langle \text{List\_Order\_Status} \rangle.$

The following predicates also hold:

$\text{product}(t_1, p_1, T) \qquad \text{order}(t_3, o_1, T) \qquad \text{query}(t_5, 1, T)$
$\text{product}(t_2, p_2, T) \qquad \text{order}(t_4, o_2, T)$

The first constraint is specified by the predicate q_1.

$q_1(s) \Leftrightarrow \forall s', T, x : s' \in prefix(s) \land entity\_traces(s', T) \land x = last(s') \land$
$\qquad action(x) = \text{Invoice\_Order}$
$\qquad \Rightarrow$
$\qquad \exists t : order(t, order\_id(x), T) \land$
$\qquad \#(t \upharpoonright \{\text{Add\_Item}\}) > \#(t \upharpoonright \{\text{Remove\_Item}\})$

The predicate q_1 states that any prefix s' of the well-formed input sequence s, such that s' is terminated by input $x = \langle \text{Invoice\_Order}, \_ \rangle$, contains a trace t, specific to the entity of type order with the key extracted from x, for which the number of items added to this order is greater than the number of items removed from this order. The function $action$ extracts the action of an input element. This formula also includes the attribute name $order\_id$ used in the declaration of several operations (*e.g.*, Add_Item). An attribute name can be used as a projection function to extract the attribute value of an input element. Moreover, the term $t \upharpoonright \Delta$ denotes the restriction with respect to set Δ of some input actions and $\#s$ the length of s.

The second and third constraints are formalized by predicate q_2 in a similar fashion. It requires that the items of an order be considered as a *weak* entity type (a marsupial entity type in JSD's terminology; it also corresponds to a weak entity type in Chen's entity relationship diagrams). Therefore, the following predicates hold for the input sequence in Table 11.1.

$\text{item}(t_6, \langle o_1, p_1 \rangle, T) \qquad \text{item}(t_7, \langle o_1, p_2 \rangle, T) \qquad \text{item}(t_8, \langle o_2, p_1 \rangle, T)$

where

$t_6 = \langle \text{Add\_Item}, o_1, p_1, 3\rangle,$
$t_7 = \langle \text{Add\_Item}, o_1, p_2, 1\rangle,$
$t_8 = \langle \text{Add\_Item}, o_2, p_1, 5\rangle \cdot \langle \text{Invoice\_Order}, o_2\rangle.$

The behaviour of the item with the key $\langle oId, pId\rangle$ is described by the process expression $item(oId, pId)$ introduced in the previous section.

$q_2(x) \Leftrightarrow \forall s', T, pId : s' \in prefix(s) \wedge entity\_traces(s', T)$
$\Rightarrow$
$stock(s', T, pId) \geq 0,$

where

$Add = s' \lceil \{\langle \text{Add\_Stock}, pId, \_\rangle\},$
$Remove = s' \lceil \{\langle \text{Remove\_Stock}, pId, \_\rangle\},$
$Invoiced\_Items = \{i \mid \exists t_1, t_2, oId : order(t_1, oId, T) \wedge$
$\quad action(last(t_1)) = \text{Invoice\_Order} \wedge$
$\quad item(t_2, \langle oId, pId\rangle, T) \wedge$
$\quad i = last(t_2 \lceil \{\text{Add\_Item}, \text{Remove\_Item}\}) \wedge$
$\quad action(i) = \text{Add\_Item}\}$

$$stock(s', T, pId) = \sum_{k=1}^{\#Add} quantity(Add[k]) - \sum_{k=1}^{\#Remove} quantity(Remove[k]) - \sum_{i \in Invoiced\_Items} quantity(i).$$

The quantity in stock for the product pId is calculated from the sequence s' by adding the quantities in all $\langle \text{Add\_Stock}, pId, \_\rangle$ and subtracting the quantities in all $\langle \text{Remove\_Stock}, pId, \_\rangle$. Furthermore, the quantities of items added to any invoiced order, but not removed, are also subtracted. The term $s' \lceil \Delta$ denotes the restriction of sequence s' to alphabet Δ and $s[i] \in X$ the ith element of sequence s.

11.3.4 Specification of Input-Output Behaviour

Question 18: What is the output of the operation List_Order_Status for a valid input sequence?

Answer: It is a list of all orders, that have been not deleted, sorted with respect to their key.

$s \vdash \langle \text{List\_Order\_Status} \rangle \in \textbf{Valid}_E \wedge entity\_traces(s, T) \wedge$
$O = \{o \mid (\exists oId, t : order(t, oId, T) \wedge action(last(t)) = \textsf{Invoice\_Order} \wedge$
$\qquad\qquad o = \langle oId, Invoiced \rangle) \vee$
$\qquad (\exists oId, t : order(t, oId, T) \wedge action(last(t)) \neq \textsf{Invoice\_Order} \wedge$
$\qquad\qquad\qquad\qquad\qquad\qquad action(last(t)) \neq \textsf{Delete\_Order} \wedge$
$\qquad\qquad o = \langle oId, Pending \rangle)\} \wedge$
$sorted(out, \pi_1, O)$
$\Rightarrow$
$s \vdash \langle \text{List\_Order\_Status} \rangle \triangleleft R \triangleright out$

The set $\textbf{Valid}_E$ includes all well-formed input sequences that satisfy predicates q_1 and q_2 defined in the previous section. This input-output axiom establishes a set O of pairs according to the definition of set Y_9. A pair is constructed by selecting an entity trace t of an order. If its last input is the operation Invoice_Order, then the order is invoiced. If its last input is neither the operation Invoice_Order nor Delete_Order, then the order is pending. The sort criteria and the transformation of the set into a sequence according to the sort criteria are expressed using the predicate $sorted(out, \pi_i, O)$, which is informally defined as out is a list of all elements of O sorted on the ith attribute given by projection function π_i.

11.4 The Natural Language Description of the Specification

11.4.1 Case 1

The system provides only one operation, Invoice_Order. This operation accepts as input an order and the stock. An order consists of an order identifier, a set of items, and an order status. An item is a product identifier with an ordered quantity. The status of an order is either *Pending* or *Invoiced*. The stock associates a quantity in stock with each product identifier. This operation produces an output message "Order xxx invoiced" when the next three conditions are satisfied: i) the order status is *Pending*; ii) the quantity in stock is greater than the ordered quantity, for each item on the order; and iii) at least one item has an ordered quantity greater than zero. The operation can be successfully invoked only once for each order.

11.4.2 Case 2

The system provides nine operations. Two operations allow product units to be added or removed from the stock. Two other operations allow orders to be created or deleted. Items may be added to or removed from an order. A product appears at most once in an order. An order may be invoiced if the next three conditions are satisfied: i) its status is *Pending*; ii) it contains at least one item with a strictly positive quantity; and iii) there is enough stock for each item. An invoice can be cancelled. When an order is invoiced, items can not be added or deleted. The quantity in stock for a product is increased by the operation Add_Stock and decreased by the operation Remove_Stock. The operation Invoice_Order also decreases the stock for each item of the order. The quantity in stock must never be negative. Finally, a query operation provides status information about orders.

11.5 Conclusion

Cleanroom's black box specifications describe the behaviour of a system in terms of sequences; they abstract from the internal system state. In this chapter, we have shown how these sequences can be described in terms of entities inspired from the JSD method. A special process algebra is used to describe the input sequences that an entity may accept. The outputs are described in terms of entity traces.

The black box approach was less suitable for Case 1, because the problem is stated at a lower level of abstraction. It refers to the internal system state (*i.e.*, the order status); hence, it is essentially a state box problem. To model Case 1 with a black box, the system state has to be included both as input and output parameters of the operation Invoice_Order. Moreover, the output of the invoice operation depends only on the last input; the history of inputs is not used at all. A black box is more suitable for Case 2, because the behaviour of each operation can be described in terms of the input history.

Using JSD's entities to describe a Cleanroom black box provides a quite intuitive means to describe system dynamics. Entity traces are explicitly illustrated by structure diagrams; these diagrams can be automatically extracted from a formal description of entities.

The method promotes modular descriptions through entities and process abstraction. It is also resilient to some specification changes, due to the use of traces. For instance, creating a new inquiry operation seldom induces a modification in entity descriptions. In Case 2, adding an operation that lists the items of orders, whether they are deleted or not, induces no changes in the structure of entities of type order. It suffices to add a new input-output axiom to describe the behaviour of this new inquiry. The same change applied to a state box would induce several changes: if no state variable contains the required information, a new state variable must be defined. The transition relation must also be modified to change the value of this new state variable as required. Similarly, adding a new constraint typically does not induce any change in entities or old constraints. For example, suppose that one would like to invoice orders in the sequence in which they are created. It suffices to add a new constraint to fulfil this new requirement; there is no need to change the rest of the specification. In contrast, the same change applied to a state box would probably require a new state variable and modifications to the transition relation for the operations Create_Order, Delete_Order, and Invoice_Order.

In general, the information in a black box is more localized than in a state box. For instance, the function *stock* introduced in Case 2 is completely defined in one expression. In a state box, *stock* would typically be represented by a state variable maintained in three different places: operations Add_Stock, Remove_Stock, and Invoice_Order.

References

1. Bolognesi, T. and Brinksma, E. (1987) Introduction to the ISO Specification Language LOTOS. Computer Networks and ISDN Systems 14(1):25–59
2. Cameron, J. R. (1989) JSP and JSD: The Jackson Approach to Software Development, Second Edition. IEEE Computer Society Press, Washington
3. Frappier, M., St-Denis, R. (1999) Specifying Information Systems through Structured Input-Output Traces, Université de Sherbrooke, Département de mathématiques et d'informatique, Technical Report 233
4. Hoare, C. A. R. (1985) Communicating Sequential Processes. Prentice Hall, Englewood Cliffs, NJ
5. Jackson, M. (1983) System Development. Prentice Hall, Englewood Cliffs, NJ
6. Milner, R. (1989) Communication and Concurrency. Prentice Hall, Englewood Cliffs, NJ
7. Mills, H. D., Linger R. C., and Hevner, A. R. (1986) Principles of Information Systems Analysis and Design. Academic Press, Orlando, FL
8. Prowell, S. J., Trammell, C. J., Linger, R. C., Poore, J. H. (1999) Cleanroom Software Engineering: Technology and Process. Addison-Wesley, Reading, MA

Part III

Other Formal Approaches

12 Algebraic Specification in CASL

Hubert Baumeister and Didier Bert

12.1 Overview of the CASL Notation

The acronym CASL stands for *Common Algebraic Specification Language* [1]. It is a language designed by the IFIP WG1.3[1] working group to provide a unified notation for writing algebraic specifications. For an easy introduction to the language see [5].

Two main principles underlie the algebraic specification technology. The first one is *representation independence*. This means that data representation is not known and does not need to be known early in the specification process. Fixing actual implementation of data is deferred as much as possible. This was made popular by the *abstract data type* paradigm. All the data defined in the algebraic formalism are "abstract" in that sense. The second principle is a consequence of the previous one. Because representation is not given the only way to use data values is to provide *sets of operations* on these data. By way of illustration, the data type integer, available in usual programming languages, is an example of an abstract data type. Its values are accessible only via constants $(0, 1, \ldots)$ and operations $(+, \times, \ldots)$. Data abstractly defined with functional operations are called *algebras* in mathematics, which explains the word "algebraic" in the formalism name. For the underlying theory of algebraic specification one can see [3,2,7]. For examples of applications see [4] among others.

A simple algebraic specification contains a part called the *signature* where new names are declared. The names can be data names, called *sorts*, operation and predicate names. Operation and predicate names are declared together with a *profile* which indicates the expected sorts of arguments and, for the operations, the sort of the result. So a signature provides a way to form expressions, also called *terms*, by combining operations, constants and variables. Terms are *well-formed* if the sorts of the arguments are compatible with the profiles of the operations. All the well-formed terms denote "values" of a given sort. The CASL language also admits declaration of subsorts to characterize subsets of values.

Once a "discourse domain" is defined through a signature one can declare *properties* on it. Properties are expressed in a standard logic formalism very close to the Z or B specification notation. They are introduced in a specification by declarations of *axioms*.

---
[1] Foundations of System Specification, URL: www.brics.dk/~pdm/IFIP-WG1.3/.

In CASL specifications may be *structured*, that is built by using structuring primitives. This provides a very powerful mechanism to reuse specification modules and to adapt old specifications in order to match with new requirements. The main structuring primitives are renaming, hiding, union and extension. Specifications can also be generic, that is parameterised by other specifications. Thus, new specifications can be built by instantiating generic specifications. Semantic relations between specifications are achieved by declarations of *views*. However it has been noticed that structuring choices at the specification level does not always yield a good structure at the program level. So the CASL language provides primitives to build *architectural specifications* which are intended to reflect the program structure.

To conclude this overview notice that CASL is a *property-oriented* specification language. That means that a specification does not build directly a model of the problem. Rather it is intended to express the properties which must hold in the final realisation. So the semantic meaning of a specification is a *class of models*, not one model only.

12.2 Analysis and Specification of Case 1

The given requirements of the case study clearly settle the aim of the final software product: "the subject is to invoice orders". Not all the used words are defined in the requirements, but the domain is assumed to be known by the specifier. When some details are missing in the requirements, the expression "*we assume*" indicates what are the hints given by the user. When several solutions are possible to specify a part of the problem, the expression "*we choose*" indicates a choice made by the specifier.

In the algebraic specification method the first task is to identify "sort" names that denote data (i.e. sets of values) of the problem and operations and predicates on these sorts. If some data do not refer to any standard data types, then new sorts are introduced. All names should be derived from the informal requirements for the sake of traceability.

Question 1: What are the data of the invoicing problem?

Answer: The requirements introduce the data of orders, stock and products. Moreover, there is a notion of *quantity* because the ordered quantity must be compared to the quantity in stock.

For the three first data we choose to use new sorts, respectively called *Order*, *Stock* and *Product*. For the "quantity" data we have two possibilities in CASL: we can introduce a new sort, say "*Qty*", and a total order predicate "$\leq$" to denote the quantity values and the ordering, or we can use a data specification of the predefined library [6]. In that case an obvious solution is to take the data type of natural numbers defined in the specification *NAT*, with the sort "*Nat*" and all the usual operators and predicates. We assume that a quantity cannot be negative, otherwise we should take the sort *"Int"* from the specification of integers.

Question 2: What is the state of an order?
Answer: The state of an order is either *"pending"* or *"invoiced"*.

So the order set denoted by the sort *Order* is divided into pending orders and invoiced orders. This can be specified by two predicates characterizing disjoint sets of order values. In the CASL texts below, keywords are boldfaced; comments are introduced by "%%" and terminate at the end of line:

> **preds** %% declaration of two predicates
>   *is_pending, is_invoiced* : *Order* %% on the orders.
> **axiom** %% declaration of an axiom:
> $\forall o : Order \bullet \neg\, is\_pending(o) \Leftrightarrow is\_invoiced(o)$

Another view of this notion would be to define the state as an *attribute* of the orders. In that case *state* becomes an operation from *Order* to *State*, where *State* is the sort of the state values: *pending* and *invoiced*. In CASL an enumerated set of values can be directly introduced with the sort declaration:

> **free type** *State* ::= *pending* | *invoiced*;

The operation *state* and the axioms relating it to the predicates are then:

> **op**   *state* : *Order* → *State*   %% declaration of an operation
> **var** *o* : *Order*   %% declaration of variables for the axioms
> • *is_pending*(*o*) ⇔ *state*(*o*) = *pending*
> • *is_invoiced*(*o*) ⇔ *state*(*o*) = *invoiced*

From now on we only consider the predicative description of the state, not the description by an attribute.

Question 3: What are the operations on the orders?
Answer: The requirements indicate the operations that observe the content of the orders. They are the "reference" to a product and the "quantity" of the ordered product.

We assume that the quantity of the ordered product is not zero (otherwise it is useless to order the product). The requirements are a bit ambiguous on the point of the references. An interpretation of the sentence: "On an order, we have one and one only reference to an ordered product of a certain quantity" is that there is one reference on an order. Another interpretation is that there may be several references, but it is forbidden that the same reference should occur several times on an order. We choose here the first interpretation which seems confirmed by the sentence "according to the reference of the ordered product".

We have stressed that an algebraic specification contains sorts, operators and predicates. A good specification-writing method is to gather all the strongly connected declarations into a specification module. So the specification $ORDER$ below declares the sorts $Order$ together with the "observer" operations. Nothing is said about the effective construction of the $Order$ values. The specification also introduces the sort $Product$, needed to define the reference attribute. In CASL the set of positive natural numbers is denoted by the sort Pos, which is a subsort of Nat. A specification module can be built as an *extension* of other specifications. Here the $ORDER$ specification needs the specification NAT, which must be "imported".

    spec $ORDER\ =\ NAT$ %% NAT is imported.
    then   %% extension by new declarations.
      sorts $Order,\ Product$;
      ops $reference$: $Order\ \rightarrow\ Product$;
                $ordered\_qty$: $Order\ \rightarrow\ Pos$;
      preds $is\_pending,\ is\_invoiced : Order$;
      vars $o : Order$ %% axiomatisation of the predicates.
        • $\neg\ is\_pending(o) \Leftrightarrow is\_invoiced(o)$
    end

Question 4: What about the stock?

Answer: In the requirements one can find the expressions "the references in stock" and "the quantity (of a product) which is in stock".

We infer that there is an operation qty which, given a reference to a product and a (current value of the) stock, returns the quantity of the product. We assume that there are operations to add and to $remove$ product items in the stock. We specify also a predicate p is_in s which holds if the product p is referenced in the stock s. The operations qty, add and $remove$ are partial, that is, are only defined on the domain of the products which are effectively in the stock. Moreover, the remove operation can be applied only if there are enough items of the product. The function symbol of partial operations is denoted by "$\rightarrow ?$". The definition domain of partial operations is specified through a "definedness predicate" introduced by the keyword **def**. The notation "ϕ_1 **if** ϕ_2" is just another way to write "$\phi_2 \Rightarrow \phi_1$". The axiomatisation of add and $remove$ is achieved by their effect on the result of the operation qty. This is called an *observational* specification of the operations. So the specification of the stock is given by:

  spec $STOCK\ =\ NAT$ **then**
    sorts $Stock,\ Product$;
    ops qty : $Product \times Stock \rightarrow ?\ Nat$;
           $add, remove$: $Product \times Pos \times Stock \rightarrow ?\ Stock$
    pred $\_\_is\_in\_\_$: $Product \times Stock$
    vars $p, p' : Product$; $n : Pos$; $s : Stock$
    • **def** $qty(p, s)\ \Leftrightarrow\ p\ is\_in\ s$
    • **def** $add(p, n, s)\ \Leftrightarrow\ p\ is\_in\ s$

- **def** $remove(p,n,s) \Leftrightarrow p\ is\_in\ s \wedge qty(p,s) \geq n$
- $qty(p, add(p,n,s)) = qty(p,s) + n$ **if** $p\ is\_in\ s$
- $qty(p', add(p,n,s)) = qty(p',s)$ **if** $p'\ is\_in\ s \wedge p\ is\_in\ s \wedge p' \neq p$
- $qty(p, remove(p,n,s)) = qty(p,s) - n$ **if** $p\ is\_in\ s \wedge qty(p,s) \geq n$
- $qty(p', remove(p,n,s)) = qty(p',s)$ **if** $p'\ is\_in\ s \wedge p\ is\_in\ s \wedge p' \neq p$

end

Question 5: What are the inputs and outputs of the main operation that we shall call *"invoice_order"*?

Answer: Clearly the operation *"invoice_order"* gets an order and the stock as inputs, because the quantity of the ordered product must be compared to the quantity in stock. The operation may modify the order and the stock, because the state of the order can change and the stock is modified; more precisely, the quantity in stock of the product must be updated if this quantity is large enough.

Because the algebraic formalism is *functional*, the read (or input) values are the parameters of the operation and the modified (or output) values are the results. However in CASL, the profile of an operation gets only one result. So the regular solution is to gather both values into a new one, the sort of which is a product type of the two respective sorts. It is easy to define a specification of a sort which is a product type of several other sorts. Similar as for enumeration types like *State* above, CASL provides an abbreviation for product types which generates all the declarations of a product at once. In the *OrdStk* declaration below *"mk_os"* is a new operation that takes two values of sort *Order* and *Stock* respectively and returns a value of sort *OrdStk*. It is called a *constructor* operation. The operations *order_of* and *stock_of* select the corresponding information from an *OrdStk* value. They are called *selectors*.

free type $OrdStk ::= mk\_os(order\_of : Order;\ stock\_of : Stock);$

This free type declaration generates the following signature and axioms:

ops
$mk\_os : Order \times Stock \to OrdStk;$
$order\_of : OrdStk \to Order;$
$stock\_of : OrdStk \to Stock;$

vars $o : Order;\ s : Stock;\ os : OrdStk$
- $mk\_os(order\_of(os), stock\_of(os)) = os$
- $order\_of(mk\_os(o,s)) = o$
- $stock\_of(mk\_os(o,s)) = s$

Question 6: What are the required conditions to invoice an order?

Answer: At a first glance, the requirements indicate that an order can be invoiced if at least three conditions are satisfied: (1) the state of the order is "pending" (2) "the ordered references are references in stock" and (3) "the ordered quantity is either less or equal to the quantity which is in stock".

All these conditions can be expressed by CASL formulas on the two parameters of the operation *invoice_order*, $o : Order;\ s : Stock$. The first one is obviously: *"is_pending(o)"*. For the other conditions new predicates are introduced through "definitions", that is, profile and meaning at the same time. For instance the second condition can be expressed by the definition:

pred $referenced(o : Order; s : Stock) \Leftrightarrow reference(o)$ is_in s

which is a short form of: **pred** $referenced : Order \times Stock$
vars $o : Order; s : Stock$
- $referenced(o, s) \Leftrightarrow reference(o)$ is_in s

Then we define the predicates $enough\_qty$ (condition (3)) and $invoice\_ok$ which formalize the precondition of the $invoice\_order$ operation.

$enough\_qty(o : Order; s : Stock) \Leftrightarrow ordered\_qty(o) \leq qty(reference(o), s);$
$invoice\_ok(o : Order; s : Stock) \Leftrightarrow$
$\qquad is\_pending(o) \wedge referenced(o, s) \wedge enough\_qty(o, s);$

In the sequel of the specification we choose a "defensive" style, that means the operation $invoice\_order$ is defined to be total on its parameters. The profile is then:

$invoice\_order : Order \times Stock \rightarrow OrdStk$

However we could choose a "generous" style with partial operation and preconditions. Of course, this style requires that the preconditions are checked by the calling programs. For this operation the conditions (1) and (2) would be left as preconditions.

Question 7: What is the effect of the operation "$invoice\_order$"?

Answer: Within the conditions defined above, the state of the order becomes invoiced and the quantity of the ordered product in the stock is reduced by the ordered quantity. The requirements do not prescribe the behaviour of the operation when the conditions are not fulfilled. We assume that the parameters are not changed in that case.

Following again the observational specification style, the effect of the operation $invoice\_order(o,s)$ is determined by the modification of the attributes of the order o ($reference$, $ordered\_qty$) and of the stock s (qty). However, for the stock we can use the modification operations already defined. The first set of axioms state what happens when the conditions for invoicing an order hold:

- $is\_invoiced(order\_of(invoice\_order(o, s)))$ **if** $invoice\_ok(o, s)$
- $stock\_of(invoice\_order(o, s)) = remove(reference(o), ordered\_qty(o), s)$
  if $invoice\_ok(o, s)$

If the conditions are not fulfilled, the order and the stock are not modified:

- $invoice\_order(o, s) = mk\_os(o, s)$ **if** $\neg$ $invoice\_ok(o, s)$ $\quad (*)$

Moreover, the other attributes of the order are not changed by the $invoice\_order$ operation. We need to make these properties explicit through extra axioms:

- $reference(order\_of(invoice\_order(o,s))) = reference(o)$
- $ordered\_qty(order\_of(invoice\_order(o,s))) = ordered\_qty(o)$

Assume now that we want that messages are issued for the various cases of the results of the *invoice_order* operation. This is not expressed by the requirements, but can be useful for the users. The messages are defined by the following free type:

free type $Msg ::= success \mid not\_pending \mid not\_referenced \mid not\_enough\_qty$

The profile of the operation *invoice_order* becomes:

free type $OSM ::= mk(order\_of: Order;\ stock\_of: Stock;\ msg\_of: Msg);$
op $invoice\_order: Order \times Stock \to OSM$

The axiom (*) from above needs to be changed and the following axioms have to be added to the specification.

- $msg\_of(invoice\_order(o,s)) = success$ **if** $invoice\_ok(o,s)$
- $msg\_of(invoice\_order(o,s)) = not\_pending$ **if** $\neg\, is\_pending(o)$
- $msg\_of(invoice\_order(o,s)) = not\_referenced$
  if $is\_pending(o) \wedge \neg\, referenced(o,s)$
- $msg\_of(invoice\_order(o,s)) = not\_enough\_qty$
  if $is\_pending(o) \wedge referenced(o,s) \wedge \neg\, enough\_qty(o,s)$

All the definitions from Question 5 should be gathered in a specification module named *INVOICE* to achieve the specification which concludes the first part of the case study.

12.3 Analysis and Specification of Case 2

In Case 2 we have to take into account the "dynamics" of the invoicing system and to specify the "two entry flows (orders, entries in stock)".

Question 8: What are the operations involved in this part?

Answer: On the orders, it is said that we have to specify:
- "*new_order*" to introduce a new pending order.
- "*cancel_order*" to cancel an order.

On the stock, the operation requested by the requirements is:
- "*add_qty*" to add a certain quantity of a product in the stock.

The requirements do not mention another fundamental operation that we shall name "*deal_with_order*". This operation tries to invoice a pending order. If invoicing succeeds, the order becomes an "invoiced" order. It is the heart of the invoicing process. This operation should use the already specified operation "*invoice_order*". In addition, a constant "*init*" is needed to represent the initial state of the invoicing system.

Question 9: Could you explain the scenario of the invoicing process?

Answer: The invoicing process evolves from the initial state by invocation of the four operations: *new_order*, *cancel_order*, *deal_with_order* and *add_qty*. Firstly, orders are put in a set of pending orders, then they can be transferred to the set of invoiced orders if the invoicing operation can be applied. A question arises when an order cannot be invoiced by lack of product quantity in the stock. In that case the order remains pending, but the system must be aware that there are orders which have not been invoiced for the reason of lack of product quantity. Independently, the stock can be supplied. Finally, orders can be cancelled at any time.

Question 10: Is there an ordering to choose the orders which must be invoiced by the system?

Answer: This point is left open in the requirements. The usual treatment is to invoice orders on the basis of the first-in first-out policy. However, the orders not invoiced by lack of product quantity should be invoiced as soon as the ordered product is supplied in the stock.

This ordering assumption is an important design decision. The scenario is now much more defined. The pending orders should be organized in a queue, at least at the abstract level. The oldest orders are the first ones in the queue. So the invoicing system must try to invoice the oldest orders which satisfy the conditions to be invoiced.

The next step now is to specify the queue data type. As explained in the introduction, this is not an implementation decision, because the specification is independent from the concrete data structures which will be used later. These queues are matter of thinking of the problem, not of giving an implementation. In CASL queues are not provided as basic data types [6]. However, there is a specification of the generic data type "*LIST*" which can be adapted to our purpose. This provides an example of using structuring primitives to build new specifications. The heading of the "*LIST*" specification presents the minimal signature required for the instantiations (here the sort of the elements).

$$\textbf{spec } LIST\,[\textbf{sort } Elem] = \ldots$$

The body of the *LIST* specification contains declarations and axioms about lists. The operations are as usual: *nil*, $a :: l$ (for *cons*), *first*, *last*, *rest*, $l_1 + l_2$ (for concatenation), etc. Inside the generic module, the sort of element list is denoted by "*List[Elem]*". We instantiate *LIST* by the *ORDER* specification. The sort generated by the instantiation mechanism is *List[Order]*. Then we build a new specification by renaming (keyword **with**) the sort *List[Order]* into *OQueue*. The operations and predicates on lists are inherited and their profiles are changed accordingly. Finally, we declare a new infix predicate "$\in$" and give the specification the name *ORDER_QUEUE*. Note that we must be able to decide if two orders are equal or not ("=" predicate).

spec *ORDER_QUEUE* =
  { *LIST* [*ORDER* **fit** *Elem* ↦ *Order*] **with** *List*[*Order*] ↦ *OQueue* }
then
  pred __ ∈ __ : *Order* × *OQueue*;
  vars o, o' : *Order*; oq : *OQueue*;   %% This predicate is specified
    • $\neg\, o \in nil$ %% by the case for *nil*, then by
    • $o' \in (o :: oq) \Leftrightarrow o' = o \vee o' \in oq$ %% the case for *cons*.
end

In the next specification named *QUEUES*, we define three subsorts of *OQueue*: the subsort *UQueue* of queues with uniquely identified, distinct orders; the subsort *PQueue* of queues with pending orders and the subsort *IQueue* of queues containing only invoiced orders. This will be done using the subsorting facilities of CASL, which allows us to declare subsorts defined by predicates.

spec *QUEUES* = *ORDER_QUEUE* **then**
  preds *unicity, pqueue, iqueue* : *OQueue*;
  vars o : *Order*; oq : *OQueue*;
    • *unicity*(*nil*)
    • *unicity*($o :: oq$) $\Leftrightarrow \neg\, (o \in oq) \wedge$ *unicity*(oq)
    • *pqueue*(oq) $\Leftrightarrow \forall x$: *Order* · ($x \in oq \Rightarrow$ *is_pending*(x))
    • *iqueue*(oq) $\Leftrightarrow \forall x$: *Order* · ($x \in oq \Rightarrow$ *is_invoiced*(x))
  sorts
    UQueue = { oq : *OQueue* • *unicity*(oq) };
    PQueue = { uq : *UQueue* • *pqueue*(uq) };
    IQueue = { uq : *UQueue* • *iqueue*(uq) };
end

Question 11: What is the global state of the invoicing process and what are the conditions which should be fulfilled by the global state values?

Answer: The global state is composed of the orders and of the stock. The requirements state that "all the ordered references are references in stock". Moreover, we have seen that if orders can be cancelled then they must be uniquely identified.

From now on, specification texts are expressed within a specification module named *WHS* (for warehouse). In our analysis of the problem, we divide the orders in two distinct queues: the pending orders and the invoiced orders. The global state can be defined through a free type product declaration:

free type *GState* = *mk_gs*(*porders* : *PQueue*; *iorders* : *IQueue*;
                  the_stock : *Stock*);

The requirements state that all orders in the queues are distinct and that the references are references in the stock. Therefore, we define the predicate *consistent* on queues yielding true if and only if the requirements are satisfied and declare the subsort *VGS* (valid global state) of *GState* containing only consistent queues. Notice the overloading of the predicate *referenced*. The distinction between both predicates is made from the sort analysis of the arguments. The same mechanism is applied to disambiguate overloaded operation symbols. The first line below is an *operation definition* in CASL.

op $the\_orders(gs : GState) : OQueue = porders(gs) + iorders(gs)$
preds $referenced(oq : OQueue; s : Stock) \Leftrightarrow$
$$\forall x : Order \cdot (x \in oq \Rightarrow referenced(x, s));$$
$consistent(gs : GState) \Leftrightarrow unicity(the\_orders(gs))$
$$\land\ referenced(the\_orders(gs), the\_stock(gs))$$
sort $VGS = \{gs : GState \bullet consistent(gs)\}$

Question 12: What is the effect of the operations identified at the very beginning of this section (Question 8)?

Answer: Their effect is mainly to change the global state according to the given scenario.

We are now able to write the specification of the operations identified at Question 8. As in the first part of the case study, parameters specify the sorts of the values that are read and the result specifies the sort of the values that are modified. So each operation takes as one parameter a global state value and returns a global state value.

$$
\begin{array}{ll}
new\_order & : Product \times Pos \times VGS \to VGS; \\
cancel\_order & : Order \times VGS \to VGS; \\
add\_qty & : Product \times Pos \times VGS \to VGS; \\
deal\_with\_order & : VGS \to VGS;
\end{array}
$$

Following the recommendations of the defensive specification style we have declared all operations as total. However, if some conditions on parameters are not fulfilled, the operations may do nothing (this will be made clear by the axioms). In the first part of the case study, the operation *invoice_order* was axiomatised through its effect on the attributes of the order to be invoiced and on those of the stock (observational specification method). Here because all the operations return a value of sort *VGS*, we could axiomatise them by giving the values of the global-state attributes, that is to say, the values of *porders*, *iorders* and *the_stock* after the execution of the operations. Instead, we shall use the *constructive* method, which means that the value of the global state after each operation will be effectively built through the constructor operation *mk_gs*. The constructive method is very close to a "model-oriented" specification style for the operations. The observational method is more abstract in the sense that the axioms defined by this method can be deduced as logical consequences of the constructive axiomatisation while the inverse is usually not possible. For the axiomatisation below we use the following variables:

vars $o : Order;\ p : Product;\ n : Pos;\ vgs : VGS;$

The $new\_order(p, n, vgs)$ operation takes as parameters an ordered product p, a quantity n and the global state. The global state is not modified if the product is not referenced in the stock. Otherwise a pending order ordering n units of the p product is added at the end of the queue of the pending orders. We need a new operation:

$$mk\_order : Product \times Pos \times VGS \rightarrow Order$$

such that $mk\_order(p, n, vgs)$ builds a pending order with product p and ordered quantity n which is different from those already in vgs. More formally:

- $is\_pending(mk\_order(p, n, vgs))$
- $\neg\ mk\_order(p, n, vgs) \in the\_orders(vgs)$
- $reference(mk\_order(p, n, vgs)) = p$
- $ordered\_qty(mk\_order(p, n, vgs)) = n$

Moreover, we use the operation: "$q \leftarrow a$" that appends an element a at the end of the queue q. Let t be of sort s', then the notation "t **as** s" forces t to be of subsort s of s' provided that t satisfies the subsorting constraints. In the second axiom below, the constructive axiomatisation makes clear which parts of the global state are modified or not.

- $new\_order(p, n, vgs)\ =\ vgs\quad \textbf{if}\ \neg\ p\ is\_in\ the\_stock(vgs)$
- $new\_order(p, n, vgs)\ =$
  $\quad mk\_gs((porders(vgs) \leftarrow mk\_order(p, n, vgs))$ **as** $PQueue,$
  $\quad\quad iorders(vgs),$
  $\quad\quad the\_stock(vgs))\quad \textbf{if}\ p\ is\_in\ the\_stock(vgs)$

Question 13: The meaning of *cancel_order* is clear when the order in pending. But what does it mean to cancel an order which has already been invoiced?

Answer: This corresponds to the case when a product is not accepted by the customer and when it is returned at the warehouse. So, the order is cancelled and the stock is updated.

The operation *cancel_order*(o, vgs) removes the order o from the queue it is on in the global state vgs. Moreover, if the order is invoiced, the stock is supplied by the ordered quantity of the referenced product. The operation which removes an order o from an order queue q is denoted by $remove(o, q)$. If the order o does not belong to the orders of the global state, then the state is unchanged. We can notice that the *unicity* property on the orders is needed to make the specification of *cancel_order* sound. Actually, the following property holds:

$$o \in porders(vgs)\ \wedge\ unicity(the\_orders(vgs))\ \Rightarrow\ \neg\ o \in iorders(vgs)$$

and symmetrically with the *iorders* queue. The axiomatisation of *cancel_order* is given through three cases, the last one being the case: $\neg\,(o \in the\_orders(vgs))$. It uses the *add* operation of the stock data type. The notation: "t_1 **when** c_1 **else** t_2 **when** c_2 **else** ..." is a "conditional term". It means that when the condition c_1 holds then the value of the whole term is t_1, otherwise when c_2 holds, then the value is t_2 and so on.

- $cancel\_order(o, vgs) =$
   $mk\_gs(remove(o, porders(vgs))$ **as** $PQueue, iorders(vgs),$
   $the\_stock(vgs))$ **when** $o \in porders(vgs)$
   else $mk\_gs(porders(vgs), remove(o, iorders(vgs))$ **as** $IQueue,$
   $add(reference(o), ordered\_qty(o), the\_stock(vgs)))$
   when $o \in iorders(vgs)$
   else vgs

The operation $add\_qty(p, n, vgs)$ adds the quantity n to the product p, if the reference is in the stock. This operation uses again the *add* operation on stocks. So the axioms of the operation *add_qty* are simply:

- $add\_qty(p, n, vgs) = vgs$ **if** $\neg\,p\ is\_in\ the\_stock(vgs)$
- $add\_qty(p, n, vgs) =$
   $mk\_gs(porders(vgs), iorders(vgs),$
   $add(p, n, the\_stock(vgs)))$ **if** $p\ is\_in\ the\_stock(vgs)$

The operation $deal\_with\_order(vgs)$ tries to invoice a pending order. The order which is invoiced is the oldest order in the pending order queue for which the quantity in stock is greater than the ordered quantity. By the consistency property of the global state, the references of the pending orders are references in the stock. So *invoice_ok* is satisfied and the invoice operation succeeds. The order is put in the queue of the invoiced orders. It is clear that if there are orders older than the invoiced one, then these orders are waiting for the stock to be supplied with a large enough quantity of the ordered product. We need to define the condition on which an order in the pending queue can be invoiced, "*invoiceable*", and what is the first order which should be dealt with.

preds $invoiceable(pq : PQueue;\ s : Stock) \Leftrightarrow$
   $\exists o : Orders \cdot (o \in pq \land enough\_qty(o, s));$
op $first\_invoceable : PQueue \times Stock \to?\ Order$
vars $o : Order;\ pq : PQueue;\ s : Stock;$
- **def** $first\_invoceable(pq, s) \Leftrightarrow invoiceable(pq, s)$
- $first\_invoceable((o :: pq)$ **as** $PQueue, s) = o$ **when** $enough\_qty(o, s)$
   else $first\_invoceable(pq, s)$

If no order in the pending queue is invoiceable then the operation *deal_with_order* leaves the global state unchanged (first axiom). Otherwise the first invoiceable order of the pending queue is effectively invoiced (second axiom). The *invoice_ok* conditions are well fulfilled, because the order is pending, the product is referenced in stock (property of the global state) and the product quantity has just been checked. The notation "$u = \text{let } x : s = t \text{ in } v$" is a readable shortcut for the formula: $\forall x : s \cdot (x = t \Rightarrow u = v)$.

- $deal\_with\_order(vgs) = vgs$
  if $\neg\, invoiceable(porders(vgs), the\_stock(vgs))$
- $deal\_with\_order(vgs) =$
  let $o_1 : Order = first\_invoceable(porders(vgs), the\_stock(vgs))$
  in let $os : OrdStk = invoice\_order(o_1, the\_stock(vsg))$
      in let $o_2 : Order = order\_of(os)$ %% the order after invoicing
                  $s_2 : Stock = stock\_of(os)$ %% the stock after invoicing
          in $mk\_gs(remove(o_1, porders(vgs))$ **as** $PQueue$,
                  $(iorders(vgs) \leftarrow o_2)$ **as** $IQueue, s_2)$
  if $invoiceable(porders(vgs), the\_stock(vgs))$

One can notice that within the condition $\neg\, isEmpty(porders(vgs))$, if we have:

$$first\_invoiceable(porders(vgs), the\_stock(vgs)) \neq first(porders(vgs))$$

then there are orders for which the number of items of the ordered product is not sufficient in stock. If required by the user (see answer to Question 9) this information can be exploited to specify a notification mechanism for such sold out products.

12.4 Architectural Specification

A feature that distinguishes CASL from other specification languages is its possibility to specify the design of a software system by defining the program modules that have to be implemented and how these modules are combined to an implementation of the specification.

The specifications given in the previous sections denote a signature and a class of algebras; the use of structuring methods on this level does not imply any structure for the program satisfying the specification. However, it is also desirable to be able to specify, in an abstract way, the construction of the resulting program from program modules. In CASL this is done using architectural specifications. The following architectural specification specifies a possible design of a program implementing the case study.

arch spec *Warehouse* =
  units
    NatAlg : *NAT*;
    OrderFun : *NAT* → *ORDER*;
    OrderAlg = *OrderFun*[*NatAlg*];
    StockFun : *NAT* → *STOCK*;
    StockAlg = *StockFun*[*NatAlg*];
    InvoiceFun : *ORDER* × *STOCK* → *INVOICE* **given** *NatAlg*;
    QueuesFun : *ORDER* → *QUEUES*;
    WhsFun : *QUEUES* × *INVOICE* → *WHS* **given** *OrderAlg*, *StockAlg*;
  result *WhsFun*[*QueuesFun*[*OrderAlg*],
                    InvoiceFun[*OrderAlg*, *StockAlg*]]
  end

The notation *NatAlg* : *NAT* means that *NatAlg* is some algebra satisfying the *NAT* specification and implies the task of providing such an implementation. The notation *OrderFun* : *NAT* → *ORDER* corresponds to the implementation task of providing a module that imports an implementation of *NAT* and produces an implementation of *ORDER*. Thus *OrderFun* applied to *NatAlg*, *OrderFun*[*NatAlg*], is an algebra satisfying the *ORDER* specification. Similarly, the definition of *StockFun* implies the task of implementing a module taking an implementation of *NAT* and yielding an implementation of *STOCK*. Identically, the definition of *QueuesFun* represents the task of implementing a module taking an implementation of *ORDER* and yielding an implementation of *QUEUES*. Here the implementation of *QUEUES* does not need to reflect the building steps of the specification itself. The only required thing is that it satisfies the signature and the axioms of this specification.

With *InvoiceFun* the situation is more complex since its arguments, an implementation of *ORDER* and an implementation of *STOCK*, share the specification *NAT*. The construction of an implementation of *INVOICE* by *InvoiceFun* only makes sense if both arguments to *InvoiceFun* use the *same* implementation of the natural numbers. This is assured by requiring that the implementation of the *NAT* subpart of *STOCK* and *ORDER* is given by *NatAlg*.

The result of the architectural specification *Warehouse* is a construction of an implementation of *WHS* using the modules defined before.

12.5 The Natural Language Description of the Specification

12.5.1 Case 1

The specification of the orders declares the *Order* data type and two disjoint predicates characterizing the pending orders and the invoiced orders. It provides two operations on the orders which respectively return the reference to the ordered product and the ordered quantity. The specification of the stock provides the *Stock* data type, a predicate which asserts if a product is referenced in the stock and three operations: the first two change the number of items of a product in stock and the third returns the number of items of a product in stock. Then the *invoice_order* operation takes an order and the stock as parameters. If the order is pending and the referenced product is in stock and the quantity in stock of the product is sufficient enough, then the invoicing operation changes the state of the order and removes the ordered quantity from the stock. Otherwise the operation is without effect. Moreover, messages are issued to inform the user about the success or failure of the invoicing operation together with the reasons for any failure.

12.5.2 Case 2

The invoicing software system is specified using a global state and four operations changing the global state. The global state consists of a queue of pending orders, a queue for the already invoiced orders and the stock. The operation *new_order* creates a new order and puts it at the end of the queue of pending orders. The operation *cancel_order* removes an order from the queue it is on and does nothing if the order is not on some queue. Moreover, if the order is removed from the queue of invoiced orders then the ordered quantity of that order is added to the stock. The third operation, *add_qty*, supplies the stock with new items of a product if the product was referenced in the stock; it has no effect otherwise. Finally, the operation *deal_with_order* invoices the first invoiceable order on the queue of pending orders, which is also the oldest invoiceable order, and puts it at the end of the queue of invoiced orders. If such an order does not exist, *deal_with_order* does nothing.

12.6 Conclusion

In the case study, no particular problem has been encountered for the specification of data types given in the requirements: *Order*, *Stock*, *OQueue*, etc. The CASL language allows data types and operations to be specified either in an *observational* or a *constructive* style. Examples of the former style are given in the *STOCK* specification and in the axioms of *invoice_order*. Examples of the latter style are the axioms of the operations on the global state in the second part. We stress that the observational style is very useful at the very beginning of the specification phase. It allows the specifier to formulate some assertions about the model without building it at all. This set of formal assertions can be discussed with the user or the customer, in order to validate the first assumptions made about the model.

Some particular features of the CASL language have been revealed as being very useful in the specification process. One of them is the notion of partial or total operations. It forces the specifier to be aware of the definition domains of operations. Definedness conditions provide guarantees about operation call correctness through the proof of lemmas (proof obligations). Another powerful feature, the subsort mechanism, is well designed to impose constraints on some data in the same way as invariant properties for model-oriented languages. Subsort checking proofs increase the confidence on a sound usage of the subsorted values. CASL environments do not yet provide proof-obligation generators, so our specifications were not checked for this aspect.

However, the functional style of the algebraic specifications makes the description of states (in the usual sense) painful. A state is often described by a tuple of variables. In CASL this tuple must be a part of the parameters and of the result of the operations. So the profiles might look rather strange compared with the final implementation of the operations in an imperative programming language. Theoretical and practical research is in progress to facilitate description and axiomatisation of states in the algebraic formalism. The CASL language is open to such extensions.

The invoicing case study is not a large problem, at least not at the very high specification level. So, few CASL structuring primitives have been exemplified. Only simple mechanisms, such as extension (importation) and instantiation, were needed. Finally, we showed how to build an architectural specification of the case study in the last part of the chapter.

References

1. The CoFI Task Group on Language Design (1998) CASL The Common Algebraic Specification Language Summary.
URL: http://www.brics.dk/Projects/CoFI/Documents/CASL/Summary
2. Bergstra, J. A., Heering, J., Klint, R. (1989) Algebraic Specification. Addison-Wesley, Reading, MA
3. Ehrig, H., Mahr, B. (1985) Fundamentals of Algebraic Specification 1. EATCS Monograph 6, Springer-Verlag, Berlin
4. van Horebeek, I., Lewi, J. (1989) Algebraic Specifications in Software Engineering. Springer-Verlag
5. Mosses, Peter D. (1999) CASL: A Guided Tour of its Design. In José Luiz Fiadeiro (ed.), Recent Trends in Algebraic Development Techniques, Proceedings, LNCS 1589, Springer-Verlag, pp. 216-240
6. Roggenbach, M., Mossakowski, T., Schröder, L. (2000) Basic Datatypes in CASL, Version 0.4. URL: http://www.brics.dk/Projects/CoFI/Notes/L-12
7. Wirsing, M. (1990) Algebraic Specifications. In J. van Leeuwen (ed.), Handbook of Theoretical Computer Science, North-Holland, Elsevier, pp. 675-788

13 An Abstract and Constructive Specification in Coq

Philippe Chavin and Jean-François Monin

This chapter is an attempt to provide a formal specification which is as faithful as possible to the informal one and consistent. The powerful type system of Coq is used to make our specification both very abstract and eventually executable. This ensures that an implementation can be found. Indeed, we *construct* mathematical structures or functions whenever possible, instead of specifying them with axioms. If the axiomatic way turns out better, we look for structures satisfying the axioms we need. We also insist on the quest for proof opportunities in order to get further confidence that specified objects are the right ones.

13.1 Introduction to Coq

Coq is a tool for developing mathematical specifications and proofs. Specifying an application using Coq is then just writing a (hopefully relevant) piece of mathematics. The main difference with other techniques like algebraic specifications [3] or Z is that Coq is not based on set theory, but on constructive type theory, which naturally deals with computational objects like data structures and algorithms. Using Coq we can put emphasis on verification: Coq includes a proof checker and a means to build formal proofs.

As a specification language, Coq is both a higher order logic—quantifiers may be applied on natural numbers, on functions of arbitrary types, on propositions, predicates, types, etc.—and a typed lambda-calculus enriched with an extension of primitive recursion. For instance the 0 has the type **nat** which has itself the type **Set**. This is formally written 0 : **nat** and **nat** : **Set**. Besides objects like natural numbers we have logical objects, like propositions. Explanations come below with the use of new notions. The reader may find further details in [2] and [5].

Let us stress some practical consequences of the use of type theory instead of set theory. First, recall that set theory is essentially untyped. Using type theory, we gain accurate and decidable type checking (note that Z and B [1] use restricted versions of set theory endowed with a limited notion of type). Conversely, subsets are sometimes less easy to represent with types. Here is an interesting illustration of the accuracy of type theory, due to the fact that functions are a primitive notion. If f is a function from A to B, we know not only that f is a binary relation between A and B, as in the type system of Z or B, but also that for any x in A there is a unique y in B related to x by f. Moreover existence and uniqueness are given for free (no proof obligation is raised), as type checking is decidable. Lemmas about f are then simpler to prove. This is used here, for formalizing sentences like "on an order, we have one and one only reference to etc." The type of functions from A to B is denoted by $A \to B$.

The main pitfall in a specification is to introduce personal assumptions (sometimes unknowingly) over data structures, system properties, implementation requirements ... Here, we are asked not to provide an implementation, but to formalize the terms of a problem written in natural language. Using Coq greatly eases this purpose: higher order logic, unusual in other formal methods, allows one to reason in a very abstract way, without yielding the consideration of implementation; for instance we pack together some sets with the few hypotheses we make on them and then hide this behind an *ad hoc* notion of separable sets; we are even able, as shown in Section 13.4.2, to quantify over abstract algebraic structures when needed, without additional complications in the specification. Still, we are able, given succinct refinement, to provide specification animation through scenarios, see Section 13.5.1. This freedom is due to the fact that we are not *a priori* coerced into any model, as opposed to B for instance, where we have to work within a particular model of set theory.

13.2 Terms Analysis

13.2.1 Stock and Orders

Informally, we have two sets (order and stock), an operation (invoice), and two attributes referring both to orders and to the stock (reference and quantity). The notion of product seems abstract here: a product will be represented by a reference. In fact references can serve as identifiers of products, while they cannot serve as identifiers of orders, because "the same reference can be ordered on several different orders". The original statement says that an order has a state, which we call *status* below. This status can take at least two values, pending and invoiced. Now we express mathematical properties on the aforementioned types.

Question 1: Does an order consists of exactly one reference, or of several references?

Answer: In our understanding of the sentence "the state of the order will be changed into 'invoiced' if the ordered quantity is either less than or equal to the quantity which is in stock according to the reference of the ordered product", an order has exactly one reference.

The sentence "the same reference can be ordered on several different orders" seems to be there only to state that the relation between orders and references is not one-to-one. We consider that this sentence has been added only in order to prevent references to be used as identifiers for orders (see Question 9), hence we simply discard it in our informal version of the specification (and similarly for "the quantity can be different to other orders").

Besides orders, we have a notion of stock.

Question 2: What is a stock?

Answer: stock defines for each reference the quantity (of the corresponding product) in stock.

Formalizing this notion is easy: we simply use a function.

13.2.2 Operations

The world is not static: the status of an order can change, new orders can arise, and so on. Then we consider operations, which are transformations from a world to a new world. We will define a type state of worlds, and operations will be functions from state (and possibly further arguments) to state.

Question 3: Can operations be applied to any state?

Answer: Operations can be applied only if their preconditions are satisfied; in a high level specification, we are concerned with intended normal behaviour. Further considerations like exception raising should be postponed until implementation-level refinement.

The first operation to be considered is invoice, which changes the status of an order from pending to invoiced. The other operations are considered in "Case 2"; they are: adding an order, cancelling an order, and entering quantities in the stock. Pre- and post-conditions are studied later.

Question 4: What is the ordering for operations?

Answer: The terms do not say anything about this issue; we can consider sequential or parallel composition. For the sake of simplicity, we chose a sequential ordering.

Question 5: Do we have a fairness requirement? Should every pending order be invoiced at some time?

Answer: The sentence "the state of the order *will be* changed into invoiced *if* ... " can be interpreted as a requirement for fairness, or as the formulation of the existence of a precondition to invoice. Again, nothing is said about ordering, triggering or whatever concerning timings, so we consider it a precondition.

If we wanted to interpret it as a requirement for fairness of behaviours of the system, we would introduce a temporal logic, using Coq-Unity for instance [4].

13.2.3 Requirements on Quantities

Question 6: What are quantities? Mathematically speaking, what operations are available on quantities?

Answer: Since nothing is said about the nature of the products, we only assume the customer uses a "traditional" notion of quantity.

We should respect a preservation principle: no operation considered in this case study may "create" or "destroy" quantities—the sum of quantities of a given product after an operation should be equal to the sum of quantities of this product before this operation. Hence, we need an addition on quantities. We also know, from the description of invoicing, that quantities can be compared. Altogether, we suppose that the type for quantities (called **quant**) is endowed with a binary relation **leq** which is reflexive, antisymmetric and transitive (it is a total order relation). We also consider that the mathematical structure of quantities includes a zero (a neutral element for addition) which is also less than or equal to any quantity. We call such a structure a *measure system*.

Question 7: Do all products share the same measure system?

Answer: We stick to the terms, which make no assumption on this point. We just attach a measure system to each reference in stock.

Actually, there is no reason to compare a quantity of kiwis to a quantity of oil, even if both are represented by natural numbers. Moreover, oil may perfectly be measured with real numbers. There is even no point in adding kilograms of potatoes to pieces of kiwis. Therefore we consider in Section 13.4.2 a *family* of types of quantities, one for each reference, where each instance of **quant** is endowed with its own version of **leq**, **zero**, **+**, etc. Natural numbers are an obvious model for quantities and we stick to this model in our first specification.

13.3 A Specification for Case 1

13.3.1 Basic Types

Coq uses a type theory: every value inhabits a (unique) type. For instance we need a type for the status of an order, a type for references, a type for quantities and a type for orders. They are respectively called **status**, **ref**, **quant** and **order**. From them we can construct more complex types, e.g. for stocks (**ref** → **quant**) or for worlds (**state**, see below).

The type **status** has exactly two inhabitants, **pending** and **invoiced**. Here we declare an enumerated type, like in Pascal but with a different syntax.

    Inductive status : Set := **pending** : status | **invoiced** : status.

The standard library of Coq constructs in the same way the type **bool**, inhabited by **true** and **false**, as well as the type **nat** of natural numbers, whose constructors are **O** (zero) and **S** (successor).

    Inductive nat : Set := **O** : nat | **S** : nat → nat.

Here we understand better the name *inductive*, because natural numbers are constructed in a recursive way. Inductive types are actually the fundamental way of constructing data types in Coq. An important property of inductive types is that the *only* values in them are constructed by their constructors, e.g. true and false for bool. Coq automatically infers induction principles for these types.

Question 8: Should the sets of references and their associated quantity measure system be considered as constant during the whole system lifetime?

Answer: We consider them as parameters of the system.

Indeed, there is no requirement for an operation which could add, or delete, a reference. The set of references seems constant: they are available for this system as well as for a user of this system.

Parameter ref : Set.

In this section, quantities are just natural numbers (the general case for quantities is postponed to Section 13.4.2). Indeed, the standard library of Coq defines the traditional operations on them, as well as a number of useful lemmas. This makes nat a good candidate for the type of quantities:

Definition quant := nat.

Now we can express a stock as an inhabitant of ref → quant. The operation invoice takes such a function s, and it returns a function that, given a reference r, yields $s(r)$ except for one reference—the ordered reference. To this effect we clearly need a computable function for testing whether two elements of ref are equal or not. We call a type endowed with such a function a *separable* type. For instance, finite types like status and bool are separable; nat is also separable, though it is infinite; but functional types over infinite sets (even separable) like nat → bool are not separable. Formally, we say that a type A is separable if

$$(x, y : A)\{x = y\} + \{\neg x = y\},$$

which reads as follows: for all x and y of type A, we can compute an inhabitant of $\{x = y\} + \{\neg x = y\}$, that is a Boolean whose value is true if $x = y$ and false if $\neg x = y$. Sep is then defined as the type of separable sets.

Given a separable type A, a type B, a function f from A to B, a value a in A and a value b in B, we can define the function f' of type $A \to B$ such that $f'(a_0) = f(a_0)$ if $a_0 \neq a$ and $f(a_0) = b$ if $a_0 = a$. As functions are first class objects, it is easy to define a (higher order) function assign which, applied to f, a and b (A and B are then implicit) yields f'.

To sum up, we need to assume a type ref and to ensure that it is separable.

Question 9: Should we specify identifiers for orders?

Answer: Using Coq we do not need to build up an order identification system; we can let orders be an abstract type and work directly with it.

We must avoid a pitfall: formalizing an order by a triple $\langle r, q, s \rangle$, where r is a reference, q a quantity and s a status is not satisfactory, because we do not necessarily want to confuse two different orders with the same components! We could try to identify orders in some way, but how?

Question 10: What is the space of all possible orders?

Answer: We are not given size limit or other properties for the set of orders. We make as few assumptions as possible in order to fit the terms: orders is just a separable set.

13.3.2 State and Operation

Now we can define a type for the states (of the world) we consider. It is just a mathematical structure composed of a stock, a set of orders and information saying that each order has one and only one reference, quantity and status. We know that functions are just the ticket for the latter requirements. The type of orders must be separable, because the operation invoice will change status_of_ord in the same way as stock.

> **Structure state** : Type := mkstate {
>   stock : ref → quant ;
>   orders : Sep ;
>   ref_of_ord : orders → ref ;
>   quant_of_ord : orders → quant ;
>   status_of_ord : orders → status }.

It is actually just syntactic sugar for an inductive type with one constructor (mkstate here) and related projections (stock, order, ref_of_ord, etc.). For instance, if st is a state, (stock st) yields the stock in state st (Coq uses the notation (f x y) for applying a function to arguments).

13.3.3 Operation "invoice"

Each operation is modelled by a function that takes an initial state, additional arguments (e.g. an order) and required properties on them, and returns a new state. Then, for each operation, we have to ask "what is the initial state?", "what are the possible values for arguments", etc. In the sequel we make such questions explicit only when the answer is not clearly stated in the terms. The first of them concerns the new state returned by invoice.

Question 11: Does invoicing an order affect the stock?

Answer: This operation could change the state only by changing the status of the order, or it could also have side effects on the stock by withdrawing the ordered quantity. We consider the latter: the ordered product is not available from the stock after invoicing.

This prevents the system invoicing twice the same instance of a product. Moreover, invoice seems to be the only operation considered in "Case 1", so we decide it is up to this operation to maintain the consistency of the stock with relation to invoiced orders. This point is also raised when we specify operations using a preservation principle.

Question 12: What is the precondition of the invoicing operation ?

Answer: It is easy to show that in order to respect the preservation principle, the ordered quantity of product should be in stock when we attempt to deliver it: on non-negative numbers, $x - a + a$ is equal to x only if $a \leq x$; this is exactly the precondition formalized below on invoice.

Given a state st and an order o in st, we have to specify the quantity q of ordered product remaining in stock after invoicing. By the preservation principle mentioned above, q is a quantity such that q, added to the ordered quantity (quant_of_ord st o), yields the quantity in stock just before invoicing (stock st (ref_of_ord st o)). We can use the type of elements x of A such that $(P\ x)$, which is denoted by $\{x : A \mid (P\ x)\}$, with suitable x, A and P:

{ q:quant | (q + (quant_of_ord st o)) = (stock st (ref_of_ord st o))}.

Let us denote this type simply by (spec_remains st o). Therefore we define a function with two arguments st and o, using the following notation:

Definition spec_remains :=
[st:state] [o:(order st)]
{ q:quant | (q + (quant_of_ord st o)) = (stock st (ref_of_ord st o))}.

Assume a function remains taking as arguments a state st, an order o (in st) satisfying a suitable precondition (see below) and yielding a result of type (spec_remains st o). The type of remains is more precisely[1],[2]:

(st:state)
(o:(orders st))
(quant_of_ord st o) ≤ (stock st (ref_of_ord st o))
→ (spec_remains st o).

---

[1] Let A and B be two types, then $A \to B$ is the type of functions from A to B. We may want to give a name to the argument (not only to its type): then we use the notation $(a : A)B$ instead of $A \to B$. This is especially useful if B is itself an expression depending on a. In the example considered here, the type of the second argument depends on the first, the type of the third and the type of the result depend on the two first arguments.

[2] The type of the third argument is a proposition. This means that the function should be applied to a state, an order, and a *proof* of the precondition: in Coq proofs are also considered as objects, this is why the syntax is uniform. But we can simply interpret $(a : A)(P\ a) \to B$ as the type of functions taking an argument a of A such that $(P\ a)$ and returning an element of B.

The operation invoice is then simply specified by:

Definition invoice :
  (st:state)
  (o:(orders st))
  (status_of_ord st o)=pending →
  (quant_of_ord st o) ≤ (stock st (ref_of_ord st o))
→ state
:=
[st,o,pre1,pre2]
(mkstate
  (assign (stock st) (ref_of_ord st o) (pr1 (remains st o pre2)))
  (order st)
  (ref_of_ord st)
  (quant_of_ord st)
  (assign (status_of_ord st) o invoiced)).

The part of this expression before := is the type of invoice; the second, the content of the definition, exhibits an inhabitant of this type.

We have to explain the rôle of the function pr1. The type $\{x : A \mid (P\ x)\}$ is not a subtype of A, it is an inductive type with one constructor taking two arguments, an x of A and a proof of $(P\ x)$. When we apply the projection pr1 to an element of this type, we get the underlying element of type A (in our case, A is quant), satisfying the predicate P. Thanks to the definition of spec_remains above, the value of q returned by the function remains is:

(stock st (ref_of_ord st o)) - (quant_of_ord st o).

We forbid negative values for quantities, therefore we need the precondition

(quant_of_ord st o) ≤ (stock st (ref_of_ord st o))

in order to prove that q does satisfy the equality specified in spec_remains. This explains why remains has an argument for this precondition.

13.4 A Specification for Case 2

13.4.1 Using General Operations over Sets

In Case 1, the set of orders and the stock were considered as constants. But including operations like adding orders, adding quantities in stock, etc., leads us to consider deeper possibilities of Coq.

We could introduce a set orders representing the set of all possible orders—including non-existent ones, at a given state. Instead, we make explicit the assumption that we can always find a fresh order. More precisely, given a (separable) Set A, we assume we can get a new (separable) type (add_fresh_elt A) which is A extended with a new element. We also assume that given a type B, a function f from A to B and an element b of B, (extend f b) is a function which extends f and which takes the value b on the fresh element. Similarly, we assume that we can remove an element from a type. Given a in A, (rem_one_elt a) is the type of inhabitants of A which are different to a. The function (restrict a f) is the restriction of f to (rem_one_elt a). The functions add_fresh_elt, extend, rem_one_elt and restrict can actually be constructed in type theory.

Now we can stick to the specification of state considered in Section 13.3.2. The definition of invoice is the same as previously. The operation add_order has a very simple definition thanks to add_fresh_elt and extend.

Definition add_order : state → ref → quant → state :=
 [st] [r] [q]
 (mkstate
  (stock st)
  (add_fresh_elt (orders st))
  (extend (ref_of_ord st) r)
  (extend (quant_of_ord st) q)
  (extend (status_of_ord st) pending)).

We rely on the mathematical possibility to enrich a type with an additional abstract element. Note that it implies that the set of orders can become arbitrarily large. This deserves a discussion that we postpone to the refinement step.

An interesting point is that *the type discipline prevents us from defining* add_order *without asking what is the status of the new order*. Here, it is just impossible to reuse the old value of status_of_ord because the *type* of this function is not the same in the new state: its domain is (add_fresh_elt (orders st)) instead of (orders st). And, as $A \to B$ is the type of *total* functions from A to B, we are obliged to declare what is the value returned by the function on the fresh element. Of course the best way to do this is to use a higher order function defined once for all, extend. This is yet another illustration of the interest of abstract (higher order) devices.

Question 13: What is the initial status of a new order?

Answer: We consider that the initial status is pending.

This is to be confirmed by the customer. The definition of cancel_order is in the same spirit.

Question 14: Can invoiced orders be cancelled?

Answer: In real life, an order is usually invoiced only after the ordered product has been delivered, and the action, by a buyer, of giving back an ordered product and getting a refund is not called "cancelling an order". So we decided that invoiced orders could not be cancelled.

Definition cancel_order :
(st:state) (o:(orders st)) (status_of_ord st o)=pending → state :=
[st] [o] [pre]
(mkstate
  (stock st)
  (rem_one_elt o)
  (restrict (ref_of_ord st))
  (restrict (quant_of_ord st))
  (restrict (status_of_ord st))).

In the specification of add_in_stock, it is enough to consider that only one product is entered at a time.

Definition add_in_stock : state → (r:ref)(quant r)→ state :=
[st] [r] [q]
(mkstate
  (assign (stock st) (ref_of_ord st o) ((stock st r) + q))
  (orders st)
  (ref_of_ord st)
  (quant_of_ord st)
  (status_of_ord st)).

13.4.2 Reference-Dependent Measure Systems

In this section we show how to define measure systems and attach a measure system to each reference in stock, as suggested in Section 13.2.3. Dependent types come naturally into the picture.

The first step is to define a structure for order relations[3].

Section def_ord_rel.
  Variable A : Set.
  Structure ord_rel : Type := mkord {
    Leq :> A → A → Prop ;
    refl : (reflexive Leq) ;
    antisym : (antisymmetric Leq) ;
    trans : (transitive Leq)   }.
End def_ord_rel.

Prop is the type of propositions. When a section is closed, all variables are abstracted: the type of ord_rel is Set →Type when def_ord_rel is closed. The symbol :> declares Leq as a coercion. Given a set A and an object R of type (ord_rel A), R can be considered right away as a relation over A.

---

[3] Logical implication between propositions is denoted by →. The same symbol is used for functional types. The reason is that proofs are considered as objects (see Footnote 2 and [2]). Similarly, we have seen that the typewriter notation for ∀s:A (P s) is (s:A) (P s).

The above piece of specification shows how properties and distinguished elements can be attached to a mathematical structure inside a record-like object. In order to mimic usual mathematical practice ("let A be a set endowed with ...") the same name is used for the underlying structure thanks to a coercion. Our notion of measure system is defined in the same way. It is a set endowed with an order relation, an addition, a subtraction and a neutral element:

Structure measure : Type := mkmeas {
  base :> Set ;
  leq : (ord_rel base) ;
  add : base → base → base ;
  subtract : base → base → base ;
  zero : base;
  add_sub : ∀x,y:base (leq x y) → (add (subtract y x) x)=y ;
  zero_min : ∀x:base (leq zero x) ;
  neutral_r : ∀x:base (add x zero)=x ;
  neutral_l : ∀x:base (add zero x)=x   }.

Again, base is a coercion: an object with type measure can be seen as a Set.

It is important to check that we are building a consistent theory. Whenever we specify a mathematical structure, we should be able to find an inhabitant of this structure. This is straightforward here, using nat for base and ≤ for Leq.

We can now specify states and operations according to these dependent quantities. We declare a measure system for each reference:

Variable quant : ref → measure.

Now we adapt the definition of state introduced in 13.3.2. We just have to provide the right argument for quant in function of adequate parameters.

Structure state : Type := mkstate   {
  stock : (r:ref)(quant r) ;
  orders : Sep ;
  ref_of_ord : orders → ref ;
  quant_of_ord : (o:orders) (quant (ref_of_ord o)) ;
  status_of_ord : orders → status }.

Let us explain (r:ref)(quant r); previously, stock had type ref→quant, meaning "to every reference, we associate a quantity". Here, the type means "to every reference, we associate a quantity in the measure system associated to this reference". The use of dependent types requires generalizing functions like extend.

A quantity may be equal to zero. In the stock, this means that no product for the considered reference is available. But what does it mean for operations?

Question 15: Is it possible to order or add in stock a null quantity of a reference?

Answer: In real life this is usually not the case, but we have decided that it is.

The reason is that the specification is simpler that way, (there is no additional precondition for add_in_stock and add_order) but the final decision is up to the customer. It is a typical question that can hardly be seen on an informal specification, but arises during formalization.

Definition add_order : state → (r:ref) (quant r) → state :=
[st] [r] [q]
(mkstate
  (stock st)
  (add_fresh_elt (orders st))
  (extend (ref_of_ord st) r)
  (extend_q (quant_of_ord st) q)
  (extend (status_of_ord st) pending)   ).

13.5 Experimenting with the Specification

13.5.1 Refining

The above specification, though very abstract, can be made executable. We consider it an important step from a methodological standpoint, as it helps us to see the behaviour of our specification in particular cases, thus it may reveal errors in types definition, forgotten preconditions ... and it often turns out very useful for providing scenarios to be discussed. The purpose of this section is to show how we can, to some extent, turn a specification into a prototype. Assumptions made in the sequel are not drawn from the terms; they are our own, and are intended to serve as examples to be discussed with the customer. Refinement is based on Case 2 with reference-dependent measure systems.

We need a system for naming orders: recall that in the above specification, the type of orders depends on the state. This proves useful in the specification, but naming instances of such orders becomes quite heavy. Moreover, orders are considered as an internal notion of the system. In real life, users handle orders using an identifier—let us call it a *key*—, and after all keys should not be confused with the orders they represent. Then, we will use a state-independent set of keys, in bijection with the state-dependent set of orders. A key is used to name an order: in operations, arguments of type order will then be replaced by arguments of type key. The actual type of keys should actually be decided with the customer. Our only requirement is that it is separable (two keys can be distinguished by computational means). We need to define the first key to be used and a way for computing a new key on request. Though it is quite easy to leave the type of keys as a parameter, there is little point in doing so and we readily implement keys by natural numbers. However they are used in an abstract way in the sequel, using first_key, new_key and the function for testing equality on keys. The lemma eq_nat_dec, from the Coq library, states that nat is separable.

Definition key := (mkSep eq_nat_dec).
Definition first_key : key := O.
Definition new_key : key→ key := S. (* successor *)

Then we define a type of states "able to communicate" (using keys) as an extension of states defined in Section 13.4.2. Note that the new structure is constrained by predicates (they are invariants of the states we consider).

Structure state_pub : Type := mksp{
  underlying_state :> state ;
  next_key : key ;
  key_of_ord : (orders underlying_state) → key ;
  ord_of_key : key → (option (orders underlying_state)) ;
  key_max : (o:(orders underlying_state)) ((key_of_ord o) < next_key) ;
  ord_key_ord : (is_left_inverse key_of_ord ord_of_key) }.

This state is "public": it offers a user interface thanks to the keys. Keys can be associated to orders, or to a special element not in orders: this is why ord_of_key is defined in (option (orders underlying_state)), instead of (orders underlying_state). A key associated to this special element may thus be freely associated to an order.

The main invariant is key_of_ord. The predicate is_left_inverse means that key_of_ord and ord_of_key are inverse functions, i.e. key_of_ord is injective: one and only one key is associated to each order. We say that a key is good (predicate good_key) if an order is associated with it. Indeed, in the initial state where no order has been added, keys are associated to no order—no key is good; when adding a fresh order, a key associated to no order is chosen (using new_order) and becomes good; when an order is cancelled, the key associated to it becomes not good—it is no longer associated to an order.

Operations are defined interactively: we show that we can construct an inhabitant of state_pub by applying (command **Apply** in interactive proof mode) mksp, the state_pub type constructor to the result of the corresponding operations on states and to appropriate values for the key system, and by proving that invariants key_max and ord_key_ord are actually preserved. For instance, invoicing consists of applying invoice to the underlying state, leaving the set of keys unchanged.

Definition invoice_pub :
  (sp:state_pub)
  (k:key) (g:(good_key sp k))
  (status_of_ord sp (retrieve g))=pending →
  (quant_of_ord sp (retrieve g)) ≤ (stock sp (ref_of_ord sp (retrieve g)))
  → state_pub.

Intros sp k g pre1 pre2.
Apply (mksp (invoice pre1 pre2) (next_key sp) (key_of_ord sp) (ord_of_key sp)).
  (* proofs of invariants... *)
Defined.

The functions cancel_order_pub and add_in_stock_pub are defined in the same way. The operation add_order_pub is slightly more complicated, because we want it to return the new state *with* the key of the new order (and a proof that this key is good). The type of the intended result is:

Structure state_and_key : Type := mksk{
    sp_sk : state_pub ;
    k_sk : key ;
    gk_sk : (good_key sp_sk k_sk) }.

Then we define the order-adding operation in two steps. First, we define add_order_pub_aux in the same way as other operations.

Definition add_order_pub_aux: state_pub → (r:ref)(quant r) → state_pub.
Intros sp r q.
Apply (mksp (add_order sp q)
            (new_key (next_key sp))
            (extend (key_of_ord sp) (next_key sp))
            (refresh_add_new_opt (next_key sp) (ord_of_key sp))).
(* proofs of invariants... *)

Then we define the three components of (add_order_pub sp r q) as, respectively, (add_order_pub_aux sp q), (next_key sp) and a proof that the latter is a good key (to this effect, we provide the appropriate witnessing order; the remaining proof is found automatically).

Definition add_order_pub : state_pub → (r:ref)(quant r) → state_and_key.
Intros sp r q.
Exists (add_order_pub_aux sp q) (next_key sp).
Exists (fresh_elt (orders sp)); Auto.
Defined.

As goodness is required on keys occurring as arguments of some operations, we also prove that each operation preserves the goodness of keys.

13.5.2 Running an Example

Now we can produce various scenarios for the intended application. Our interface is the interactive Coq toplevel, which provides us with particular type-checking information and performs reductions (i.e. computations).

Consider a store selling a finite set Ref of products comprised of potatoes, oil and kiwis: each reference is associated to a unit of measure (respectively kilos, gallons and pieces); we use simply integers for them.

Definition quant : Ref → measure :=
    [r:Ref]**Cases** r of potatoes ⇒ kilos | oil ⇒ gallons | kiwis ⇒ pieces **end**.

Our initial state is empty:

Definition null := [r:Ref](zero (quant r)).
Definition init_state_pub : state :=
  (mkstate null empty_sep
           (f_empty ref) (f_empty_f quant (f_empty ref))(f_empty status)).
Definition Init_state := (init_state_pub quant).

We can now perform a transition, which adds an order for two gallons of oil.

Definition sk1 := (add_order_pub Init_state (qt_of (2) oil)).
Definition s1 := (sp_sk sk1).
Definition ks1 := (k_sk sk1).

The state sk1 has type (state_and_key quant). The state we will consider afterwards is s1, the underlying state from sk1. The key of this order is ks1. We check that the goodness of keys is preserved: **Lemma g1_1** : (good_key s1 ks1).
We can perform reductions in order to check, interactively, the status of the order.

  Coq < **Eval Compute in** (Status_of_ord (retrieve g1_1)).
    = **pending** : status

13.6 Terms Rephrasing

From our analysis and first attempt of specification, we can rephrase the terms more precisely than the original ones.

We are given orders, references to products and a notion of quantity for each reference. Quantities for the same reference can be added, subtracted and compared using an order relation, informally denoted by "less than or equal to". Quantities are also endowed with a zero, such that adding zero to any quantity yields the same quantity; zero is less than or equal to any quantity.

Orders have the following properties: each order has one and only one reference, one and only one quantity for this reference and one and only one status, which can be pending or invoiced.

We are also given a stock, which defines, for each reference, one and only one quantity. When this quantity is equal to zero, it means that no product is available for the considered reference in the physical stock.

We have to specify a system whose state is defined by the knowledge of the stock and of the set of orders. This state evolves through the following operations:

invoice: given an order, whose status is pending and such that the ordered quantity is less than or equal to the quantity in stock, then its status is changed to invoiced and the quantity in stock is updated in a way such that the total quantity remains invariant: adding the ordered quantity to the new quantity in stock yields the quantity in stock before invoicing.
add_order: given a reference r and a quantity q, a new order o is added; the reference corresponding to o, is r, the quantity corresponding to o is q and the status of o is pending.

cancel_order: given an order, whose status is pending, then this order is discarded in the new state.

add_in_stock: given a reference and a quantity, the stock is updated by adding this quantity to the one in stock for that reference.

Case 1: consider only invoice.
Case 2: consider all operations.

13.7 Conclusion

The ability of Coq to describe new (and potentially arbitrarily complex) *ad hoc* theories proves useful, for instance when formalizing abstract notions of quantities and of keys. Note also that the abstract view of orders developed here leads us to a clear separation between orders and their names, giving us the opportunity to ask questions about the space of possible orders.

Type theory has also specific interests. Some properties can be automatically checked in this way, e.g., existence and unicity of the status of a given order for relations like status_of_ord. More surprisingly, type theory can force us to be complete in some sense: in Section 13.4, we cannot escape the question of the initial value of the status of a new order.

We consider it important to state (and prove) theorems about the specification, in order to check that our specification has better chances of making sense. Here, we take care to ensure that specified objects do exist, at least from a mathematical point of view. This is illustrated in the proof that natural numbers satisfy the properties we require on abstract quantities.

A further tool for checking that a specification is the intended one is prototyping. The computational features of Coq can be used to this effect, to some extent. The next step in this direction would be to use program extraction as provided by Coq, yielding a program which is correct by construction.

As a last interesting methodological point, note that a preservation of matter principle helps us to express the pre- and post-conditions for invoice.

References

1. Abrial J.-R. (1996) *The B-Book*. Cambridge University Press
2. Barras B. *et al* (1999) *The Coq Proof Assistant Reference Manual. version 6.3.1*. INRIA, December 1999
3. Bidoit M., Kreowski H.-J., Lescanne P., Orejas F., Sanella D. (Eds.) (1991) *Algebraic System Specification and Development, a Survey and Annotated Bibliography*. volume 501 of *LNCS*, Springer Verlag
4. Heyd B., Crégut P. (1996) A modular coding of Unity in Coq. In von Wright J., Grundy J., Harrison J (Eds.) *Theorem Proving in Higher Order Logic*. volume 1125 of *LNCS*, Springer Verlag, 251–266
5. Huet G., Kahn G., Paulin-Mohring C. (1996) The Coq proof assistant, a tutorial, V6.1. Technical report, INRIA Rocquencourt et CNRS-ENS Lyon

14 Petri Nets: A Graphical Tool for System Modelling and Analysis

Annie Choquet-Geniet and Pascal Richard

14.1 Overview of Petri Nets

Petri nets have been defined in 1962 by C.A. Petri [9,10] in order to model or to specify sequential and parallel systems including resources, data and events management, sequential evolution of the program counter. They are used either as a specification tool, or for analysing a previously designed system. In the first case, the system to design is modelled by a net, which is then implemented. In the second case, an existing system is modelled by a net, and its properties are then deduced, verifications are performed. One can verify that the system meets the requirements expressed in the specification, or can use the nets for performance analysis. Petri nets constitute a compromise between finite automata and the Turing machine.

There are two kinds of definitions concerning Petri nets:

- Definitions related to the structure of the nets, which are correlated to the static description of the system: what are the different parts of the system, what actions are performed by the system, what conditions are required for an action to be feasible, what effects does an action have on the different parts of the system?
- Definitions related to the behaviour of the net, which describe the dynamic evolution of the system: what are the possible actions according to the current state, what happens when some of them are performed, what kinds of situations are then possible to reach, what further evolution can be considered...

A very nice aspect of Petri nets is that they support a graphical representation, which enables a good general view of the modelled system and a rather intuitive perception of its different components.

A Petri net (or Place/Transition net) is an oriented graph with two kinds of vertexes (see Figure 14.1). It consists in a finite set of places (P), viewed as circles, a finite set of transitions (T), viewed as rectangles (corresponding to the different actions), a set of labelled arcs from places to transitions or from transitions to places, which express the conditions required for an action to be feasible and its consequences when it occurs. The valuation function W, is defined from $P \times T \cup T \times P$ in N, the set of natural numbers.

A marking function $M : P \to N$ is added to the previous description of the net, which represents the current state of the system, while the graph represents only the topology of the net, i.e. its different parts, and the connections between these parts. For each place p, $M(p)$ is interpreted as the number of tokens held by p.

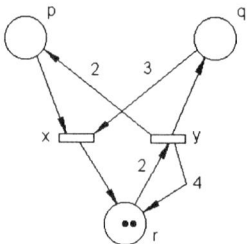

Fig. 14.1. There are three places (p, q, r) and two transitions (x and y). The firing of x requires one token in p and three in q, and it produces one token in r. The firing of y requires two tokens in place r, and it produces 2 tokens in p, one in q and 4 in r. In the initial state, p and q are empty, and r holds two tokens.

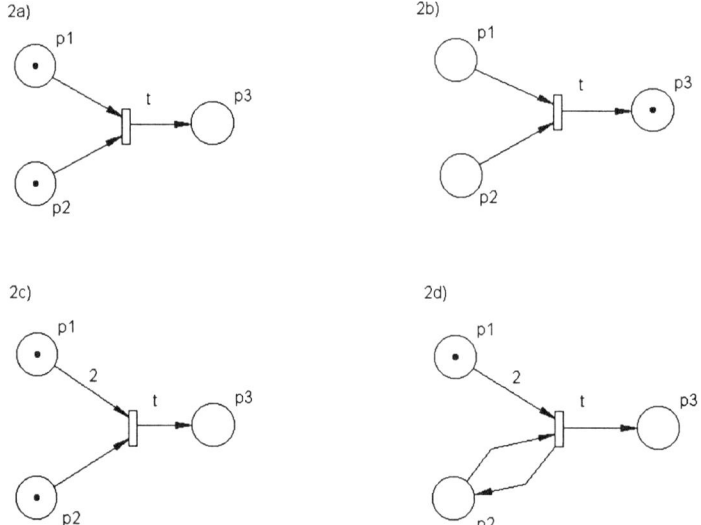

Fig. 14.2. The firing rule: on Figure 14.2.a, the transition t can fire, and its firing produces the marking of Fig 14.2.b. On Figure 14.2.c and 14.2.d, the transition t cannot fire because one token is missing, in place p1 (Figure 14.2.c) or p2 (Figure 14.2.d).

The dynamics of the system is described by means of the firing rule (Figure 14.2): a transition can fire (or is enabled) if each of its input places p contains at least as many tokens as indicated by the valuation of the arc from p to t. These tokens are removed from the input places when the transition fires, and tokens are added to the output places, again according to the valuation of the arcs from t to these places.

The firing of transitions can straightforwardly be extended to the firing of sequences of transitions. For instance, if we consider the net of Figure 14.1, the sequence $yyyx$ can fire and leads to the marking M so that $M(p) = 5, M(q) = 0$ and $M(r) = 9$.

Let us finally mention that there exist a large number of tools for editing and analysing Petri nets. As an example, we can mention Design/CPN [4], which provides both an editor of Petri nets, and an analysis environment. And let us also mention that an ISO norm 15909 for Petri nets is currently in preparation, and will be useful in the future.

14.2 Analysis and Specification of Case 1

We first present a brief overview of the different semantics which can be attached to the different components of a Petri net for the purpose of modelling. A place may be associated to: a class of resource, a counter, an event, a buffer (possibly with capacity), a condition. Transitions are generally connected to actions concerning: resources (allocation / deallocation), the evolution of a process (incrementation of the program counter), the processing induced by the occurrence of an event or by the verification of a condition, a buffer (production / consumption). Finally, tokens can represent: instances of a resource, contents of a buffer (in these two cases, tokens are associated to data), occurrences of an event (tokens are here associated to signals), the position of the program counter, the fact that a condition holds.

As we show next, there may be several approaches for modelling a system, according to the way the analysis of the system is approached. We present in the next section two approaches. In the first case, we treat a single instance of an order, but we can specify the ordered quantity. In the second case, we can specify the number of instances of an order, but not the ordered quantity.

14.2.1 One Order with a Data/Action Approach

We have assumed that quantities for each reference of a product are expressed as integer number. We deal with one single order, and we take into account neither arrival of new orders nor restocking. In Subsection "One Order - One Reference", we consider that the stock contains only one reference of a product, and in Subsection "One Order - Several Reference", we enlarge our hypothesis and consider several references.

One Order - One Reference.

Question 1: What are the basic data ?

Answer: We have defined four types of data:

- the stocked products, which constitute the stock;
- the ordered products, which define the pending order;
- the invoiced order;
- the non satisfied order.

The last two data are semantically connected to the condition "the order can be invoiced", and correspond to the two possible values of this condition.

Question 2: What actions are performed by the system ?

Answer: The processing of the order, which consists in invoicing it, either completely, or partially. An order may not be completely invoiced, due to the lack of the required amount of product.

Question 3: What does the invoicing of the order require ? What are its effects ?

Answer: There must be enough products in the stock, i.e. at least as many as mentioned in the order. If it is the case, the corresponding quantity of the reference is removed from the stock, the order is deleted, and an invoiced order is produced. Otherwise the stock is emptied, the order remains partially pending (there is a partial invoicing), and a "non satisfied order" is produced. Two pieces of information are thus represented: the status of the order when processed, and, if it has not been completely invoiced, the amount of products which could not be handed over (Figure 14.3).

Once the analysis of the system is achieved, we define the corresponding Petri net. From our analysis four places appear, each of them corresponding to a type of data: one place represents the stocked products (ST), one the ordered products (OP), one the invoiced order (IO) and one the non satisfied order (NSO). Initially, the marking of the place ST corresponds to the amount of products held in the stock, the marking of OP the quantity of products ordered, and both places IO and NSO are empty since the order has not still been processed.

Question 4: Which functionality must be supported by the net ?

Answer: The net must be able to compare two markings: the marking of the place ST must be greater than or equal to this of the place OP for the order to be invoiced. If it is not the case (and only in this case) a non satisfied order must be produced.

Since the test to zero is required, we will use the extension of Petri net which integrates inhibitor arcs since they explicitly implement the test to zero.

Nets with inhibitor arcs (Figure 14.4) are Petri nets where the firing rule has been modified in order to explicitly integrate the test to zero. An inhibitor arc

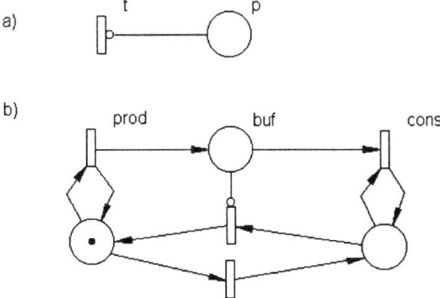

Fig. 14.3. (a) Representation of an inhibitor arc (b) this net models the activity of a producer which produces some objects and lays them down in a store. After a while, a consumer starts to consume the objects, and the producer goes on producing only when the store is empty.

enables the firing of a transition only when its input places are empty (i.e. it inhibits the firing when the input places hold tokens). The valuation function W is defined from $P \times T \cup T \times P \to N \cup \{\Theta\}$ (where Θ is a symbol, which does not belong to and model the inhibitor arc) and the firing rule becomes: t can fire if $M(p)$ is greater than or equal to $W(p,t)$ for each p so that $W(p,t) \in N$ and $M(p) = 0$ for each p so that $W(p,t) = \Theta$.

We introduce three transitions: a classical transition HO which corresponds to the handing over of products. Its firing requires one token in both places OP and ST. It means that each time a product is taken within the stock, it is removed from the order. This transition can fire until either the stock is empty or the ordered products have been completely handed over. Two further transitions (Error and OK), connected to inhibitor arcs enable the production of a token within either the place IO or the place NSO.

First case: $n < q$. After n firings of HO, Error will fire since the marking of ST is 0 and the marking of OP is still positive. In the final marking, ST is empty, OP contains still $q - n$ tokens (the ordered quantity which could not be invoiced), IO is empty since the order has not be completely invoiced and NSO holds one token.

Second case: $n \geq q$. After q firings of HO, the transition OK will fire since the marking of OP is 0. In the final marking, ST holds $n - q$ tokens (the quantity still present in stock), OP is empty, IO holds one token (the order has been completely invoiced) and NSO is empty. The net of Figure 14.4 presents our solution.

One Order - Several References. We now enlarge our hypothesis, and assume the existence of several references. The stock as well as the order are thus defined by the quantities of each of them, either stocked or ordered.

Question 5: What is an order composed of ?

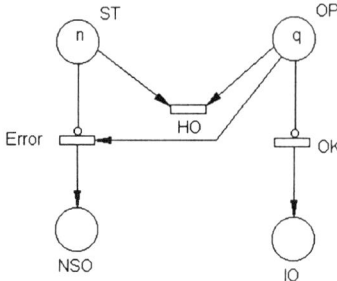

Fig. 14.4. A solution using inhibitor arcs. Legend: ST: stock; OP: ordered products; IO: invoiced order; NSO: non satisfied order; HO: handing over of product; Error: the order could not be satisfied; OK: the order is invoiced. n is the quantity present in the stock and q is the ordered quantity.

Answer: It consists of a list of pairs (reference, quantity), where a given reference appears at most once. The amount of each reference is still assumed to be known.

The number of places representing either the stock or the order increases: if there are n possible references, n places ST1, ST2, ... , STn model the stock, and n places OP1, ... , OPn model the order. The transition HO is split up into n transitions HO1,... , HOn, each of them concerning one reference and having the same semantics as the transition HO of Figure 14.4.

The order is then invoiced if and only if every place OPi is empty. Finally, the transition Error is also split up into Error1, ... , Errorn. After the complete treatment of the order, either IO contains one token if the order could be completely handed over, or the place NSO contains as many tokens as there are (partially) missing references. This extended solution is presented on Figure 14.5, for two references.

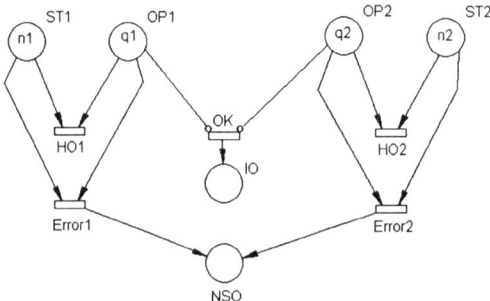

Fig. 14.5. A solution for the problem of one order with two references using inhibitor arcs

14 Petri Nets: A Graphical Tool for System Modelling and Analysis

14.2.2 One Order with a Structural Approach

In this section, we analyse the system differently, and consider that we deal with an unique kind of order: the ordered quantity cannot be chosen, i.e. it is a constant of the system, while the stocked quantity remains a parameter. In our first approach, we were able to consider any order, but only one instance. In this second approach, we take into account several instances of a given order: the number of instances is a parameter (expressed through the initial marking), but not the ordered quantities.

If we assume the ordered quantity to be known before we proceed to the construction of the Petri net, we can avoid the use of inhibitor arcs. In this case, the comparison of integers is supported by the firing rule (which integrates it explicitly). The ordered quantity is included within the topology of the net.

One Order - One Reference. Here again, we first deal with one single reference, and afterwards, we will assume several ones.

Question 6: What are now the data, and what does the net model do here?

Answer: The data in this approach are: the stocked products, the pending orders, the invoiced orders. An order is here considered in its whole, thus it is either invoiced, or it remains pending. The partial handing over of the ordered products cannot here be modelled.

Using this approach, we define three places: one models the stocked products (ST), one the pending orders (PO) and one corresponds to the invoiced orders (IO). The marking of ST corresponds again to the amount of products held in the stock. The marking of PO corresponds to the number of pending orders. Finally, the initial marking of IO is 0. It will afterwards represent the number of already invoiced orders.

There is one single transition (HO), corresponding to the handing over of the order, considered in its whole. It can fire only if there are enough products within the stock. This condition is expressed by means of the valuation of the arc between ST and HO. It then removes the number of tokens corresponding to the ordered quantity from the place ST, one token from PO, and adds one token to the place IO (Figure 14.6).

In the first solution, the modification of the order does not affect the topology of the net, but is taken into account by a new marking. In the second approach, the modification of the order induces the modification of the net which has thus to be recompiled after any modification of order. Furthermore, in our second approach, we can express only the fact that an order can be invoiced, but if it can not, we have no information about the missing amount of products.

One Order - Several References. Here again, we enlarge the system by taking several references into account. Our assumption about the composition

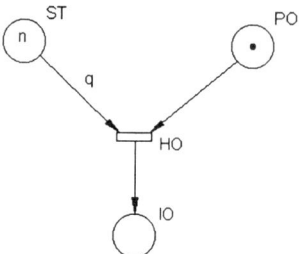

Fig. 14.6. A solution to the problem of one order for one reference, using a structural approach

of an order is the same as in the previous section and we still suppose that the ordered quantity for each reference is known before the design of the net is carried over.

The only change brought to the net of Figure 14.6 concerns the modelling of the stock. Again, the place ST is split up into n places (if there are n different references). The arcs between STi and HO are valuated by the amount of the i-th reference which is ordered (see Figure 14.7).

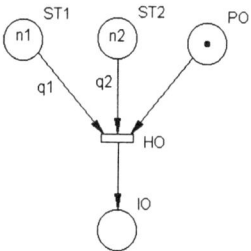

Fig. 14.7. A solution for the problem of one order, with two references

In the next section, which deals with Case 2, we will focus on this second approach. However, whatever the chosen approach, we will have to use a high level net. The structure of the net when using the first approach, would be more complex: we would have used fifos for modelling the file of pending orders; then, for each order, we would start to hand it over, but, in the case of non satisfaction, we would have to restore the stock, and then to delete the order from the fifo. This would have required the use of several inhibitor arcs. For the sake of simplicity, we have chosen to present only the solution corresponding to the second approach here.

14.2.3 Several Orders

In this section we complete the model in order to take into account several orders. As in the previous section, orders and products are completely defined at the modelling step.

Question 7: How to model several orders ?

Answer: We consider different references of products, which differ by the ordered quantities and, for each kind, there may exist several instances. In the sequel, order will mean « kind of order ». Since an order is modelled through the structure of the net, the associated subnet must be repeated for every order. New places « pending » and « invoiced » must be created and also a new transition for changing the state of the order and consuming products in the stocks. Consider two orders: order 1 requires three products A and two products B, and order 2 requires one product B. As shown in Figure 14.8, adding a new order increases the size of the net with two places, one transition and at most $n + 2$ arcs (where n is the number of different products). The size of the net is polynomially bounded in the number of orders.

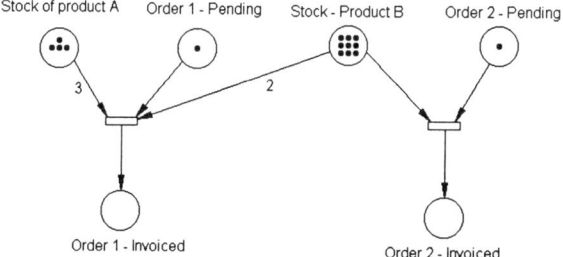

Fig. 14.8. Low-level net modelling the system with two orders

This modelling approach leads to the problem of the growth of the size of the net. It cannot be avoided with classical low-level nets since every order is modelled by new places, transitions and arcs. The size can be decreased using high level nets such as coloured nets [6]. Coloured nets have been defined in order to give a concise model even for complex systems, while keeping the same expressiveness (i.e. every coloured net can be unfolded into a classical low-level net). It allows to merge all identical parts of a low-level net into only one structure. We now only present basic coloured net concepts used hereafter.

A coloured net is defined by a finite set of colours, let us denote it C. A colour can also be considered as a data type (e.g. a type of order). Colours are totally ordered and every token is coloured. To every transition is associated C or a subset of C, and to every arc is associated a function which models colour changes when a transition is fired (in practice the arcs are only labelled by the name of the functions). As example we give three classical functions that are widely used (n is the number of colours in the set C, and the symbol | denotes the modulo operation):

- Identity: $Id < Colour_i >=< Colour_i >$
- Successor: $Succ < Colour_i >=< Colour_{i+1|n} >$
- Predecessor: $Prec < Colour_i >=< Colour_{i-1|n} >$

Figure 14.9 gives an example of a coloured net with the set of colours:

$$C = \{<r>,<b>,<j>,<v>\}$$

Note that the ordering of colours is very important. For instance $<b>$ is the successor of $<r>$, and conversely $<r>$ is the predecessor of $<b>$. Furthermore the functions Successor and Predecessor behave cyclically: precisely $Succ <v>=<r>$, and $Prec <r>=<v>$.

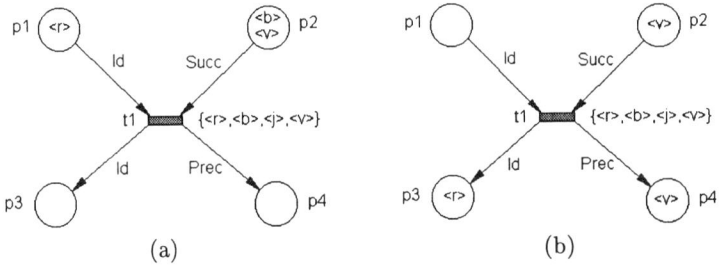

Fig. 14.9. (a) Structure of a coloured net with the set of colours C={<r>,<b>,<j>,<v>}; (b) The net after the fire of transition t1 with colour <r>

We describe next the behaviour of a coloured net. We first define the enabling process of a transition and then the firing process. Let t be a transition and c be a colour belonging to the set associated to t, we check that the required coloured tokens (computed with functions using the colour c) are available in every input place of t. If it is not the case, we proceed in the same way with an other colour associated to t until the previous condition holds for a colour a. We say that the transition is enabled for the colour a. The firing is processed in two steps. First tokens in the input places of t are removed using the functions on the arcs connecting the places to t, and then coloured tokens are added to the output places of t according to the functions labelling output arcs of t.

Consider Figure 14.9, we first show that the transition $t1$ is enabled using the functions on arcs connected to the input places of $t1$. For $p1$ $Id < r >=< r >$, since $p1$ contains a token with colour $<r>$, the condition is satisfied. For $p2$, $Succ < r >=< b >$, since such a token is available in $p2$, the condition is also satisfied. As consequence $t1$ is enabled for the colour $<r>$. During the firing, $Id < r >$ is removed from $p1$, $Succ < r >$ is removed from $p2$, $Id < r >$ is added to $p3$ and $Prec < r >$ is added to $p4$.

Question 8: How to model the products and their stocks ?

Answer: The places ST1,...,STn are merged into one single place ST. One colour is created per product. The colour can be viewed as the name of the product. The stocks are modelled by tokens of the corresponding colours and quantities.

Question 9: Question: How to model the orders ?

Answer: Here again places PO1,...,POq are merged into one single place PO and one colour is associated to each order. An order becomes a coloured token. All these tokens must have a different colour. The set of pending orders (coloured tokens) are stored in the place PO. The quantities of products required in the orders are defined by a function which gives the number of tokens in the colours associated to the products. The places modelling invoiced orders are also merged into a place IO. For instance, consider an order <1> of three units of product A and two units of product B, and an order <2> which only requires one unit of product B. The function (Qty) modelling these orders is defined as follow:

Qty <1> = <A><A><A><B><B>

Qty <2> = <B>

Functions, as the set of colours, are not directly integrated within the structure of the net (i.e. places, transitions and arcs). But they are rather stored within a table associated to the net. In the following O denotes the set of colours associated to the set of orders, and P denotes the set of colours associated to the set of products. Figure 14.10 gives the whole model of the system.

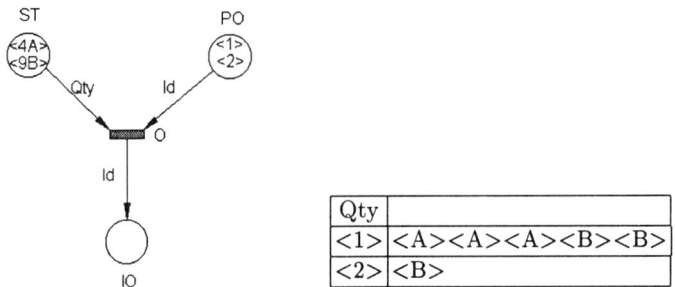

Fig. 14.10. Coloured net modelling the order system, with its table of functions

As said before every coloured net can be unfolded into an equivalent low-level Place/Transition net. The unfolded net of the net presented Figure 14.10 is exactly the net of Figure 14.8.

Question 10: Can we schedule the orders with a given policy ?

Answer: In the net of Figure 14.10, all orders that can be invoiced correspond to the selected colours that enable the transitions. Scheduling orders is equivalent to schedule enabled transitions. Moreover, if a given order cannot be satisfied because there are not enough products in stock, it must be delayed in order to pass to the next order with respect to the policy. So we need first to test that the selected order can be satisfied. If not, it is delayed, else it is invoiced.

But as explained before, such tests cannot be done with low-level nets. And since coloured nets have the same modelling power as low-level nets, then it cannot be done with them. To implement a scheduling policy of orders with our approach, we need an extension of Petri nets including inhibitor arcs and fifos or priority nets. But these extensions increase the expressiveness power, and as consequence, most of the classical properties that can be verified on classical Petri nets fall indecidable (the model becomes as powerful as a Turing machine).

14.3 Analysis and Specification of Case 2

Up to now the system studied is fully static: all orders and products are known at the modelling step. We now extend the previous case to model the flow of orders and the entry flow of products in stocks. Without loss of generality, we only consider that new orders can arrive in the system, but not new references. For the other cases, the principles would be the same and are left to the reader.

14.3.1 Entry Flow in Stocks

Question 11: How to model an entry flow in stocks ?

Answer: We need a special transition that can be enabled without any condition. Such transitions are called source transitions, since they do not have any input place. Source transitions are always enabled and can fire at any time. So for modelling entry flow of products in stocks, we add a source transition, noted later EFO, connected to the place ST. The set of colours that labelled the transition is the subset of colours dedicated to the products. The function associated to the corresponding arc is Identity. So that at any time every colour of P satisfies the enabling condition and the corresponding product is added to the stock.

Question 12: How is the entry flow controlled ?

Answer: The entry flow is nondeterministic, in the sense that the reference introduced in the stock is not controlled. If the source transition fires three times with colour <A> then three coloured tokens are added to the Stock. But the selected colour is always chosen arbitrarily. With these nondeterministic choices, the analysis deals with all possible behaviours of the system. Figure 14.11 gives the model of the entry flow of products.

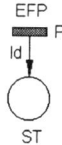

Fig. 14.11. Order systems with entry flow of products EFP

14.3.2 Flows of Orders

Question 13: How to model new orders ?

Answer: As for the entry flow of products, we need a new source transition. It is connected to the place that holds pending orders. In practice the order system can deal with an infinite behaviour and so with an infinite set of orders. Distinguishing the orders requires to generate one new colour that must not exist in the system. This source transition, noted later EFO, is in fact a generator of new colours in order to deal with an infinite number of orders. Furthermore quantities of products indicated in the order are defined by extending the Quantity function (noted Qty in the net). The table containing the function Qty can become infinite.

But the unfolding of a Coloured Net with an infinite set of colours produced an infinite set of places and transitions. So the graph of the unfolded net is infinite. It has been shown that the expressiveness of the model becomes in that case equivalent to a Turing machine. But in practice the number of orders in the system can be kept finite by destroying invoiced orders. As a consequence the set of colours and the size of the function Quantity are finite.

Question 14: How to cancel pending orders or destroy old invoiced ones ?

Answer: In that case we have to consume tokens. The only way to proceed is to use a sink transition (i.e. a transition without output place). When a sink transition fires tokens are removed from the input places. Since no output place exists no new token is generated. Removed tokens from the entry places have been destroyed. So in the final model we need two sink transitions, DIO and CO, for modelling respectively the deleted invoiced orders and the cancelled orders.

The choices of cancelled orders or destroyed invoiced orders are nondeterministic. We include all feasible behaviours of the order system. When an order is destroyed, the table of function Qty must be updated and the corresponding removed colours can be reused later. Figure 14.12 gives the final model of Case 2.

14.4 Validation of the Specification

Petri nets analysis consists in verifying two kinds of properties: behavioural properties and structural properties [1,8]. Behavioural properties depend on the

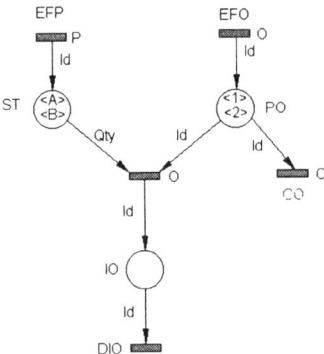

Fig. 14.12. Final model

initial marking (initial distribution of tokens in the places) and by opposition structural properties focus on the structure without any initial marking consideration. Generally solving these problems requires exponential time and space, even for simple net structures [3]. The main behavioural properties are reachability, liveness, boundedness, deadlock-freeness. And the main structural properties are invariants and structural liveness, structural boundedness and also structural deadlock-freeness.

Obviously when coloured Petri nets are used the objective is not to unfold the net because of it usually enormous size (even if it is always possible). Some specific algorithms have been developed. But in order to be clear, we do not detail such specific solutions and we only present the analysis of a low-level net.

Behavioural properties can be checked by building the reachability graph from the Petri net. In this graph vertexes are markings and edges are labelled by transitions that change one marking into another. If the system has an infinite number of different states, then the reachability graph is infinite.

The reachability property consists in verifying that a marking (a given state of the system) is reachable from the initial marking. The problem is very complex to solve, the decidability proof has held for ten years. So deciding if a marking is reachable can be decided by searching the according vertex in a finite reachability graph (otherwise a complex algorithm is required). The path from the initial marking to the searched marking produces a feasible firing sequence that proves the reachability. Liveness consists in verifying that every transition can always fire in the system. More precisely, there is for every reachable marking a fireable sequence, containing at least once each transition. This property ensures that every operation (modelled by transitions) can always be performed in the system. So there is no partial deadlock of the system. If the number of different markings is finite, then a live net has a strongly connected reachability graph. That graph property can be checked in $O(n^2)$ in the size of the reachability graph (which usually has itself an exponential size in comparison with the size of the net). For instance the net of Figure 14.12 is live. The third property is boundedness: there is no place that can have an infinite number of tokens while playing the token game. In order to have an infinite number of tokens in a place, there must be an infinite firing sequence producing them. So an unbounded net has an infinite reachability graph. But it has been shown that a reachability graph is infinite if and only if, it has infinite paths. These paths can be cut by identifying repetitive firing sequences. The obtained graph is called the Karp's graph [7] and is finite for every net. If the number of tokens increases while firing a repetitive sequence, then the places in the corresponding vertex is marked by a the symbol ω. So verifying boundedness consists in searching this symbol in the Karp's graph. For instance the net of Figure 14.9 is bounded and has a finite reachability graph. The last behavioural property presented is deadlock-freeness. A marking is deadlocked if it enables no transition. So in a deadlock-free system, there always exists a transition to fire (i.e. an operation to do). That property can be checked using the finite reachability graph: it is sufficient to check that there is no leaf in the graph (i.e. a vertex without any successor).

Structural properties are studied by using an algebraic representation of the net. From the structure of the net an incidence matrix can be defined (as in a classical graph theory). Markings are vectors which are indexed on the set of places. The number of transitions in a firing sequence can be stored in a characteristic vector. Let us denote C the incidence matrix, X a characteristic vector, and M_0 the initial marking of the net. Every reachable marking M verifies the marking equation: $M = M_0 + CX$. Every reachable marking satisfies a linear algebraic system of equations [5]. But take care, the converse is not true: computing M and/or X using the marking equation can lead to spurious solutions (i.e. markings and sequences that are not feasible on the net while playing the token game). As a consequence many algorithms working on structural properties are semi-decision algorithms (verifying a necessary or a sufficient condition but not both).

Invariant (also called semiflows) refers to stable situations in the net behaviour whatever the initial marking is. The weighted sum of tokens in a set of places is called place invariant. It is always the case for a set of places modelling renewable resources or mutual exclusion sub-systems. Computing place-invariants can be easily done by solving the system $^tCX = 0$ (i.e. the kernel of the transposed matrix C in classical linear algebra) with the Fourier-Motzkin's algorithm [2]. For instance in Figure 14.6 the places pending and invoiced constitute a place-invariant since no orders are introduced or deleted in the system. Another kind of invariant deals with repetitive firing sequences (that lead from one marking to the same marking). These invariants based on transitions can be easily computed by solving the system $CX = 0$. Since it is the dual system of the place invariant one, it can be solved by the same algorithm. Structural properties can then be efficiently semi-decided using classical linear programme solvers.

14.5 The Natural Language Description of the Specifications

14.5.1 Case 1

An order is defined by a set of references of products. For each reference is known the ordered quantity, inventory levels and its status which are natural numbers. The status of the order is defined by two different variables upon natural numbers. The first variable contains one if the order is not invoiced, and zero otherwise, and the second variable stores one if the order is invoiced and zero otherwise. The system provides an operation (invoice order) that can be executed if, and only if, every reference is available according to the ordered quantity. When the operation is completed, the operation decrements the pending order variable, increments the invoiced order variable and updates the quantities in stocks.

14.5.2 Case 2

The ordering system is an extension of Case 1, that allows dynamic arrivals and cancellations of orders, and dynamic arrivals of raw of materials (i.e. products in the stock). The definitions of orders and stocks are the same as in Case 1. The system provides four new operations to input new products in the stock, to input new orders, to cancel orders not yet invoiced, and to delete invoiced orders. The operation introducing products in stock increases the value of the variables associated to these references. The operation which introduces new orders defines a set of references and their ordered quantities. Both cancellation operations decrease the status variables, as defined in Case 1. An operation that invoices an order is defined per order in the same manner than in Case 1.

14.6 Conclusion

Through this chapter, we have outlined the strong points as well as the weaknesses of the Petri nets. When the order flow is completely defined at the modelling step, Petri nets provide a very nice and concise modelling of the system. The graphical support is very helpful, since it gives a good synthetic view of the system in its whole, points out the different objects which constitute it, and describes their interactions.

The structural approach is here completely suitable to the problem, since it uses the firing rule in order to model the invoicing of orders. Moreover, the model we get with this approach can be analysed, using all the analysing facilities of Petri nets. The limits of this approach come from the fact that the orders have to be specified in the model. If we want to consider any possible order, that is to consider the order as a parameter, our previous approach does not work anymore, and we stumble to the main weakness of the model: the test to zero fails, so does any comparison between markings. Thus we have to change the power of the model, and to integrate inhibitor arcs. But we get then the power of a Turing Machine, which forbids any analysis of the model.

Thus, the data/action approach can be used only in order to play the token game (in our case, the process will end, so does the token game). Now, if we take an order flow into account, we use a high level coloured net, here again, any analysing facility fails. But we can get an instantaneous description of the system, at any time, and perform some analysis or play the token game, from the state of the system at that time. Finally, we did not present any solution including the scheduling of the orders, since it would have required the use of fifos or of priorities and inhibitor arcs, and would have supposed a rather complicated net, dedicated to the deletion of the unsatisfied order, and the restoration of the stock, after a partial handing over of products for a finally non satisfied order.

As a general conclusion, Petri nets seem to be rather suitable for the modelling of the first case (since the invoicing of order is directly modelled by the firing rule), but for the second case, their weaknesses (no comparison between markings, the structure cannot dynamically be modified) are too important, and we cannot provide a good solution, unless we use an extended model with the power of the Turing machine. Thus, for the second case, the modelling with Petri nets is not really suitable.

References

1. Choquet-Geniet A., Vidal-Naquet G. (1993) Petri nets and parallel systems. Armand Colin (in french)
2. Colom J.M., Silva M. (1991) Convex Geometry and Semiflows in P/T Nets. A Comparative Study of Algorithms for Computation of Minimal P-Semiflows. In: Advances in Petri nets'90, 79–112, Springer Verlag
3. Desel J., Esparza J. (1995) Free-Choice Petri nets. Cambridge Tracts in Computer Science n° 40, Cambridge University Press
4. Design/CPN, tool Homepage: http://www.daimi.au.dk/designCPN/
5. David R., Alla H. (1992) Petri nets and Grafcet. Prentice-Hall
6. Jensen K. (1997) Coloured Petri nets, Basic concepts, Analysis Methods and Practical Use. Monographs in Theoretical Computer Science, Springer Verlag
7. Karp R.M., Miller R.E. (1969) Parallel program schemata. Journal of Computer System Sciences 3:147–195
8. Murata T. (1989) Petri nets : Properties, Analysis and Applications. Proceedings of the IEEE 77(4):541–580
9. Peterson J.L. (1981) Petri net theory and the modelling of systems. Prentice-Hall
10. Petri C.A. (1962) Kommunikation mit Automaten. (German) Schriften des Rheinisch-Westfälischen Institutes für instrumentelle Mathematik an der Universität Bonn, Nr. 2, Bonn

15 Using Petri Nets and Objects: A Formal yet Expressive Approach

Christophe Sibertin-Blanc

15.1 Introduction

Petri nets are a formalism well suited for modelling the behaviour of concurrent systems, thanks to many valuable features such as a graphical representation, the possibility to reason about both the states and the operations, a well-defined semantics allowing formal analysis, and the possibility to make simulation or to generate code. However, the expressive power of Petri nets makes difficult the precise modelling of large systems, because of the lack of concepts for dealing with the structure of systems and with their data processing dimension. Thus, there is a need to improve the expressive power of Petri nets, and introducing concepts from the Object-Oriented approach can do this. Object-Orientation and Petri nets complement very well since the former provides efficient concepts to cope with the global organisation of systems and with their data processing aspects, while the latter provides efficient concepts to cope with their behaviour. Throughout this chapter, Petri net refers to High-Level Petri Net formalisms such as [3,6,8,9,1] allowing to handle tokens which may be identified, and more precisely to the *Petri Net with Objects* formalism [9,11].

In order to produce a formal model of a system, the designer needs to have some knowledge of the system under consideration, whatever Formal Description Technique is used. He acquires this knowledge from a domain specialist which is a potential user of the system. However, this knowledge transfer is effective only if the formalism specialist and the domain specialist share a *conceptual framework* giving a rigorous meaning to terms that are commonly used to discuss about systems, to understand their structure, their behaviour and their finality. Using such a conceptual framework, the domain specialist can state in a precise way his informal but concrete knowledge of the system, while the formalism specialist is able to understand this natural language description and to avoid ambiguities.

In addition, the designer needs a set of correspondence rules that relate the terms of the conceptual framework and the terms of the formalism. Then it becomes possible to translate a conceptual description of the system into a formal model, and conversely to provide a formal model with a concrete meaning. Thanks to both a conceptual framework and translation rules, the relationships between the real system and the formal model become clear.

The *conceptual framework* introduced in this chapter relies upon a few basic concepts commonly used by designers. According to this framework, any system handles some *Entities* to which its activity is applied to and is capable of doing some *Operations* to process these Entities – creation, deletion or transformation in any way. Moreover, any system includes some *Actors*, or processors able to perform Operations and to keep Entities. These three kinds of components define the structure of the system, and they are related through the concept of *Action*, which occurs when an Actor performs an Operation with Entities. To become an active device, a system must in addition be provided with a *Control Structure* that defines under which cases Actions may occur.

Accordingly, the conceptual model of a system may be presented as the answers to a set of questions about the Entities, Operations, Actors, Actions and the Control Structure of this system. The designer asks the questions and the user provides the answers. Although the answers are expressed in natural language, it is possible to check that they satisfy the main properties of a specification (completeness, consistency and avoidance of ambiguity, see [4] Chapter 5.2) because the conceptual framework is well founded. Afterwards, the designer issues the formal model: applying correspondence rules between the conceptual framework and the Petri net formalism, he translates the answers in terms of the formalism. Consequently, the conceptual model and the formal model are organised in the same way, since the latter is just a formal answer in reply to the questions.

The second section of this chapter introduces the conceptual framework shared by the domain and formalism specialists. On the other hand, the correspondence rules are not explicitly given; they are just applied in the treatment of the case study. The remaining sections follow the structure of the conceptual framework: the system's interface, identification of the system's components, study of Entities, Operations, Actors and of the Control Structure. A few remarks about properties of the issued model are given as a conclusion.

15.2 A Conceptual Framework for the Representation of Systems

The designer and the user have to agree upon the meaning of the terms they use in questions and answers, and this meaning is defined by the conceptual framework. According to this framework, Entities, Operations and Actors constitute the system's structure, while the Control Structure defines how these components interact to perform the system's behaviour.

The Entities: any system handles some concrete or abstract things that make the result of its activity usable; these things, referred to as Entities, are the matter or the resource of the system activity.

The Operations: an Operation is a transformation which can create or delete entities, or change their value, state, location or whatever property.

The Actors: actors are both containers for keeping entities and engines able to perform operations. They maintain entities, execute the work done by the system, and use some energy as a counterpart. An Actor is also able to interact with other Actors by means of entities or operations. Interactions by means of entities are *asynchronous* communications: an Actor supplies an entity, which is then retrieved by another Actor. Interactions by means of operations are *synchronous* communications: two Actors perform an operation together.

The Entity, Operation and Actor concepts feature two noteworthy properties. First, we may distinguish *types* and *instances* (or occurrences), where a type is a frame defining some virtual features, while an instance is a concrete element that enacts these abilities in a given point of space and time; for instance, an *Operation type* is the description of a process while an *Operation occurrence* is an actual and located execution of this process. When there is no ambiguity, we will use "Entity", "Operation" or "Actor" for types, and "entity", "operation" or "actor" for instances. The other common property of Entity, Operation and Actor is that they may be described at different abstraction or detail levels, and therefore are amenable to a *refinement* process. For instance, an Actor may be the system under consideration, a sub-system, its environment or even the system plus the environment.

The three collections of Entities, Operations and Actors define the *structure* of a system, and they are related through **Actions**. An Action is the association of an Actor, an Operation and a set of Entities; when "a clerk invoices an order", the "clerk" Actor performs the Action (it is the subject), the "to invoice" Operation is the processing (it is the verb), while the "order" is one of the Entities affected by the Action (it is the complement). We again find the type / instance distinction, and an Action occurrence is the association of one instance of the Actor, one occurrence of the Operation and one instance of each Entity. The dynamic dimension, or *behaviour* of a system is the set of sequences of (sets of) actions which may occur, and it is defined by a Control Structure.

The Control Structure: the control structure of a system defines the behaviour of the system, how it operates, by stating under which conditions an Action occurrence may or must take place. These conditions often refer to a special attribute of Entities and Actors, referred to as their state.

The Control Structure of a large system cannot be described as a whole and needs to be structured. To this end, we distinguish on the one hand the internal behaviour of each Actor type, referred to as its *activity*, and on the other hand the composition of the activity of the Actor types, referred to as their *interaction*. Then it becomes possible to organise the model of a system as the description of each Actor – with the Entities it handles, the Operations it performs and the part of the Control Structure concerning its own behaviour –, together with the description of the interactions among these Actors. Therefore, *the model of a system is organised as a collection of Actors that interact according to some composition mechanisms*.

15.3 Case 1

A separate treatment of the two cases would lead to raise twice the list of questions suggested by our conceptual framework. To spare the reader a boring repetition, the questions about the first case are skipped and they are raised only on the second case. However, the answers give first the information related to the first case and then the information related to the second case. As for the model of Case 1, it mainly comes down to Figures 15.1, 15.2 and 15.5.a.

15.4 The System's Interface

Many methodologies advise to start the modelling process of a system by drawing a Communication Diagram (CD) [12,2]. A CD shows the Actors of the system and the Actors of its environment, together with the flows of Entities that move among Actors. Such a chart highlights the interactions between the system and its environment, and thus how the system and the environment use each other.

Question 1: How does the Company interact with its environment?

Answer: The statement of the case provides no much information about the interaction of the Company with its environment. However, we may assume that the Company interacts with Customers and Suppliers and that peoples doing the work belong to the Actor type Clerk. They communicate in an asynchronous way as shown in the CD of Figure 15.1, without synchronous interaction.

A CD is a good starting point of a modelling process since it is quite easy to draw even at an early step when designers have few insights into the system. Moreover, this diagram shows fundamental features of the system's structure and enables one to identify:

- the Actors of the system and of its environment;
- the Entities which are communicated;
- important states of these Entities, since each flow is nothing else than a state where entities are moving through a communication channel;
- the Operations that send and receive the flows, and so enable the system to communicate with other Actors;

15.5 The Components of the System's Structure

The aim of this step is to identify the types of Entities, Operations and Actors of the Company, and then to identify the Actions to which the Control Structure of the system is applied.

Question 2: What are the Entities?

15 Petri Nets and Objects: A Formal yet Expressive Approach

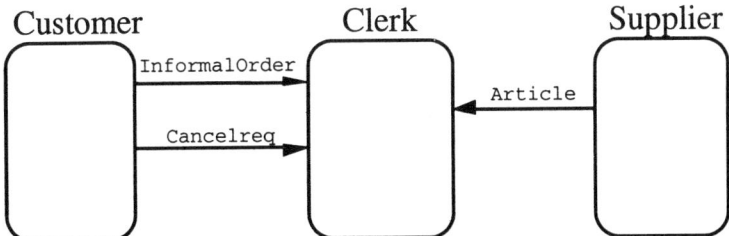

Fig. 15.1. The communication diagram of the system

Question 2.1: What are the names of Entities?

Answer: Six Entity types have to be considered: Order, Invoice, Product, InformalOrder, Cancelreq and Article.

Question 2.2: What is the role of each Entity, what is it intended for?

Answer:

1. Order stores the wish of a customer mentioned in an informalOrder, and causes the delivery of some amount of an article, if possible.
2. Invoice causes a financial flow, in compensation to the flow of goods.
3. Product keeps information about the articles sold by the Company, namely the currently available quantity.
4. InformalOrder corresponds to the information provided by a customer intending to order some Article.
5. Cancelreq corresponds to the information provided by a customer intending to cancel an informalOrder previously sent.
6. Articles are the goods that the Company sells to customers and receives from suppliers.

No additional questions are raised, because the instances of these types are easy to identify.

Question 3: What are the Operations?

Question 3.1: What are the names of Operations?

Answer: to invoice, to receiveO, to cancel and to receiveA.

Question 3.2: What is the role of each Operation, what is it intended for?

Answer:

1. to invoice reserves the articles ordered by an order, and accordingly creates a new invoice;
2. to receiveO accounts for the arrival of an InformalOrder by creating a new order;

3. to cancel accounts for the arrival of a cancelReq, by nullifying the effect of operation to receiveO, if possible;
4. to receiveA accounts for an in-flow of articles.

This set of Operations implies that an order may be cancelled only when it is in the state pending and not when it is in the state invoiced. If an order could be cancelled from both states, we would have to consider two Operations – to cancel a pending order and to cancel an invoiced order – because different processing have to be done in each case.

Question 4: What are the Actors?

Answer: As already mentioned, we have little information about the organisation of the Company and we assume that it includes the only Actor type Clerk. Thus the Company is just a set of clerks.

Now we are ready to identify the Actions that may occur within the system. By the way, we will know which Entities, Operations and Actors are in relationship. In addition, the list of Actions will be the starting point to describe the Control Structure of the system.

Question 5: In which Actions the Actors, Operations and Entities take part?

Answer: The four following Actions can be realised by the system:
- act1 : (Clerk, to invoice, {Order, Invoice, Product})
- act2 : (Clerk, to receiveO, {InformalOrder, Order})
- act3 : (Clerk, to cancel, {Cancelreq, Order})
- act4 : (Clerk, to receiveA, {Article, Product})

It turns out that each Operation appears in only one Action, but if an Actor Warehouseman could also receive articles, we would have an additional Action (Warehouseman, to receiveA, {Article, Product})

Once the types of Entities, Operations and Actors are identified, they have to be studied more deeply. For each type, we need to know what is its structure and what are its relationships with other types.

15.6 The Entities

The aim of the first question is to obtain a definition of each Entity type, which will be modelled as a passive Object class. Consequently, we will be able to design the Database of the system.

Question 6: What is the structure of Entities?

Question 6.1: What are the meaningful properties, or attributes, of each Entity: how do you name them and what is their domain of value?

Answer: An order has three attributes of interest:

1. no refers to nothing, it only serves to identify each order;
2. product is the reference of the ordered article, thus its value has to be the ref of a known instance of type Product;
3. qtity is a positive integer, the quantity that is ordered.

A product has two attributes of interest:

1. ref refers to one article and is used to identify each product;
2. amount is a positive integer recording the number of items of the article that are available.

An invoice is characterised by:

1. object is the no of the related order and allows to identify each invoice;
2. amount is the total sum to be paid by the customer of the order.

As for the other Entity types, the question does not lead to a precise answer, because their instances are not managed by the Company's Information System. In addition, these Entities are created by the Environment and not by the Company. The important facts are the following:

1. An informalOrder includes information (which may be received by telephone, by fax or by any means) allowing to extract values for the attributes of an order.
2. A cancelReq includes information allowing to identify the order that has been created upon reception of an InformalOrder.
3. Articles are in one-to-one correspondence with products, and each article is a set of physical items stored by the Company.

Question 6.2: What are the elementary functions associated to each Entity to read or to modify the value of its attributes: how do you name them, what are their parameters and what do they do?

Answer: One function allows to create a new order from an informalOrder, and another one allows to create a new invoice from an order. As for Product, the functions takeout and increase allow to decrease and increase the value of attribute amount. The detail of the computation achieved by these functions is not relevant for the case; it could be expressed by some mathematical expressions or in a programming language.

We have enough information to draw a schema defining the structure of Entities and how they are related. Figure 15.2 presents such a schema according to very usual O-O notations showing the attributes and functions, or methods of each Entity type; another notation such as UML could alternatively be used [2].

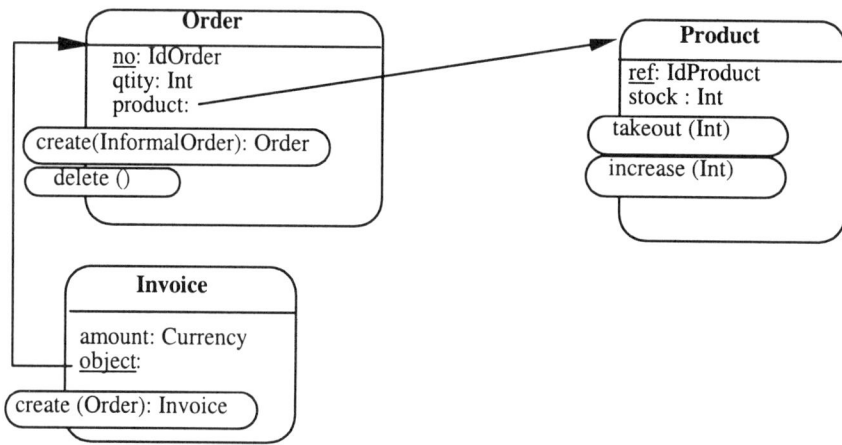

Fig. 15.2. The structure of entities

Entities that are not recorded in the Database of the system have been avoided. The system's database schema can easily be deduced from this schema.

Questions about Entities such as the number of instances of each type, where they are located, how they are stored and so on are not relevant for the conceptual model we intent to draw. The same holds for questions concerning the Database Entities, such as the key attributes, Integrity Constraints, the public or private nature of attributes and functions, and so on.

The following questions serve to understand what relationships the Entities have with Operations and Actors.

Question 7: What are the relationships between Entities and Operations?

Answer: The answer is summarised in Table 15.1 that indicates how Operations act upon Entities for creation, deletion, access for reading the value, and access for changing the value or the state. A more detailed description could provide a graph indicating which Operations access each attribute and function of Entities.

Table 15.1. The use of entities by operations

	Informal Order	Cancelreq	Order	Invoice	Product	Article
to invoice			change state	create	change value	
to receiveO	delete		create			
to cancel		delete	delete			
to receiveA					change value	change state

Question 8: What are the states of Entities, and which state changes are produced by Operation occurrences?

Answer: To invoice an order produces the change from the pending to the invoiced state, and puts the created invoice into the to be collected state. To receiveO an order places it into the pending state. To receiveA an article produces the change from the receivedA to the warehouse state. Products remain in the stock state.

This information defines how entities may be used. It can be collected into the *life cycle* of each Entity type that describes (1) the state space of each instance of this type, (2) under which state(s) an operation may be applied to an instance, and (3) the state change resulting from an occurrence of this operation. A Petri net as shown in Figure 15.3 for Entity Order describes a life cycle. Each *place* (represented by a circle) corresponds to a possible state of an instance and each *transition* (represented by a box) corresponds to an Operation. The fact that an entity is in a certain state is represented by a *token* (a black dot) within this place. Places and transitions are connected through directed *arcs*. When an entity is in the input state of an operation, this operation is *enabled* and may occur with this entity. When an enabled operation occurs, the entity is moved from the input state to the output state. The Petri net of Figure 15.3 shows that the initial state of an order is to be created; to receiveO is the only enabled operation, and its occurrence moves the order into the pending state. The life cycle of an Entity allows checking that each state is reachable from the initial state and whether a final state may be reached from any state. Modelling a life cycle with a Petri net instead of a State Diagram (or Automaton) allows accounting for the fact that an Entity may be involved in several concurrent procedures; for instance, Products take part both in the Customer-Company procedure and in the Company-Supplier procedure.

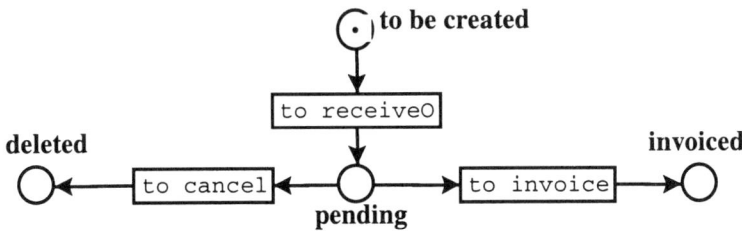

Fig. 15.3. The life cycle of entity order

Question 9: What are the relationships between Entities and Actors?

Answer: Since the system includes a single Actor type, clerks are responsible for all tasks regarding entities, such as creation, deletion or keeping. In addition, the Clerk instances share all the Entity instances, that is to say:

when a `clerk` can perform an Operation with some Entity instances, any other `clerk` can do this Operation with the same instances.

15.7 The Operations

We will now study the Operations of the system. As for Entities, the first question is about the definition of Operation types.

Question 10: What is the structure of Operations?

Question 10.1: What are the parameters?
Answer: See Table 15.2

Table 15.2. The parameters of operations

	In parameters	Out parameters	InOut parameters
to invoice	Order	Invoice	Product
to receiveO	InformalOrder	Order	
to cancel	CancelReq, Order		
to receiveA	Article		Product

Question 10.2: How are they defined? More precisely, how do the values of parameter Entities change?
Answer: The statement of the case provides no detail about the processing achieved by Operations. For instance, we may assume the following:

    to invoice (o: Order, i: Invoice, p: Product)
      is i=Invoice.create(o); p.takeout(o.qtity) **end**.
    to receive0 (io: InformalOrder, o: Order)
      is o=Order.create(io) **end**.
    to cancel (cr: CancelReq, o: Order)
      is o.delete() **end**.
    to receiveA (a: Article, p: Product)
      is p.increase(a.qtity) **end**.

A more detailed answer is useless to draw a conceptual model.

Question 11: What are the relationships between Operations and Actors?
Answer: Since the system includes a single Actor type, `clerks` play all the roles of the Actor-Operation relationships. Namely, they are responsible for triggering, executing and monitoring all Operations. `Clerks` are assumed to be continuously in the `ready` state, so that Operation occurrences do not produce state changes.

Relationships between Operations and Entities have been already addressed (See Question 7).

15.8 The Actors

We have now to study the Actors of the system, which will be modelled as active Object classes. We will again ask questions about the structure of Actors, while questions about their relationships with Entities and Operations have been already addressed (See Question 9 and 11).

Question 12: What is the structure of Actors?
Answer: ???

The statement of the case is not suitable to discuss this issue because it does not account for the organisation of the system and who is doing the work (To do so would lead to widen the case in a very large extent). This situation is quite common, when the designer draws a *functional* model that ignores the Actor component of Actions.

An Actor is described in the same way as an Entity, by means of attributes and functions together with a Petri net describing its activity, or *Task*. Here, clerks have neither attribute nor function, and their Task is shown in Figure 15.4.

One may wonder what is the real difference between Entities and Actors, and in fact, to classify a component as an Entity or as an Actor is a modelling choice that depends on the purpose and the abstraction level of the model. The status of their behavioural structure makes the difference: an Entity is a *passive* component and its Life Cycle shows constraints on its use, while an Actor is an *active* component and is responsible for achieving the activity described by its Task. The behaviour of the system is determined by the Tasks of the Actors (and how they interact), while life cycles mainly serve documentation purpose.

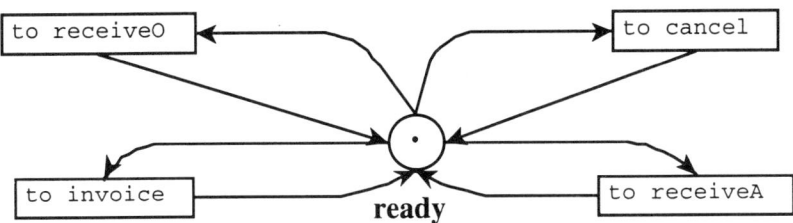

Fig. 15.4. The task of actor clerk

Question 13: What about the interactions among Actors?
Answer: Since there is just one Actor type, only `clerks` are concerned by the question. There are no synchronous interactions among `clerks`, that is no Action requires that several actors intervene together to perform an instance of this Action. There are also no asynchronous communications among Actors since `clerks` share all the Entity instances (see Question 9).

However, `clerks` communicate with the Company's environment, that is with `customers` and `suppliers`, as shown by the Communication Diagram in Figure 15.1.

No questions have been raised about the relationships among Entities and among Operations. The relationships among Entities (an Entity may include, refer or inherit another one) are described through their structure (see Figure 15.2). As for the relationships among Operations (an Operation can include another one), it is obvious that the Operations of the case are not related.

15.9 The Control Structure

Once the components of the structure of the system have been defined, its Control Structure may be addressed. First, each Action is examined in order to know under which cases it may occur and what is the effect of its occurrences. Then issues related to the concurrent and sequential occurrence of Actions are addressed. Finally, the Control Structure of the system is described by means of Petri nets. To this end, the *Activity net* of each Actor type is drawn that describes the concurrent activity of all the instances of this type; then, these activity nets are *composed* (by places and/or transitions merging) into a global net modelling the Control Structure of the whole system. Since the system under consideration includes only the `Clerk` Actor, it does not allow illustrating the composition of activity nets.

Question 14: In which cases an Action instance may or must occur?

Answer: Any action that may occur has to occur, except if the occurrence of another action produces a situation where it is no longer enabled. It is the clerks' duty to actually trigger the occurrence of an action that may occur. According to this rule, it is enough to define when an action may occur. Let c, io, o, i, p, cr, a be an instance of the type `Clerk`, `InformalOrder`, `Order`, `Invoice`, `Product`, `CancelReq` and `Article` respectively.

1. An action (c, to receive0, {io, o}) may occur as soon as the Company receives io.
2. An action (c, to invoice, {o, i, p}) may occur whenever the order o is pending, if the product referred by o is p, p is in the state stock and p.stock is greater than o.qtity.
3. An action (c, to cancel, {cr, o, i, p}) may occur as soon as the Company receives cr, if the corresponding order o is in the pending state.
4. An action (c, to receiveA, {a, p}) may occur as soon as the Company receives a, if the product p is in the state stock and refers to a.

This answer indicates that no Action is triggered by a *temporal event* caused by the elapsing of time. To deal with such events, arcs would be labelled by

15 Petri Nets and Objects: A Formal yet Expressive Approach 271

minimum and maximum delays, which determine the period within which a token must be used by a transition occurrence.

Question 15: What about the effect of each Action occurrence?

Answer: The state change caused by each Action is the same as the one caused by the Action's Operation, and it has already been defined (Cf. Questions 7, 8 and 11).

Enough information is now available to formalise the enabling and the resulting state of each Action. This is achieved by designing, for each Action, a small Petri net that includes:

- One transition corresponding to the Action (if an Action is enabled under different states, the net includes one transition for each enabling state); the name of this transition is the name of the Action, while its body is a call to the Action's Operation; in addition, the transition may be guarded by a Boolean expression involving its input variables.
- One place for the Action's Actor if the execution of the Action does not change the state of the Actor, and in the opposite case one input place and one output place that respectively correspond to the state of the Actor before and after the execution of the Action; The type of the place (written in italic characters) is the type of the Actor while its name is the one of the corresponding state.
- Places corresponding to the state of Entities involved in the Action, according to the rules illustrated in Figure 15.4 and the relationships between the Operation and its parameter Entities (cf. Questions 7 and 8, an operation may create, delete, change the state or change/read the value of an entity); the name and the type of these places are defined like for the Actor's places.
- There is an arc from an (input) place toward a transition if this place corresponds to a state of an Actor or an Entity that enables an occurrence of the Action, and there is an arc from a transition toward an (output) place if this place corresponds to the state reached by an Actor or an Entity after an Action's occurrence. These arcs are labelled by variables that act as formal parameters of the transition and receive the type of the connected place. Graphically, a double-headed arrow connecting a place and a transition stands for two arcs: one arc from the place to the transition and another arc in the opposite direction.

To give an overview of the semantics of such a net, let's consider the net of Action act1 (Clerk, to invoice, {Order, Invoice, Product}), Figure 15.5(a).

Each place of the net corresponds to a state variable and its value is the set of instances that are in this very state. This set is called the *marking* of the place, and its element, called *tokens*, are instances of the place's type. A *marking of the net* is the marking of all places. So, a marking of the considered net is a set of clerks in the place ready, a set of orders in the places pending, another

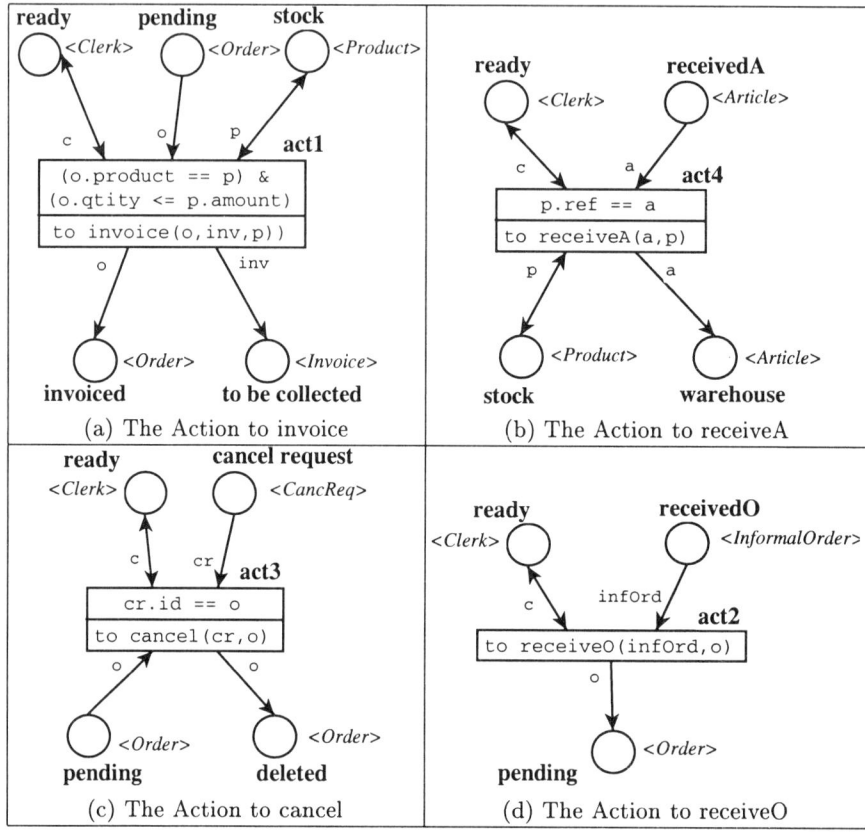

Fig. 15.5. The nets showing the enabling and resulting states of each action

one in the place `invoiced`, etc. Tokens remain in the same place until they are involved in a transition occurrence.

The transition `act1` may *occur* (or is *enabled*) under a marking of the net if:

1. there exists a binding of its variables with tokens such that the variable of each input arc is bound to a token lying in the corresponding place, and
2. this binding evaluates the guard of the transition to true.

Thus `act1` may occur under a marking including at least a `clerk c` in the place `ready`, an `order o` in the place `pending` and a `product p` in the place `stock` such that `(o.product == p) & (o.qtity <= p.amount)` holds.

When `act1` may occur, its *occurrence* (or firing) causes the execution of its body (an instance of the Operation `to invoice`) and also changes the marking of its surrounding places: tokens bound to input variables are removed from input places, and tokens bound to output variables are put into output places; an output variable that does not appear on any input arc is assumed to be bound to a "new" instance that appears in no token of the marking. Thus, the occurrence of act1 moves o from the place pending to the place invoiced, put a new invoice into the place to be collected, and changes the value of p by means of its function takeout.

If the marking of the net allows to build several bindings that involve distinct tokens, act1 may occur concurrently more that once, one time for each binding. For instance, if the places ready, pending and stock contain enough tokens to have four bindings that evaluate the guard of act1 to true, four occurrences of this transition may take place simultaneously. The same holds for bindings concerning other transitions.

Now, we need information on the Action instances that may occur concurrently and on the nondeterminism of the system.

Question 16: What about the concurrency constraints?

Answer: A clerk performs only one action at a time, he cannot concurrently perform several actions. Of course, clerks do not work in turn: different clerks can simultaneously take part to different Action instances.

An Entity instance can be involved in only one action at a time; as a consequence, an order cannot be concurrently invoiced and cancelled, two orders that refer to the same product cannot be concurrently ordered, and a product cannot be involved in concurrent occurrences of to invoice and to receiveA. But different Entity instances can take part to concurrent Action instances.

As for Operations, there is no additional constraint: if the above constraints are satisfied, any Operation may occur concurrently with others and with itself.

Question 17: When two actions can both occur but cannot occur concurrently (for instance because they involve the same clerk or the same product), what are the priority rules allowing to decide which action will occur first?

Answer: Actions involving the Operation to cancel have a higher priority than the other Actions. When two pending orders referring to the same product may be invoiced, the order that is arrived first is invoiced first. These rules do not solve all conflicts, so the system features some amount of nondeterminism that is solved by the choices of clerks.

Several nets may be combined into a single one, by merging either places or transitions. In the first case, a place of a net is merged with a place of another net, or with several such places. In the second case, transitions of the nets are merged [5]. We are now provided with all the information allowing formalising, in the net of Figure 15.6, the activity of clerks. This net is obtained by merging the nets of the Actions (Figure 15.5) through their common places.

In order to account for the communications between a net and its environment, it is possible to distinguish entry places and result places. *Entry places*, or input communication channels are intended to receive tokens from the environment of the net and have only output transitions. Conversely *result places* are

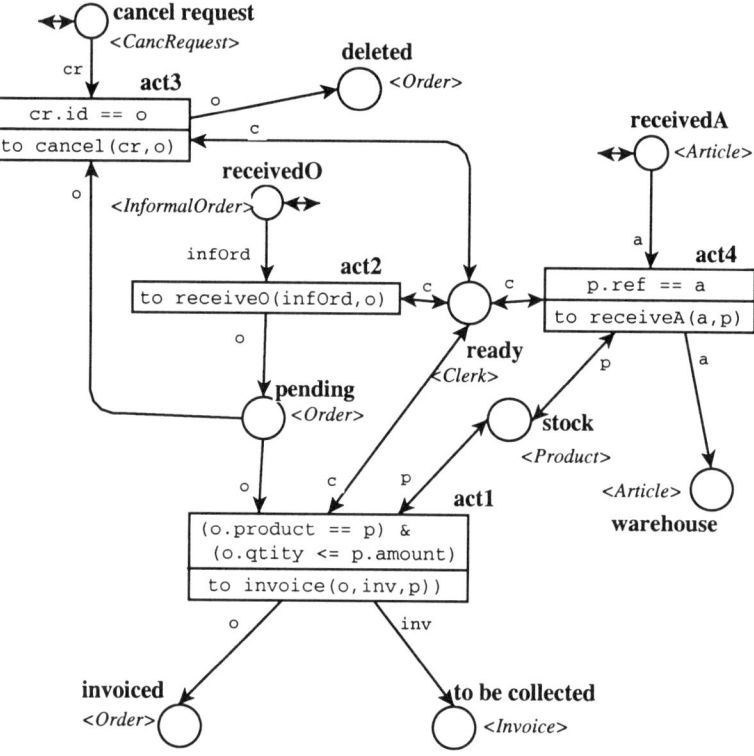

Fig. 15.6. The Activity Net of clerks (Case 2)

output communication channels intended to supply tokens to the environment and have only input transitions. Here, places receivedO, cancel request and receivedA are entry places enabling clerks to receive entities from customers and suppliers (this fact results from the answer to the first question), while there is no result place.

At the initial marking, places ready, stock and warehouse respectively contain the actual clerks, products and articles of the Company. According to the statement of the case, an order is never rejected; if the ordered product is not in the stock, or if the ordered quantity is greater than the amount of the ordered product, the order is delayed as long as this situation holds. According to concurrency constraints, several orders may be invoiced concurrently provided that they do not reference the same product, the to invoice and to receiveA Operations cannot occur concurrently for the same product. The priority rules are ensured by the following properties that do not appear on the graphical representation of Figure 15.6: the transition corresponding to Action act3 has a higher priority – the other transitions cannot occur if it is enabled; the set of orders in place pending is ranked as a queue – the first arrived order is invoiced or cancelled first, if possible.

When a system includes several Actor types, their Activity nets are composed by merging their common entry and result places (asynchronous communication) or their common transition (synchronous communication). This results in a net describing the Control Structure of the whole system.

The analysis techniques of the Petri net theory [7] may be applied either on the activity net of an Actor or on the net of the whole system. As an example, analysing the flow of tokens enables to verify that:

- the `clerks` are steadily in the state `ready`;
- the `products` are steadily in the state `stock`;
- the `articles` are in the states `receivedA` or `warehouse`;
- an `informalOrder` in the state `receivedO` gives raise either to a `deleted order`, or to an `invoiced order` and a `to be collected invoice`.

To analyse the actions that may occur within a net, its entry and exit places have to be avoided. Then it is possible to compute the sequences of sets of actions that may occur, the actions that constitute a loop, the possibility of deadlocks, and so on.

15.10 Natural Language Description of the Specifications

The purpose of our conceptual framework is to structure the informal description of a system, and the questions are just the ones allowing to obtain such a description. As a consequence, the natural language description of the case comes down to the concatenation of the answers to the questions. As for the formal model, it mainly comes down to Figures 15.2 and 15.5(a) – for Case 1, and to Figures 15.2 and 15.6 and answer 10.2 – for Case 2.

15.11 Remarks about the Treatment of the Case Study

This chapter shows how to model a simple case study using the Petri Net with Object formalism together with a conceptual framework to guide the modelling process.

The considered case study is very simple. Thus, it cannot show to what extent this approach allows to master the complexity of real systems, whereas issuing tractable and understandable models of complex systems is an essential challenge. In addition, the simplicity of the case allows illustrating only a part of the expressive power of the formalism.

The other drawback of the case is that it is not a system, while our approach is intended to cope with realistic systems that counterbalance their in-flows and out-flows. For instance, the Company would have to send the invoices, to deliver the ordered articles, to collect the Customers' payments, and so on. Consequently, the consistency of the Company's behaviour cannot be validated using the analysis techniques of Petri nets. In addition, no attention is paid to the organisational structure of the Company, so that the interactions among the Actor instances are very poor.

On the other hand, this case study is appropriate to show some essential features of the approach. With regard to the conceptual framework, we have shown that it provides the domain specialists and the modellers with a shared language, and that it defines a standard pattern for the informal description of systems. With regard to Petri Net with Objects, we have shown that this formalism allows drawing simple models of simple systems.

The questions raised by the formalism specialists are not grounded upon technical considerations related to the formalism, but on the common conceptual framework. Thus the domain specialist is only required to reply to questions that are of his concern – the knowledge of the system –, and he is not consulted for issues that are a matter for the formalism specialist. Both the domain and the formalism specialists contribute to work out the model within their scope of competence. This drastically increases the reliability of their respective contribution. The conceptual and formal models are very close to each other, so that the modeller encounters no cognitive difficulty to build a mental representation of the system. In addition, these series of questions are not specific to the system under consideration and follow a standard pattern determined by the conceptual framework (for the importance of standards in Software Engineering, see e.g. [4]).

These series of questions have to be viewed as a standard outline for presenting the informal description of a system and not as the copying out of the talk between the domain specialist and the modeller. These series are not the script of the questions actually raised by the modeller in order to gain the information he needs about the system. They are only the report of their conversation. First, the detail of the actual dialogue is of no interest, since it depends on characteristics of the involved peoples such as their ability to clearly express their thought, their experience in modelling, and so on. Second, it is unlikely that the domain specialist is able to right away provide a complete and unambiguous answer to each question. It is more likely that during the modelling process he refines his answers as he improves his understanding of the system.

The order according to which the questions are introduced in this chapter – the system's interface, the identification of the types, the Entities, the Operations, the Actors and the Control Structure –, does not correspond to a strict sequence of modelling steps. The Petri Net with Objects formalism is a notation, not a methodology.

Nevertheless, each question corresponds to a task that has to be done during any modelling process, and the order of questions is not arbitrary. In any case, the issues concerning the system's interface deserve a special attention; they are of great importance, because the interaction of a system with its environment most often deeply determines its structure and its behaviour. To avoid forward references, the identification of the types has to come before their detailed study, and the description of the Control Structure needs that the Actions' components are well defined. As for the questions about Entities, Operations and Actors, they may be introduced in any order.

Finally, we would stress the relevance of Petri nets to deal with the behavioural aspect of systems. To justify this claim, we will have a glance at other ways to use it.

First of all, let's consider the activity net of Figure 15.6: removing all places but the `ready` one results in the Task net of Figure 15.4, and removing transition `act4` and all places that have not the type `order` results in the Life Cycle net of Figure 15.3. Thus these three behavioural structures are closely related: Life Cycles and Task nets are the projection of the system's Control Structure on the Entities and the Actors respectively.

In order to break up the Control Structure of a system, we have made the choice to associate to each Actor the part of the Control Structure concerning the Action it performs. Doing so, Actors have been emphasised, because they are responsible for triggering the Action occurrences, and play a role that Entities are denied.

Another way to build the Petri net model of the Control Structure of a system is to start from the life cycle nets of Entities and to compose them. To this end, these nets are combined by merging the transitions corresponding to the same Action, after an eventual renaming of variables labelling the arcs. The resulting net is the same than the one obtained by composing the activity nets of Actors.

Yet another solution to build the Petri net of the Control Structure is to consider the *Procedures*, or *Use Cases* [2], since the activity of a system may often be breakdown into Procedures. As an example, the Operations `to receive0`, `to cancel` and `to invoice` of our Company are certainly steps of a Procedure `process order`, which starts upon the arrival of an `informalOrder` and terminates when either the `order` has been cancelled or the ordered `articles` have been delivered and paid by the customer. Thus, it is possible to break up the Control Structure of a system by drawing, for each Procedure, one net that describes the part of the Control Structure concerning the Actions of this procedure. The Control Structure of the whole system is then obtained by composing these Procedure nets through the fusion of their common places. Again, the resulting net is the same than the one obtained by the two other ways

Thus, the Control Structure of a system may be obtained by focusing the modelling process either on Actors, on Entities or on Use Cases, according to the most problematic features of the system under consideration. For instance, it is relevant to draw the nets of the Procedures in order to highlight how the system elaborates replies for environment's requests. This makes it also possible to mix these strategies, or to use them concurrently and then to verify that they lead the same model. Of course, procedure nets and actor behaviours are tightly related and the ones stem from the others, even when procedures involve several actors or an actors participate to several procedures.

As a conclusion, we have proposed a conceptual framework allowing designers to decide what are the relevant questions according to the characteristics of the case under consideration. Such a framework is usable as a map making designers aware of the ways coming to the desired model of the system, so that they can choose the modelling process which is the most appropriate. We believe that any modelling approach needs such a conceptual framework to become mature, and that the one proposed in this chapter is general enough to improve the practice of many Formal Description Techniques.

References

1. Chiola G., Dutheillet C., Franceschinis G., Haddad S. (1991) On Well-Formed coloured Nets and their Symbolic Reachability Graph. In: Rozenberg G. (Ed.) *Advances in Petri Nets 91*, Lecture Notes in Computer Science Vol. 524, Springer-Verlag
2. Fowler M., Scott K. (1997) *UML Distilled, Applying the Standard Object Modelling Language*. Addison-Wesley
3. Genrich H., Lautenbach K. (1981) System modelling with High Level Petri Nets. *Theoretical Computer Science* **13**, North-Holland
4. Ghezzi C., Jazayeri M., Mandrioli D. (1991) *Fundamentals of Software Engineering*. Prentice-Hall
5. Huber P., Jensen K., Shapiro R.M. (1990) Hierarchies in coloured Petri nets. In: *Application and Theory of Petri Nets 1990*, Lecture Notes in Computer Science Vol. 483, Springer-Verlag
6. Jensen K. (1987) Coloured Petri Nets. In: Brauer W., Reisig W., Rozenberg G. (Eds.) *Petri Nets: Applications and Relationships to Other Models of Concurrency Part I*, Lecture Notes in Computer Science Vol. 254, Springer-Verlag
7. Murata T. (1989) Petri Nets: Properties, Analysis and Applications. *Proc. of the IEEE*, 77(4):541–580
8. Reisig W. (1985) Petri Nets with Individual Tokens. *Theoretical Computer Science* 41:185–213, North-Holland
9. Sibertin-Blanc C. (1985) High Level Petri Nets with Data Structure. In: *Proceedings of the 6th european Workshop on Application and Theory of Petri Nets*, Espoo, Finland, June 1985
10. Sibertin-Blanc C. (1991) Cooperative Objects for the Conceptual Modelling of Organizational Information Systems. In: Van Assche F., Moulin B., Rolland C. (Eds) *Proceedings of the IFIP TC8 Conference on The Object-Oriented approach in Information Systems*, North-Holland, Québec, October 1991
11. Sibertin-Blanc C. (2000) CoOperative Objects: Principles, Use and Implementation. In: Agha G., De Cindio F. (Eds.) *Petri Nets and Object Orientation*, Lectures Notes in Computer Science, Springer-Verlag, 2000
12. Yourdon E., Constantine L. (1989) *Structured Design : Fundamental of a Discipline of Program and Systems Design*. Prentice Hall

Index

:=, assignment in E-LOTOS 175
;, sequence in (E)-LOTOS 175
?, set offer in (E)-LOTOS 174
[], choice in (E)-LOTOS 175
E-LOTOS, Enhancements to Language of Temporal Ordering Specification 165
LOTOS, Language of Temporal Ordering Specification 165
offspring 151
parent 151
self 151
sender 151

abbreviation definition 6
abstract data type 209
abstract machine 64
abstract state 3, 6
action 81, 261
action system 81
– execution 81
– refinement 93
– semantics 91
activity 151
actor 260
– task 269
ADT, Abstract Data Type 165
after state 3, 6, 8
algebraic specification 209
– constructive 218
– observational 212
analysis and design phase 97, 99, 106, 112
architectural specification 221
association 57
Atelier B 74
axioms 209

B method 57

basic type 5
before state 3, 6, 8
behaviour 196, 261
behaviour-driven approach 97
behavioural style 113, 129
bisimulation, in (E)-LOTOS 186
block 149
– diagram 149
– reference 151
– substructure 149
box
– black 191
– clear 191
– state 191
– structure 191

CASL 209
channel 149, 151
class diagram 97, 101, 102
Cleanroom 191
coercion 234
collaboration diagram 97, 100, 101
coloured net 249
command 81
communication
– asynchronous 151
communication diagram 262
conceptual framework 260
concurrent 113, 121
connection
– point 149, 151
constructive specification 166
control structure 261
Coq 225
CSP 81, 191

data type, in E-LOTOS 174
data type, in LOTOS 180

data-oriented specification, in (E)-LOTOS 178
dataflow style   113
deadlock   81
decision   152
– branch   152
divergence   81
domain restriction   46
domain subtraction   46

enabled action   81
entity   57, 191, 260
– life cycle   267
– structure diagram   191, 198
environment   262
environment, in (E)-LOTOS   165
error report   10
Estelle   131
event   58
event gate, in (E)-LOTOS   165
event offer, in (E)-LOTOS   166
event trace diagram   59
event, in (E)-LOTOS   166
event-based specification   81
event-driven   113, 129
explicit operation   17

FDT, Formal Description Technique   165
finite automata   241
firing rule   242, 250
flow line   152
formal specification   57
function, in E-LOTOS   178

gate, in (E)-LOTOS   165
generalised substitutions   39
given set   5
guard   81

higher order
– function   229, 233
– logic   225
horizontal schema   12

implementation   132, 137, 143, 144
implicit precondition   15
inheritance   154
inhibitor arcs   244

initial state   3
input   152
input set   193
input space   193
interaction/message   131
interaction/point   131, 133, 134, 138, 139
invariant   3, 7, 39, 48, 255

JSD   191

label
– definition   152
– join   152
lambda abstraction   46
library, in LOTOS   177
literal   148
LTS, Labelled Transition System   183

machine
– abstract   39
marking   242
model-checking   183
module, in E-LOTOS   174
module/body   131, 134, 136, 137, 142
module/header   131, 133, 134, 138
module/instance   131, 132, 134, 139, 144

noexit, in LOTOS   177
nondeterminism   85

object   97, 98
object diagram   57
OMT   57
OMT-B combination   76
one-point rule   15
operation   3, 39, 193, 260
operator   148
output   152
output set   193
override   46
overriding   10

pair construction   46
parallelism   131
partial function   6, 7
Petri net   241, 259
place   241
port
– input   151
postcondition   9

precondition 3, 9, 96
process 113, 114, 119, 121, 147
– instance 147
– reference 151
process algebra 165, 191
process, in (E)-LOTOS 165
process, in E-LOTOS 174
process, in LOTOS 177
process-oriented specification, in (E)-LOTOS 174
proof obligation 74
property 148
property, of formal specification 185

reachability graph 254
refinement 47
relation 3
requirements capture 97, 98, 103, 111, 112
requirements capture, in LOTOS 166
resolution function 114, 121

SAZ 21
scenario 57, 97, 99, 104
schema 3
schema inclusion 7
schema operators 12
semi-formal notation 57
set comprehension 6
signal 113, 114, 119, 121, 147
– definition 151
– list 149, 151
– route 149, 151
signature 209
– operation 209
– predicate 209
– sort 209
– subsort 209
simulation 113, 128, 129
sort 147
specification architecture 166
specification style, in LOTOS 166
SSADM 21
– data flow diagram 21
– entity life history 22
– entity-relationship diagram 21
– function definition 21
– Requirements Analysis module 21

– Requirements Specification module 21
state 3, 150
– initial 150, 152
– target 151
state component 6
state diagram 97, 102
state-based specification 81
state/transition diagram 57
structural style 113
substitution
– conditional 46
– elementary 44
– multiple 46
– precondition 46
substructure 151
synchronisation, in (E)-LOTOS 176
system 147
system/distributed 131, 132, 143, 144
system/systemactivity 131, 132
system/systemprocess 131

task 152
temporal logic 185
token 242, 249
total operation 3, 10
trace 194
transition 151, 241, 252, 253
Turing machine 241, 257
type 147
– abstract data type 148
– dependent 234
– inductive 229
– powerset 154
– structure 154
– syntype 153
– theory 225

UML 97
use case diagram 97, 98

validation 182
variable
– definition 152
verification 182
vertical schema 6

weakest precondition 39, 91

Z 22, 81

- error schema 26
- processing specification 26
- schema calculus 27
- state specification 24

Z notation 3–5

Z toolkit 3
Z/EVES tool 17
ZANS animator 17
ZTC type-checker 17

FORMAL APPROACHES TO COMPUTING AND INFORMATION TECHNOLOGY SERIES

Series Editor: S. A. Schuman

The series with which dependable software is built

Are you an industrial or commercial practitioner in computing and information technology? Do you want to improve your professional effectiveness? If so, then this series is for you!

FACIT offers a range of textbooks, case studies and reference works which address the same basic need: to develop an understanding of formal methods and apply them effectively, in order to produce dependable software.

All books are, of course, available from all good booksellers (who can order them even if they are not in stock), but if you have difficulties you can contact the publishers direct, by telephoning +44 (0) 1483 418822 (in the UK & Europe), +1/212/4 60/15 00 (in the USA), or by emailing orders@svl.co.uk

www.springer.co.uk   www.springer.de
www.springer-ny.com

REFINEMENT IN Z AND OBJECT-Z
Foundations and Advanced Applications

John Derrick and Eerke Boiten

Series: **FACIT**

Refinement is one of the cornerstones of the formal approach to software engineering and - over the last few years - its use in various domains has led to research on new applications and generalisations.

Refinement in Z and Object-Z reviews recent research developments in the refinement of state-based formal specifications, focusing in particular on refinement and its application in Z and Object-Z.

Each section of this book looks at a different theme:
- data refinement and its applicability in Z;
- recent generalisations;
- the theory of refinement and its use in the context of object-orientation;
- a comparison of the use of refinement in Z/Object-Z and other languages.

400 pages
Softcover
ISBN: 1-85233-245-X
Please see page 283 for ordering details.

www.springer.co.uk   www.springer.de
www.springer-ny.com

UNDERSTANDING FORMAL METHODS

J. F. Monin
Translation Editor: **M. G. Hinchey**

Series: **FACIT**

Understanding Formal Methods is an excellent introduction to formal methods which will bring anyone who needs to know about this important topic right up to speed. It is all-inclusive, giving the reader all the information needed to explore the field of formal methods in more detail.

Special features include:

- a comprehensible guide to the mathematics required;
- easy-to-understand introductions to various methods;
- a run-down of how formal methods can help to develop high-quality systems that come in on time, within budget and according to requirements.

Understanding Formal Methods is aimed at advanced undergraduate students, postgraduate students and computing professionals who need to know how formal methods can help to improve the quality of the systems they build.

Originally published in French, this version has been revised and updated to include recent work and improved coverage of Z.

328 pages
Softcover
ISBN: 1-85233-247-6
Please see page 283 for ordering details.

www.springer.co.uk   www.springer.de
www.springer-ny.com

FORMAL ASPECTS OF COMPUTING

The International Journal of Formal Methods

Editor-in-Chief:
C. B. Jones, Manchester, UK
Associate Editor:
J. Cooke, Loughborough, UK

Published in association with the British Computer Society

Formal Aspects of Computing promotes the growth of computing science, showing its relationship to practice, and stimulating applications of apposite formalisms. In particular, the scope of the journal includes the following areas:

- Well-founded notations for system description (specification);
- Verifiable designs;
- Proof methods;
- Transformational design;
- Formal approaches to requirements analysis;
- Results on algorithm and problem complexity;
- Fault-tolerant design;
- Descriptions of relevant "Project Support Environments";
- Theories of objects used in specifications and implementations;
- Methods of approaching development.

ISSN: 0934-5043 (Print Version)
ISSN: 1433-299X (Electronic Version)
6 Issues per year

For journal information or to subscribe, please visit:
http://link.springer.de
Special discounted rates are available.

www.springer.co.uk   www.springer.de
www.springer-ny.com